Armin Größlinger

The Challenges of Non-linear Parameters and
Variables in Automatic Loop Parallelisation

The Challenges of Non-linear Parameters and Variables in Automatic Loop Parallelisation

Armin Größlinger

2009-07

Eingereicht an der Fakultät für Informatik und Mathematik der Universität Passau als Dissertation zur Erlangung des Grades eines Doktors der Naturwissenschaften

Submitted to the Department of Informatics and Mathematics of the University of Passau in Partial Fulfilment of Obtaining the Degree of a Doctor in the Domain of Science

Betreuer / Advisor:
Prof. Christian Lengauer, Ph.D.
Universität Passau

Zweitgutachter / External Examiner:
Prof. Albert Cohen
INRIA Saclay–Île-de-France
Parc Club Orsay Université

Fakultät für Informatik und Mathematik

Armin Größlinger
Fakultät für Informatik und Mathematik
Universität Passau
94030 Passau
Germany

Revised first edition December 2009

The original edition is available at
http://nbn-resolving.de/urn:nbn:de:bvb:739-opus-17893

Copyright © 2009 Armin Größlinger

Cover design by lulu.com

Printed by lulu.com

ISBN 978-1-4452-5421-0

Abstract

With the rise of manycore processors, parallelism is becoming a mainstream necessity. Unfortunately, parallel programming is inherently more difficult than sequential programming; therefore, techniques for automatic parallelisation will become indispensable. We aim at extending the well-known polyhedron model, which promises this automation, beyond some of its current restrictions. Up to now, loop bounds and array subscripts in the modelled codes must be expressions linear in both the variables and the parameters. We lift this restriction and allow certain polynomial expressions instead of linear ones. With our extensions, we are able to handle more programs in all phases of the parallelisation process (dependence analysis, transformation of the program model, code generation).

We extend Banerjee's classical dependence analysis to handle one non-linear parameter p, i.e., we are able to determine precisely the solutions of the system of conflict equalities for input programs with non-linear array accesses like $A[p \cdot i]$ in dependence of the residue class of p.

We make contributions to three transformations desirable in automatic parallelisation. First, we show that using a generalised simplex algorithm, which we have developed, schedules with non-linear parameters like $\theta(i) = \lfloor \frac{i}{n} \rfloor$ can be computed. In addition, such schedules can be expressed easily as a quantifier elimination problem but this approach turns out to be computationally less efficient with the available implementation. As a second transformation, we study parametric tiling which is used to adapt a parallelised program to the number of available processors at run time. Third, we present a localisation technique to exploit scratchpad memories on architectures on which data caching has to be handled by software. We transform a given code such that it keeps values which are reused in successive iterations of a sequential loop in the scratchpad. An access to a value written in an earlier iteration is served from the scratchpad to accelerate the access. In general, this transformation introduces non-linear loop bounds in the transformed model.

Finally, we present an algorithm for generating code for arbitrary semi-algebraic iteration sets, i.e., for iteration sets described by polynomial inequalities in the variables and parameters. This is a vast generalisation of existing polyhedral code generation techniques. Although our algorithm is less efficient than polyhedral code generators, this paves the way for a code generator that can handle arbitrary parametric tilings and other transformations which introduce non-linear parameters (like non-linear schedules and the localisation we present) or even non-linear variables.

Technically, our extensions rely on results from algebra (multivariate polynomials and univariate quasi-polynomials) and logic (quantifier elimination in the reals). We prove that solutions of systems of linear Diophantine equalities with one non-linear parameter can be computed by a generalisation of a well-known algorithm for the non-parametric case to coefficients which are univariate quasi-polynomials in the parameter. Computing schedules and other transformations are directly related to quantifier elimination or can be performed by a generalisation of an algorithm for the linear case by the help of quantifier elimination. Cylindrical algebraic decomposition (originally developed as a method for quantifier elimination) is the key to generating code for iteration sets with polynomial bounds. To generate code, a suitable partitioning of the index sets is required. We observe that such partitionings are cylindrical and, based on this observation, present a code generation algorithm based on cylindrical algebraic decomposition for iteration sets with arbitrary polynomial bounds.

Acknowledgements

This thesis has only been made possible through the support of many people. First of all, I have to thank my adviser Prof. Christian Lengauer, Ph.D. for enabling me to explore the field of polynomial parameters and variables in the polyhedron model. I am grateful to him for the many discussions, the support and the many valuable suggestions on the structure and the contents of this thesis and for the many improvements of my use of the English language.

Dr. Martin Griebl has always been a valuable dialogue partner. The discussions with him gave the initial impetus to explore some of the aspects dealt with in this thesis. He offered his insights and comments on some of the topics while they came into existence.

I enjoyed the work with Stefan Schuster while he was doing his Diploma thesis about the foundations for a more general dependence analysis. The LooPo team in Passau has been a source of constant, fruitful discussion about the topics of this thesis.

I have to thank Dr.-Ing. Sven Apel, Eva Reichhart and my other friends in Passau for keeping me going with the work on this thesis.

Additional thanks go to the ALCHEMY group for the discussions and suggestions while finishing this thesis. I am indebted to Prof. Albert Cohen for providing me with a supportive environment to finish this work.

Last but not least, I have to thank my partner Thomas for his understanding and his continuous support throughout my work on this thesis.

viii

Contents

List of Figures

Chapter 1

Introduction

Until recently, parallel programming has been a niche phenomenon. Only when the demand for processing power or memory size in some special applications exceeded the resources of a single processor, a cluster of workstations, i.e., processors connected through a local area network, was used. But, in recent years, parallel computing has become increasingly main-stream. CPU power is not increasing as fast as before and the recent trend in both the desktop and the server CPU market has been towards multicore chips with several instances of the same processor or different, special-purpose processors on a single die. Processing power is increased by adding more cores, not by making a single core faster. Exploiting this processing power clearly requires parallel programming techniques. Another instance of this emerging parallelism on the small scale is general-purpose graphics processing unit (GPGPU) computing. Initially, graphics processors were special-purpose, but some modifications to the design allow them to be used as a general-purpose parallel computing hardware (cf. Section 2.2.2).

On the large scale, world-wide interconnection of computing systems has given rise to Grid computing. With the Internet becoming faster, the delay and bandwidth limitation present between sites is becoming less of a problem and enable parallel computing applications to run across the Internet. But, even with fast networks, it is necessary to exploit data locality, i.e., to arrange computations in a way such that as much data as possible is supplied to computations by local sources, e.g., by reusing data computed in preceding steps of the computation.

The peculiarities of parallel programming make it inherently more difficult than sequential programming and it has remained somewhat of a black art. To unburden the programmer from dealing with the subtleties of parallel programming like interprocess/interprocessor communication, synchronisation, deadlock avoidance, arranging computations for efficiency, etc. automatic methods are needed that perform a parallelisation in a provably correct fashion and are only guided by hints from the programmer or a parallelism expert. Of course, full automation is only achievable for restricted classes of problems due to the undecidability of most nontrivial properties of arbitrary programs. One such class of programs which has been subjected successfully to an automatic paralleli-sation is the class which satisfies the restrictions of the so-called polyhedron model. This model places several restrictions on the programs it can handle, most notably the requirement that they be for loops with loop bounds linear in the variables (and structural parameters) and with statements in the body con-sisting of array accesses with affine array subscripts. The struggle to increase the model's applicability and to repeat the success the model has had in its original domain in a broader setting, is the driving force behind several recent developments in this field (see the chapter on related work, Chapter 3).

The main point of our work has been to explore how the polyhedron model can be extended in a certain direction to handle a richer class of programs. The extension we have been pursuing allows non-linearities; the classical model allows only linear (or affine) loop bounds and array subscripts. When we will speak of "non-linear" constructs, we will always mean polynomial expressions in the variables and parameters, i.e., we do not consider array subscripts like $A[B[i]]$ or expressions like 2^i which are clearly beyond linearity as well. To achieve this extension, several techniques from different areas of algebra and logic are required. In the following sections, we give a brief, example-driven overview of the extensions we make. These sections mirror the sections of the main part of this work, Chapter 5, where we elaborate on the extensions we pursue. Chapter 2 introduces the mathematical background needed to formulate the algorithms presented in Chapter 4, which are the basis for the generalisation presented in our main chapter.

The presentation in the following sections is intended for readers familiar with automatic parallelisation to gain a quick overview of our work and its applicability. Dependence analysis (Sections 1.1 and 5.1) and code generation (Sections 1.5 and 5.5) relate to the well-known first and third step in the polyhe-dron model (cf. Section 2.2.1). In these sections, we describe how to do depen-dence analysis in the presence of one non-linear parameter and how to perform code generation for arbitrary non-linear iteration set bounds. The computation of schedules, tiling and array localisation (Sections 1.2 to 1.4 and 5.2 to 5.4) are examples of viable transformations (the second phase of the model) which introduce non-linearities into a previously linear program. This motivates the desire for non-linear transformations and the necessity of code generation for non-linear iteration sets.

1.1   Dependence Analysis

The main challenge in dependence analysis is to determine whether there are values for the loop variables such that two array accesses actually write to or read from the same memory cell. Since loop iterations are discrete and, therefore, loop variables usually are integers, generalising dependence analysis to non-linearities is difficult because of the undecidability of the theory of the integers with addition and multiplication [Dav73]. But, in the case that only one parameter is allowed to occur non-linearly, we can precisely determine the solutions of the conflict equality system in dependence of the parameter.

One common case in which non-linear parameters are used is in a library which offers functions with a stride argument. For example, many functions in the well-known BLAS linear algebra library have a stride parameter to access every p^{th} element of a vector argument. This can be used to access a row (with $p = 1$) or a column (with p equal to the row length of the matrix) of a matrix stored in row-major order. Such codes perform the strided access with array subscripts like A[p*i]. With the technique we present, the corresponding conflict equality system can be analysed exactly. As another example consider the following code (assuming $p \geq 1$):

```
for (i=0; i<=m; i++)
    for (j=0; j<=m; j++)
        A[p*i+2*j] = i+j;
```

Here, the structure of the dependence from the write access to itself depends on whether p is even or odd. This can be deduced from the fact that $2 \cdot j$ is always even. Therefore, if p is even, too, an increment of i can be "compensated" for by lowering j by $\frac{p}{2}$, i.e., the output dependence is from iteration (i, j) to $(i+1, j-\frac{p}{2})$. On the other hand, if p is odd, then i must be increased by two such that the increase can be compensated for by lowering j by p; the dependence is from (i, j) to $(i + 2, j - p)$, then. Our algorithm derives this case distinction and the solutions mechanically.

1.2 Computing Schedules

Depending on the dependence structure of a program, a linearly parametric schedule may not be sufficient to express the potential parallelism. Therefore, we present two approaches (quantifier elimination and a generalised simplex) to computing non-linear schedules. With these techniques, we can compute, for example, the schedule $\theta(i) = \lfloor \frac{i}{n} \rfloor$ for the following code with a dependence from iteration i to $i + n$ caused by the statement in its body:

```
for (i=0; i<=m; i++)
    A[i+n] = f(A[i]);
```

Our code generation techniques then enable us to generate the following parallel code:

```
for (t=⌈1-n/n⌉; t<=⌊m/n⌋; i++)
    parfor (i=max(n*t,0); i<=min(n*t+n-1,m); i++)
        A[i+n] = f(A[i]);
```

1.3 Tiling

Tiling is used to coarsen the grain of parallelism after a parallelising transformation (or it can be used as an optimising transformation in its own right). A coarsening aggregates several operations to one "big" operation. This may be necessary to distribute the otherwise too many operations of a parallel execution step across the available physical processors. To achieve this adaptation to a number of physical processors which is unknown at compile time, the tiling transformation has to refer to non-linear parameters, cf. Section 5.3. Tiling has been studied extensively in the non-parametric case and there are approaches to solving special cases with parameters. Our code generation procedure (Section 5.5) demonstrates the feasibility in the general case. In addition, our discussion of tiling reveals that the rather complex loop bounds introduced by both parametric and non-parametric tiling need not lead to increased overhead in the loop code.

1.4 Array Localisation

Under this heading, we present a method for exploiting so-called scratchpad memories, memory areas which are fast like data caches but which have to be addressed explicitly like ordinary memory. Data caching has to be organised in software, i.e., one has to generate code which moves data between the main memory and the scratchpad memory. The transformation we present requires, for an efficient use of the scratchpad, to generate loops with non-linear bounds. This is another example that a transformation which introduces non-linearities into the model is desirable.

1.5 Code Generation

Polyhedral code generation is limited to the case that the inequalities describing the iteration sets are affine expressions in the variables and parameters. Several transformations (we demonstrate non-linear schedules, parametric tiling and array localisation) introduce products between variables and parameters or we may want to deal with code which has products between variables and/or parameters. A few such codes are presented in Section 5.5. In all these cases, to be precise, in all cases in which the bounds of the iteration sets are (multivariate) polynomial expressions in the variables and parameters, we are able to generate loops to enumerate the iteration sets. The loops generated are efficient in the sense that there are no conditions (`if` statements) inside the loops.

Chapter 2

Prerequisites

In our discussion of automatic parallelisation in the polyhedron model and in the extensions and applications we present, we require several concepts from different areas of mathematics which we introduce in Section 2.1. In Section 2.2, we give an overview of the polyhedron model and describe parallel computing hardware with a focus on the special-purpose hardware (graphics processors for parallel computing) which some of the techniques presented in our main chapter (Chapter 5) target. The reader is invited to skip the mathematical prerequisites if she is not interested in the foundations of all the algorithms and methods we present in Chapters 4 and 5.

2.1 Mathematical Prerequisites

2.1.1 Notation

As usual, we denote the set of natural numbers by $\mathbb{N}$, where, by convention, $0 \in \mathbb{N}$. The set of positive natural numbers is denoted by $\mathbb{N}_+ := \mathbb{N} - \{0\}$.

We will frequently encounter vectors and the lexicographic ordering on the components of the vector.

Definition 2.1. Let $n \in \mathbb{N}$ and $\mathbf{a} = (a_1, \ldots, a_n), \mathbf{b} = (b_1, \ldots, b_n) \in \mathbb{R}^n$. The relation *vector $\mathbf{a}$ is lexicographically less than or equal to vector $\mathbf{b}$*, written $\mathbf{a} \preceq \mathbf{b}$, is recursively defined by:

$$() \preceq ()$$
$$(a_1, \ldots, a_n) \preceq (b_1, \ldots, b_n) \iff$$
$$a_1 < b_1 \vee \left(a_1 = b_1 \wedge (a_2, \ldots, a_n) \preceq (b_2, \ldots, b_n) \right) \quad \text{for } n \geq 1$$

A vector $\mathbf{c}$ is said to precede lexicographically a vector $\mathbf{d}$, written $\mathbf{c} \prec \mathbf{d}$, if $\mathbf{c} \preceq \mathbf{d} \wedge \mathbf{c} \neq \mathbf{d}$ for $\mathbf{c}, \mathbf{d} \in \mathbb{R}^n$.

Definition 2.2. For $d, n \in \mathbb{N}$, $d \leq n$ and $\mathbf{i} = (i_1, \ldots, i_n) \in \mathbb{R}^n$, we write $\mathbf{i}_{|d}$ to denote the projection of the vector $\mathbf{i}$ to the outer d dimensions, i.e., $\mathbf{i}_{|d} = (i_1, \ldots, i_d)$.

Definition 2.3. We write frac(q) for the fractional part of a rational number $q \in \mathbb{Q}$, i.e., we define frac(q) := $q - \lfloor q \rfloor$.

We use the notation $a \equiv_l b$ for $a, b \in \mathbb{Z}$, $l \in \mathbb{N}_+$ to denote that a and b are equivalent modulo l, i.e., $l \mid (a - b)$.

2.1.2 Rings

Throughout this work, we will encounter the concepts of a ring, domain and field from commutative algebra. We assume that the reader is familiar with these concepts, but review the most important properties.

Definition 2.4. A structure $\underline{D} = (D, +, -, \cdot, 0, 1)$ is called a *ring*, if $+$ and $\cdot$ are associative and commutative, $\cdot$ distributes over $+$, 0 is neutral w.r.t. $+$, $-$ is the inverse operation w.r.t. $+$, 1 is neutral w.r.t. $\cdot$ and $0 \neq 1$.[1]

Structure $\underline{D}$ is called a *domain*, if it is a ring and it has no zero-divisors, that is, $(\forall x, y : x, y \in D : x \cdot y = 0 \Rightarrow x = 0 \vee y = 0)$ holds.

Structure $\underline{D}$ is called a *field*, if it is a domain and has multiplicative inverses except for zero, i.e., $(\forall x : x \in D - \{0\} : (\exists y : y \in D : x \cdot y = 1))$.

To simplify the language we use, we will write "a ring D" to mean an algebraic structure over the set D with operators $+$, $-$, $\cdot$ and constants 0 and 1; likewise for "domain" and "field".

Definition 2.5. Let D be a ring and $a, b \in D$. a is said to *divide* b, written $a \mid b$, if and only if there exists $c \in D - \{0\}$ such that $a \cdot c = b$; a is called a *unit* if a divides 1; a is called a *zero-divisor* if it divides 0. If there exists a unit $u \in D$ such that $a \cdot u = b$, then a and b are called *associated*, written $a \sim b$.

Definition 2.6. Let D be a ring and $a, b, g \in D$. Then g is called a *greatest common divisor* (GCD) of a and b if and only if g divides a and b and any other $h \in D$ which divides both a and b also divides g.

Definition 2.7. Let D be a ring and $a, b \in D$ such that any two greatest common divisors $g \in D$ and $g' \in D$ of a and b are associated, i.e., $g \sim g'$. Then, we write $g \sim \gcd(a, b)$ to denote that g is a greatest common divisor of a and b. If the greatest common divisors of any $a, b \in D$ are associated, we say that greatest common divisors are *unique* in D (modulo multiplication with units).

Definition 2.8. Let D be a ring with unique GCDs. If, for any $a, b, g \in D$ such that $g \sim \gcd(a, b)$, there exist $e, f \in D$ such that $g = e \cdot a + f \cdot b$, then D is called a *Bézout ring*.

Let us now recall a well-known general, abstract way to compute greatest common divisors in rings which allow a kind of division with remainder. The sequence of remainders describes a unimodular matrix (i.e., a matrix whose determinant is associated to 1) which shows how to compute the GCD from the

---

[1] Some authors call this a domain and their definition of ring allows $0 = 1$; what we call a domain is then called an *integral* domain. Since we never deal with degenerate rings where $0 = 1$, we allow ourselves to use the simpler terminology.

given elements. The following lemma states implicitly that any ring, in which we can compute such remainder sequences for any two elements, is a Bézout ring. The "remainder" computation is quite abstract, i.e., the lemma does not assume that the remainder is "less than" the divisor in any sense. The only requirement is that the remainder sequence has to be finite.

Lemma 2.9. *Let D be a ring, $n \in \mathbb{N}_+$, and $g_0, \ldots, g_{n+1} \in D$, $q_1, \ldots, q_n \in D$ such that $g_{i-1} = q_i \cdot g_i + g_{i+1}$ for $1 \leq i \leq n$ and $g_{n+1} = 0$. Then g_n is a GCD of g_0 and g_1. In addition, there exists a unimodular matrix $U \in D^{2 \times 2}$ such that*

$$\begin{pmatrix} g_n \\ 0 \end{pmatrix} = U \cdot \begin{pmatrix} g_0 \\ g_1 \end{pmatrix}.$$

Proof. Let n and $g_0, \ldots, g_{n+1}$ be as stated. First, we show that g_n divides every g_i with $0 \leq i \leq n$ by a downward induction.

$i = n :$ Obviously, $g_n \mid g_n$.

$i = n - 1 :$ Since $g_{n-1} = q_n \cdot g_n + 0$ by hypothesis, $g_n \mid g_{n-1}$.

$i, i - 1 \rightarrow i - 2$ for $2 \leq i \leq n :$
   Assume $g_n \mid g_i$ and $g_n \mid g_{i-1}$. Since $g_{i-2} = q_{i-1} \cdot g_{i-1} + g_i$, it follows that g_n divides g_{i-2}, too.

Hence, g_n divides g_0 and g_1. Second, we show that any d that divides g_0 and g_1 also divides g_n. We prove by induction that d divides every g_i for $0 \leq i \leq n$.

$i = 0$ and $i = 1 :$ True by assumption.

$i, i + 1 \rightarrow i + 2$ for $0 \leq i \leq n - 2 :$
   Assume $d \mid g_i$ and $d \mid g_{i+1}$. Since $g_{i+2} = g_i - q_{i+1} \cdot g_{i+1}$, this implies $d \mid g_{i+2}$.

Hence, d divides g_n. Both properties together imply that g_n is a greatest common divisor of g_0 and g_1.

A unimodular matrix U with the stated properties can be constructed by observing that

$$U_i := \begin{pmatrix} 0 & 1 \\ 1 & -q_i \end{pmatrix}$$

for $1 \leq i \leq n$ has the two properties

$$\begin{pmatrix} g_i \\ g_{i+1} \end{pmatrix} = U_i \cdot \begin{pmatrix} g_{i-1} \\ g_i \end{pmatrix}, \quad \det U_i = -1$$

and, hence, $U := U_n \cdot \ldots \cdot U_1$ has the stated property. $\square$

Note that the lemma does not state that taking remainders is possible in D or that any remainder sequence one constructs terminates (i.e., there is no guarantee that one reaches a remainder in the sequence which is 0). This has to be proved for a given procedure which determines q_i and g_{i+1} from g_{i-1} and g_i in a given ring D for the lemma to be applicable.

2.1.3 Polynomials and Logical Formulas

Definition 2.10. Let D be a ring, X a formal unknown, $n \in \mathbb{N}$ and $a_0, \ldots, a_n \in D$. Expressions of the form $\sum_{i=0}^{n} a_i X^i$ are called univariate *polynomials* in X over D. The set of all univariate polynomials over D in the unknown X is denoted by $D[X]$. Let $f = \sum_{i=0}^{n} a_i X^i$ be a polynomial with $a_n \neq 0$. Then, we call

$$\mathrm{HC}(f) := a_n \qquad \text{the highest coefficient of } f, \text{ and}$$
$$\deg(f) := n \qquad \text{the degree of } f.$$

For several unknowns $X_1, \ldots, X_k$, the set of multivariate polynomials over D is defined by:

$$D[\,] := D$$
$$D[X_1, \ldots, X_i, X_{i+1}] := (D[X_1, \ldots, X_i])[X_{i+1}] \qquad \text{for } i \geq 0$$

The set of rational functions in the unknowns $X_1, \ldots, X_k$ over D is defined by:

$$D(X_1, \ldots, X_k) := \{\frac{f}{g} \mid f, g \in D[X_1, \ldots, X_k], g \neq 0\}$$

The polyhedron model (cf. Section 2.2.1) is based on linear and affine expressions. In the following, $\mathcal{V}$ is used to denote the set of variable names.

Definition 2.11. Let D be a ring, $n \in \mathbb{N}$, $a_0, a_1, \ldots, a_n \in D$ and $v_1, \ldots, v_n \in \mathcal{V}$. An expression of the form $a_0 + \sum_{i=1}^{n} a_i v_i$ is called *affine*. The set of all affine expressions over D in the variables $v_1, \ldots, v_n$ is denoted by $AffExpr_D(v_1, \ldots, v_n)$. A *linear* expression is an affine expression with $a_0 = 0$.

Definition 2.12. Let $n \in \mathbb{N}$, $v_1, \ldots, v_n$ be variables, $f \in \mathbb{Z}[v_1, \ldots, v_n]$ a polynomial with integral coefficients and $\rho \in \{=, \neq, <, \leq, \geq, >\}$. Then, $f \rho 0$ is called an *atomic* formula; in addition, the formulas true and false are considered atomic formulas, too. The set of all atomic formulas in the variables $\mathcal{V} = \{v_1, \ldots, v_n\}$ is denoted by $At(\mathcal{V})$.[2]

Atomic formulas are defined with coefficients from $\mathbb{Z}$ independently of the structure they will be evaluated in later. But, since every structure in which we will evaluate formulas is a ring, there is always a homomorphism from $z \in \mathbb{Z}$ to a ring element, since z is either zero or a (possibly negated) sum of 1s.

Definition 2.13. The set of *quantifier-free* formulas in the variables $\mathcal{V}$, denoted by $Qf(\mathcal{V})$, is inductively defined by:

- $At(\mathcal{V}) \subseteq Qf(\mathcal{V})$,

- if $\varphi \in Qf(\mathcal{V})$, then $(\neg \varphi) \in Qf(\mathcal{V})$,

---

[2]Note that we only use one signature, namely the operations $+, -, \cdot, 0, 1$ and the relations $=, \neq, <, \leq, \geq, >$ throughout this thesis and, hence, omit the signature in the denotation of formulas.

- if $\varphi, \psi \in Qf(\mathcal{V})$, then $(\varphi \, \nu \, \psi) \in Qf(\mathcal{V})$ for $\nu \in \{\wedge, \vee, \rightarrow, \leftrightarrow\}$.

A quantifier-free formula is *positive*, if it contains only the logical connectors $\wedge$ and $\vee$ and its atomic formulas do not use the relation $\neq$. A quantifier-free formula is in *disjunctive normal form*, if it is of the form $\bigvee_{i=1}^{m} \bigwedge_{k=1}^{l_i} \alpha_{i,k}$ where $m, l_1, \ldots, l_m \in \mathbb{N}_+$ and all $\alpha_{i,k}$ are atomic formulas. We call a formula φ *affine*, written $\varphi \in A\!f\!f(\mathcal{V})$, if the formula is positive and all the expressions in the formula are affine.

We will omit parentheses by applying the usual precedence rules, i.e., $\wedge$ binds stronger than $\vee$ and $\vee$ binds stronger than $\rightarrow, \leftrightarrow$.

Definition 2.14. The set of first-order formulas $Fo(\mathcal{V})$ in the variables $\mathcal{V}$ is inductively defined by:

- $Qf(\mathcal{V}) \subseteq Fo(\mathcal{V})$,

- if $\varphi \in Fo(\mathcal{V})$ and $x \in \mathcal{V}$, then $(\exists x \; \varphi), (\forall x \; \varphi) \in Fo(\mathcal{V})$.

The set of free variables of a formula $\varphi \in Fo(\mathcal{V})$ is denoted by $fv(\varphi)$.

In the following, we will denote implication and equivalence by $\rightarrow$ and $\leftrightarrow$, respectively, when they occur within a logical formula, i.e., $\rightarrow$ and $\leftrightarrow$ are part of formal objects. To denote a semantical implication or equivalence (when stating a lemma, for example), we will use $\Rightarrow$ and $\Leftrightarrow$, respectively. Similarly, the notation for a quantified formula as a formal object is given in Definition 2.14. When we need to quantify variables semantically, we use the Dijkstra notation for quantifiers. For example, we will write, e.g., $(\exists n : n \in \mathbb{N} : f(n) > 0)$, to denote the domain of the quantified variable ($n \in \mathbb{N}$ in this example).

Definition 2.15. For any atomic formula $\varphi \in At(\mathcal{V})$, we define the formulas φ^+ and $(\neg \varphi)^+$ by:

$$(f \neq 0)^+ := f < 0 \vee f > 0$$
$$(f \, \rho \, 0)^+ := f \, \rho \, 0 \qquad\qquad \text{for } \rho \in \{<, \leq, =, \geq, >\}$$
$$\big(\neg(f = 0)\big)^+ := f < 0 \vee f > 0$$
$$\big(\neg(f \neq 0)\big)^+ := f = 0$$
$$\big(\neg(f < 0)\big)^+ := f \geq 0$$
$$\big(\neg(f \leq 0)\big)^+ := f > 0$$
$$\big(\neg(f \geq 0)\big)^+ := f < 0$$
$$\big(\neg(f > 0)\big)^+ := f \leq 0$$

For any quantifier-free formula $\varphi \in Qf(\mathcal{V})$, we define the formula φ^+ by the following recursive procedure:

$$(\varphi\,\rho\,\psi)^+ := \varphi^+\,\rho\,\psi^+ \qquad\qquad\qquad \text{for } \rho\in\{\wedge,\vee\}$$

$$(\varphi\to\psi)^+ := (\neg\varphi)^+\vee\psi^+$$

$$(\varphi\leftrightarrow\psi)^+ := (\varphi^+\wedge\psi^+)\vee\big((\neg\varphi)^+\vee(\neg\psi)^+\big)$$

$$\big(\neg(\varphi\vee\psi)\big)^+ := (\neg\varphi)^+\wedge(\neg\psi)^+$$

$$\big(\neg(\varphi\wedge\psi)\big)^+ := (\neg\varphi)^+\vee(\neg\psi)^+$$

$$\big(\neg(\varphi\to\psi)\big)^+ := \varphi^+\wedge(\neg\psi)^+$$

$$\big(\neg(\varphi\leftrightarrow\psi)\big)^+ := \big((\neg\varphi)^+\wedge\psi^+\big)\vee\big(\varphi^+\wedge(\neg\psi)^+\big)$$

Note that φ^+ contains no negations, neither in the form of the logical connective $\neg$, nor "hidden" as the relation $\neq$ or in the connectives $\to$ or $\leftrightarrow$.

Lemma 2.16. *For any $\varphi\in Qf(\mathcal{V})$, $\varphi^+\leftrightarrow\varphi$ holds in $\mathbb{R}$ and φ^+ is a positive formula.*

Proof. Obvious from the well-known laws for negation (e.g., de-Morgan's law) and the properties of the ordering relations. $\qquad\qquad\qquad\square$

Definition 2.17. For any positive formula $\varphi\in Qf(\mathcal{V})$, we define the formula $\varphi^\vee$ by the following recursive procedure:

$$\alpha^\vee := \alpha \qquad\qquad\qquad \text{for } \alpha\in At(\mathcal{V})$$

$$(\varphi\vee\psi)^\vee := \varphi^\vee\vee\psi^\vee$$

$$(\varphi\wedge\psi)^\vee := \bigvee_{1\le i\le n,\,1\le j\le m}(\beta_i\wedge\gamma_j) \quad\text{where } \varphi^\vee=\bigvee_{i=1}^n\beta_i \text{ and } \psi^\vee=\bigvee_{j=1}^m\gamma_j$$

Lemma 2.18. *For any positive formula $\varphi\in Qf(\mathcal{V})$, $\varphi^\vee\leftrightarrow\varphi$ holds in $\mathbb{R}$ and $\varphi^\vee$ is a positive formula in disjunctive normal form.*

Proof. Obvious from the definition and because $\wedge$ distributes over $\vee$. $\qquad\square$

Corollary 2.19. *Let $\varphi\in Qf(\mathcal{V})$. Then $\varphi^{+\vee} := (\varphi^+)^\vee$ is a positive formula in disjunctive normal form and $\varphi^{+\vee}\leftrightarrow\varphi$ holds in $\mathbb{R}$.*

Proof. Follows directly from the two preceding lemmas. $\qquad\qquad\qquad\square$

2.1.4 Polyhedra

Definition 2.20. Let $n,m\in\mathbb{N}$, $\mathbf{v}=(v_1,\dots,v_n)$ be variables and $f_1,\dots,f_m\in AffExpr_{\mathbb{Z}}(\mathbf{v})$. Then the set P defined by

$$P := \{\mathbf{x}\in\mathbb{R}^n \mid f_1(\mathbf{x})\ge 0\wedge\cdots\wedge f_m(\mathbf{x})\ge 0\}$$

is called a *polyhedron*. A polyhedron P which is bounded, i.e., which satisfies the condition $\big(\exists d : d\in\mathbb{R} : (\forall\mathbf{x} : \mathbf{x}\in P : |x|\le d)\big)$, is called a *polytope*.

Most of the time, the polyhedra and related objects dealt with in the polyhedron model depend on so-called *structure parameters* $\mathbf{p} = (p_1, \ldots, p_k)$ for $k \in \mathbb{N}$, i.e., run-time constants which are unknown at compile time/parallelisation time. Therefore, we introduce the concept of parametric polyhedra.

Definition 2.21. Let $k, n, m \in \mathbb{N}$, $\mathbf{p} = (p_1, \ldots, p_k)$, $\mathbf{v} = (v_1, \ldots, v_n)$, $C \subseteq \mathbb{Z}^k$ and $f_1, \ldots, f_m \in \textit{AffExpr}_\mathbb{Z}(\mathbf{v}, \mathbf{p})$. Then the family of sets $P(\mathbf{p})$ defined by

$$P(\mathbf{p}) := \{\mathbf{x} \in \mathbb{R}^n \mid f_1(\mathbf{x}, \mathbf{p}) \geq 0 \wedge \cdots \wedge f_m(\mathbf{x}, \mathbf{p}) \geq 0\}$$

for $\mathbf{p} \in C$ is called a parametric *polyhedron*. C is called the *context*.

Note that $P(\mathbf{p})$ is a non-parametric polyhedron for every choice of $\mathbf{p} \in \mathbb{Z}^k$. The definition of parametric polyhedra is a generalisation of the definition of ordinary polyhedra, because the case $k = 0$ coincides with the definition of non-parametric polyhedra: in this case, the family of polyhedra defined by $f_1, \ldots, f_m$ consists of only one polyhedron.

Definition 2.22. A *parametric Z-polyhedron* $Z(\mathbf{p}) \subseteq \mathbb{Z}^m$ is the image of the integral points of a parametric polyhedron $P(\mathbf{p}) \subseteq \mathbb{R}^n$ under a parametric integral affine mapping $f : \mathbb{Z}^{n+k} \to \mathbb{Z}^m$, i.e., $Z(\mathbf{p}) = \{f(\mathbf{x}, \mathbf{p}) \mid \mathbf{x} \in P(\mathbf{p}) \cap \mathbb{Z}^n\}$.

For example, the Z-polyhedron containing the even numbers can be defined by $P = \mathbb{R}$ and $f(x) = 2x$.

The following lemma says that a finite union of polyhedra described by φ, which forms another polyhedron, can be described by bounds found in φ, i.e., no other bounds than those provided by φ are needed to describe the union by a conjunction of atomic formulas.

Lemma 2.23. *Let* $\varphi \in \textit{Aff}(\{v_1, \ldots, v_n\})$ *be a such that* φ *defines a polyhedron. Then*

$$\beta := \bigwedge\{\alpha \mid \alpha \text{ is an atomic formula of } \varphi, \forall v_1 \cdots \forall v_n(\varphi \to \alpha) \text{ holds in } \mathbb{R}\}$$

is equivalent to φ *in* $\mathbb{R}$.

The proof can be found in the literature [BFT01, Theorem 3].

2.1.5 Periodic Numbers

Definition 2.24. A one-dimensional *periodic number* is a function $c : \mathbb{Z} \to \mathbb{Q}$ with a period $l \in \mathbb{N}_+$, i.e., $(\forall p : p \in \mathbb{Z} : c(p) = c(p + l))$. The set of all periodic numbers is denoted by $\mathcal{P}$:

$$\mathcal{P} := \left\{c : \mathbb{Z} \to \mathbb{Q} \mid \left(\exists l : l \in \mathbb{N} : \left(\forall p : p \in \mathbb{Z} : c(p) = c(p + l)\right)\right)\right\}$$

If $l \in \mathbb{N}_+$ is a minimal period of $c \in \mathcal{P}$, then l is called the *least period* of c, written $\mathrm{lp}(c)$. To specify a one-dimensional periodic number with period l, we write $[v_0, \ldots, v_{l-1}]$ for $v_0, \ldots, v_{l-1} \in \mathbb{Q}$ meaning that the periodic number is defined as:

$$[v_0, \ldots, v_{l-1}](p) := \begin{cases} v_0 & \text{if } p \equiv_l 0 \\ \vdots \\ v_{l-1} & \text{if } p \equiv_l l-1 \end{cases}$$

For example, $c = [1, \frac{1}{2}]$ denotes the periodic number which evaluates to $c(p) = 1$ for $p \equiv_2 0$ and $c(p) = \frac{1}{2}$ for $p \equiv_2 1$. Obviously, if $l \in \mathbb{N}_+$ is a period of $c \in \mathcal{P}$, then every integral multiple of l is a period of c, too. $(\mathcal{P}, +, -, \cdot, 0, 1)$, where $+$, $-$ and $\cdot$ are defined by pointwise operations, forms a commutative ring with zero-divisors. For example, $[1, 0] \cdot [0, 1] = 0$.

Lemma 2.25. $c \in \mathcal{P}$ *is a zero-divisor in* $(\mathcal{P}, +, -, \cdot)$ *if and only if there exists* $z \in \mathbb{Z}$ *such that* $c(z) = 0$.

Proof. Let $c \in \mathcal{P}$ and $z \in \mathbb{Z}$ such that $c(z) = 0$. Let $l \in \mathbb{N}_+$ be a period of c. Let $d : \mathbb{Z} \to \mathbb{Q}$ be defined by:

$$d(p) = \begin{cases} 1 & \text{if } p \equiv_l z \\ 0 & otherwise \end{cases}$$

Then $d \in \mathcal{P}$, $d \neq 0$ and $c \cdot d = 0$ by construction. Conversely, if $c \cdot d = 0$ for $c, d \in \mathcal{P} - \{0\}$, then there exists $z \in \mathbb{Z}$ such that $d(z) \neq 0$ and, hence, $c(z) = 0$ follows. $\qquad\square$

Definition 2.26. An n-dimensional *periodic number* c with *periods* $(l_1, \ldots, l_n) \in \mathbb{N}_+^n$ is a function $c : \mathbb{Z}^n \to \mathbb{Q}$ such that either $n = 1$ and c is a one-dimensional periodic number with period l_1, or $n \geq 2$, $(\forall p_1 : p_1 \in \mathbb{Z} : c(p_1, p_2, \ldots, p_n) = c(p_1 + l_1, p_2, \ldots, p_n))$ and for every $p_1 \in \mathbb{Z}$ the function d defined by $d(p_2, \ldots, p_n) := c(p_1, p_2, \ldots, p_n)$ is an $(n-1)$-dimensional periodic number with periods $(l_2, \ldots, l_n)$.

The set of all n-dimensional periodic numbers is denoted by $\mathcal{P}_n$.

Again, $(\mathcal{P}_n, +, -, \cdot, 0, 1)$ with pointwise operations is a ring with zero-divisors.

Due to currying (i.e., the equivalence of functions on n tuples and higher-order functions with n arguments), an n-dimensional periodic number can be regarded as a one-dimensional periodic number that evaluates to $(n-1)$-dimensional periodic numbers instead of rationals. For example,

$$c = [[1, 2], [3, 4, 5]]$$

is a two-dimensional periodic number as $c(p_1) = [1, 2]$ for $p_1 \equiv_2 0$ and $c(p_1) = [3, 4, 5]$ for $p_1 \equiv_2 1$. The least period of c is $(2, 6)$ since the least common period of the second dimension is 6.

2.1.6 Univariate Quasi-Polynomials

Since the n-dimensional periodic numbers form a ring, we can form polynomial rings over them. We start with the polynomials over the one-dimensional periodic numbers.

Definition 2.27. The polynomial ring $\mathcal{P}[X]$ over the one-dimensional periodic numbers is called the ring of univariate *quasi-polynomials*. For $u \in \mathbb{N}$ and $f = \sum_{i=0}^{u} c_i X^i \in \mathcal{P}[X]$, we define the evaluation $f(p)$ of f at a point $p \in \mathbb{Z}$ by

$$f(p) := \sum_{i=0}^{u} c_i(p) \cdot p^i.$$

Any common period of $c_0, \ldots, c_u$ is called a *period* of f. The least common period of $c_0, \ldots, c_u$ is called the *least period* of f, written $\mathrm{lp}(f)$.

Note that in the evaluation the value substituted for the formal unknown X is also used to evaluate the coefficients, which are periodic numbers. Hence, the coefficients may assume different values depending on the residue class of the substituted value modulo the periods of the coefficients. We extend the notation for evaluation to objects which contain quasi-polynomials. For example, for vectors $\mathbf{v} \in \mathcal{P}[X]^m$ and matrices $A \in \mathcal{P}[X]^{m \times l}$, we write $\mathbf{v}(p)$ and $A(p)$, respectively, to denote that every entry of the vector or matrix shall be evaluated at $p \in \mathbb{Z}$ to obtain a vector or matrix, respectively, with all the evaluated polynomials as entries.

Since the coefficients are periodic numbers, a quasi-polynomial f can be described equivalently by a list of l polynomials where l is a common period of the coefficients of f. Each polynomial describes the function values of f for a certain residue class modulo l.

Definition 2.28. Let $l, k \in \mathbb{N}_+$ and $f = \sum_{i=0}^{u} c_i X^i \in \mathcal{P}[X]$. We define $\mathrm{con}_l(f, k) \in \mathcal{P}[X]$ by

$$\mathrm{con}_l(f, k) := \sum_{i=0}^{u} c_i(k)(lX + k)^i.$$

If l is a common period of $c_0, \ldots, c_u$, then we call $\mathrm{con}_l(f, k)$ for $0 \leq k < l$ the *constituents* of f.

For example, for $f = [3, \frac{1}{2}] \cdot X + [1, \frac{1}{2}]$, we have $\mathrm{con}_2(f, 0) = 3(2 \cdot X) + 1 = 6X + 1$ and $\mathrm{con}_2(f, 1) = \frac{1}{2}(2 \cdot X + 1) + \frac{1}{2} = X + 1$. Note that the coefficients of the constituents differ from the coefficients of f, because the function values of f at $p = 2 \cdot p' + k$ are mapped to the values of the kth constituent at p', i.e., $f(p) = \mathrm{con}_l(f, k)(p')$. This observation is formalised in the following lemma.

Lemma 2.29. *Let $f \in \mathcal{P}[X]$ and $l \in \mathbb{N}_+$. Then $f(p) = \mathrm{con}_l(f, k)(p')$ if $p = l \cdot p' + k$.*

Proof. The proposition follows directly from Definition 2.28. $\square$

To form a quasi-polynomial from given constituents, we introduce the following notation which is the reverse of the con operation.

Definition 2.30. Let $l \in \mathbb{N}_+$ and $f_0, \ldots, f_{l-1} \in \mathbb{Q}[X]$. Then $\mathrm{comb}(f_0, \ldots, f_{l-1})$ denotes the quasi-polynomial $f \in \mathcal{P}[X]$ defined by:

$$
f(p) := \begin{cases}
f_0(p') & \text{if } p = lp' + 0 \\
f_1(p') & \text{if } p = lp' + 1 \\
\vdots \\
f_{l-1}(p') & \text{if } p = lp' + (l-1)
\end{cases}
$$

Operation comb can be extended to constituents which are themselves quasi-polynomials.

Definition 2.31. Let $l \in \mathbb{N}_+$, $f_0, \ldots, f_{l-1} \in \mathcal{P}[X]$ and let $l' \in \mathbb{N}_+$ be a common period of $f_0, \ldots, f_{l-1}$. Then, we define:

$$
\begin{aligned}
\mathrm{comb}(f_1, \ldots, f_{l-1}) := \mathrm{comb}(&\mathrm{con}_{l'}(f_0, 0), \ldots, \mathrm{con}_{l'}(f_{l-1}, 0), \\
&\mathrm{con}_{l'}(f_0, 1), \ldots, \mathrm{con}_{l'}(f_{l-1}, 1), \\
&\qquad\qquad \vdots \\
&\mathrm{con}_{l'}(f_0, l'-1), \ldots, \mathrm{con}_{l'}(f_{l-1}, l'-1) \\
)&
\end{aligned}
$$

The quasi-polynomial created by $\mathrm{comb}(f_0, \ldots, f_{l-1})$ iterates through the first constituent of $f_0, \ldots, f_{l-1}$, then through the second constituent of $f_0, \ldots, f_{l-1}$ and so one. Since polynomials from $\mathbb{Q}[X]$ are quasi-polynomials with period 1, comb defined in Definition 2.31 is a generalisation of the previous definition (Definition 2.30).

Since integrality plays such an important role in loop parallelisation, we will deal only with quasi-polynomials which evaluate to integral function values. To this end, we introduce the class of integer-valued univariate quasi-polynomials.

Definition 2.32. The sub-ring $EQP := \left\{ f \in \mathcal{P}[X] \mid \left(\forall p : p \in \mathbb{Z} : f(p) \in \mathbb{Z} \right) \right\}$ of $\mathcal{P}[X]$ is called the ring of univariate *entire quasi-polynomials*.

In fact, $(EQP, +, -, \cdot, 0, 1)$ is a ring since the sum, difference and product of integral values are again integral. The polynomial $f = [3, \frac{1}{2}] \cdot X + [1, \frac{1}{2}]$ is an entire quasi-polynomial because, for $p \equiv_2 0$, we have $f(p) = 3p + 1 \in \mathbb{Z}$ and, for $p \equiv_2 1$, we have $f(p) = \frac{1}{2}p + \frac{1}{2} \in \mathbb{Z}$.

From the above definitions it is clear that entire quasi-polynomials are exactly those quasi-polynomials whose constituents are polynomials over the integers.

Lemma 2.33. *Let $f \in \mathcal{P}[X]$ and $l \in \mathbb{N}_+$ be a period of f. Then $f \in EQP$ if and only if $\mathrm{con}_l(f, k) \in \mathbb{Z}[X]$ for $0 \le k < l$.*

Proof. Clear from the definition of con_l and the fact that l is a period of f. $\square$

The ring EQP has zero-divisors, since, e.g., $[1,0] \cdot [0,1] = 0$. The polynomials in EQP can have zeros for two different reasons. First, the coefficients of a quasi-polynomial may vanish periodically and, hence, the zero is periodic, too. This means that a constituent of the quasi-polynomial is the zero polynomial. Second, a non-zero constituent can have non-periodic roots. For example, with $f = [1,0] \cdot X$, we have $f(p) = 0$ for every odd p, because $con_2(f, 1) = 0$. In addition, f vanishes also for $p = 0$ due to the root $p = 0$ of $con_2(f, 0) = 2X$. This observation is formalised in the following lemma.

Lemma 2.34. *Let $f \in EQP$ and $R(f) := \{p \in \mathbb{Z} \mid f(p) = 0\}$. Then there exists some finite set $M \subset \mathbb{Z}$, some $l \in \mathbb{N}_+$ and $k \in \{0, \ldots, l\}$ different integers $0 \leq n_1 < \cdots < n_k < l$ such that*

$$R(f) = M \cup (l\mathbb{Z} + n_1) \cup \cdots \cup (l\mathbb{Z} + n_k).$$

Proof. Every constituent $con_l(f, i)$ for $0 \leq i < l$ is either the zero polynomial and, hence, $f(p) = 0$ for all $p \in l\mathbb{Z} + i$, or $con_l(f, i)$ is not the zero polynomial and, hence, has finitely many zeros. $\square$

Lemma 2.35. *Let $f, g, h \in EQP$ with common period $l \in \mathbb{N}_+$. Then the following equivalence holds:*

$$f = g \cdot h \quad \Longleftrightarrow \quad \big(\forall i : 0 \leq i < l : con_l(f, i) = con_l(g, i) \cdot con_l(h, i)\big).$$

Proof. Let f, g, h, l be as stated. Assume $f = g \cdot h$ and let $i \in \{0, \ldots, l-1\}$. Then, for any $p \in \mathbb{Z}$, $con_l(f, i)(p) = f(lp+i) = g(lp+i) \cdot h(lp+i) = con_l(g, i)(p) \cdot con_l(h, i)(p)$.
Conversely, assume $\big(\forall i : 0 \leq i < l : con(f, i) = con(g, i) \cdot con_l(h, i)\big)$ and let $p, p', i \in \mathbb{Z}$ such that $p = lp' + i$. Then $f(p) = f(lp' + i) = con_l(f, i) = con_l(g, i) \cdot con_l(h, i) = g(lp' + i) \cdot h(lp' + i) = g(p) \cdot h(p)$. $\square$

2.1.7 Multivariate Quasi-Polynomials and Counting $\mathbb{Z}$-Polyhedra

We now introduce multivariate quasi-polynomials as a generalisation of univariate quasi-polynomials.

Definition 2.36. Let $n \in \mathbb{N}_+$ and $\mathbf{X} = X_1, \ldots, X_n$. The multivariate polynomial ring $\mathcal{P}_n[\mathbf{X}]$ over the n-dimensional periodic numbers is called the ring of n-variate *quasi-polynomials*. Let $E \subset \mathbb{N}^n$ be finite and $f = \sum_{\mathbf{e} \in E} c_{\mathbf{e}} X^{\mathbf{e}} \in \mathcal{P}_n[\mathbf{X}]$ with n-dimensional periodic numbers $c_{\mathbf{e}}$ for $\mathbf{e} \in E$. We define the evaluation of f at $\mathbf{p} \in \mathbb{Z}^n$, written as $f(\mathbf{p})$, by

$$f(\mathbf{p}) := \sum_{\mathbf{e} \in E} c_{\mathbf{e}} \mathbf{p}^{\mathbf{e}}$$

where $\mathbf{p}^{\mathbf{e}}$ is componentwise exponentiation (i.e., $(p_1, \ldots, p_n)^{(e_1, \ldots, e_n)} := (p_1^{e_1}, \ldots, p_n^{e_n})$).

In this thesis, we encounter multivariate quasi-polynomials when counting the number of integral points in a parametric Z-polyhedron. The following lemma is a well-known consequence of Ehrhart theory (for Ehrhart theory, see, e.g., [BR07, Chapter 3]).

Lemma 2.37. *Let $Z(\mathbf{p}) \subset \mathbb{Z}^n$ be a Z-polyhedron which depends on the (linear) parameters $\mathbf{p} \in \mathbb{Z}^k$. Then the number of integral points in $Z(\mathbf{p})$ is a piecewise multivariate quasi-polynomial, i.e., there exist $c_1, \dots, c_l \in \mathit{Aff}(\mathbf{p})$ and $\rho_1, \dots, \rho_l \in \mathcal{P}_k[X_1, \dots, X_k]$ such that*

$$|Z(\mathbf{p})| = \begin{cases} \rho_1(\mathbf{p}) & \text{if } c_1(\mathbf{p}) \text{ holds} \\ \vdots & \\ \rho_l(\mathbf{p}) & \text{if } c_l(\mathbf{p}) \text{ holds} \\ 0 & \text{otherwise} \end{cases}$$

There are algorithms [VSB+07] which compute, from the description of a Z-polyhedron $Z(\mathbf{p})$, a set of condition/quasi-polynomial pairs (c_i, ρ_i) such that the value $\rho_i(\mathbf{p})$ of the quasi-polynomial ρ_i gives the number of integral points in $Z(\mathbf{p})$ if $c_i(\mathbf{p})$ holds.

Example 2.38. The number of integral points $|Z(p,q)|$ in the parametric Z-polyhedron defined by $Z(p,q) = \{2 \cdot i \mid 0 \le i \le \min(\frac{p}{2}, q) \wedge i \in \mathbb{Z}\}$ is given by:

$$|Z(p,q)| = \begin{cases} \frac{p}{2} + [1, \frac{1}{2}]_p & \text{if } 0 \le p \le 2q \\ q+1 & \text{if } p \ge 2q \ge 0 \\ 0 & \text{otherwise} \end{cases}$$

Counting the integral points in a union of Z-polyhedra is possible, too, by computing a disjoint union of the Z-polyhedra first with one of the available libraries for Z-polyhedra.

2.1.8 Algebraic Numbers and Cylindrical Algebraic Decomposition

Code generation for non-linearly bounded index sets (cf. Section 5.5) requires to solve polynomial equalities with integral or rational coefficients. As not every solution is a rational number, we have to go beyond the rationals. But we need not go as far as to the reals, because we are not interested in transcendental numbers like π. An intermediate class of numbers is the set of algebraic numbers – exactly the numbers that can occur as real zeros of polynomials over the integers.

Definition 2.39. The set $\mathbb{A} := \{x \in \mathbb{R} \mid f \in \mathbb{Z}[X], f \ne 0, f(x) = 0\}$ is called the *set of algebraic numbers*.

Obviously, $\mathbb{Q} \subsetneq \mathbb{A} \subsetneq \mathbb{R}$, because any rational number $\frac{a}{b} \in \mathbb{Q}$ is a zero of $b \cdot x - a$, $\sqrt{2} \in \mathbb{A}$, since $\sqrt{2}$ is a root of $x^2 - 2$ and $\pi \notin \mathbb{A}$. The algebraic numbers are closed under addition, multiplication and division (except by 0, of course) and, in fact, they form a field. Algorithms for the arithmetic operations in $\mathbb{A}$ can be found in the literature [Loo83].

One way to represent an algebraic number $\alpha \in \mathbb{A}$ is by a triple (f, a, b) where $f \in \mathbb{Z}[X]$ is a square-free polynomial[3] with $f(\alpha) = 0$ and two rational numbers $a, b \in \mathbb{Q}$ such that $a < \alpha < b$ and $(\forall x : a \leq x \leq b : f(x) = 0 \rightarrow x = \alpha)$, i.e., α is the only root of f in $[a, b]$. Algorithms for computing f, a and b can be found in the literature [Loo83]. Note that, by interval bisection, on can make $b - a$ arbitrarily small. Since α is the only root of f in $[a, b]$ and f is square-free, the signs of $f(a)$ and $f(b)$ must be different and, hence, the sign of $f(\frac{a+b}{2})$ tells whether $\alpha = \frac{a+b}{2}$, $\alpha \in]a, \frac{a+b}{2}[$, or $\alpha \in]\frac{a+b}{2}, b[$.

To describe the root of a polynomial, i.e., an algebraic number, in dependence of some parameters (outer dimensions), we need the concept of a root expression.

Definition 2.40. A *root expression* is a triple (f, x, i) where f is a polynomial in the variable x and possibly other variables and $i \in \mathbb{N}_+$. The parametric algebraic number denoted by the root expression is the ith root of f in the variable x.

Note that the number of roots a polynomial f has in a variable x usually depends on the values of the other variables. Therefore, one has to be careful when dealing with root expressions. For example, cylindrical algebraic decomposition makes sure that the number of roots and their relative ordering are the same for the possible values of the outer variables for which the root expression is used. When the values of the outer variables are known (at run time), the value of the ith root can be approximated by root isolation. Since the isolation interval can be made arbitrarily small, it can be determined precisely (i.e., without using floating point arithmetic or the like) what $\lfloor r \rfloor$ and $\lceil r \rceil$ of a root r are.

We continue by giving the definition of cylindrical decomposition.

Definition 2.41. A non-empty connected subset of $\mathbb{R}^n$ ($n \in \mathbb{N}$) is called a *cell*. For a cell R, we define the *cylinder over R*, written as $Z(R)$, as $R \times \mathbb{R}$.

The cylinder over $\mathbb{R}^0 = \{()\}$ is $\mathbb{R}^0 \times \mathbb{R} = \mathbb{R}$.

Definition 2.42. Let R be a cell of $\mathbb{R}^n$. An *f-section of $Z(R)$* is the set

$$\Big\{ (a, f(a)) \mid a \in R \Big\}$$

for a continuous function $f : R \rightarrow \mathbb{R}$. An *$(f_1, f_2)$-sector of $Z(R)$* is the set

$$\Big\{ (a, b) \mid a \in R, b \in \mathbb{R}, f_1(a) < b < f_2(a) \Big\}$$

where $f_1 = -\infty$ or $f_1 : R \rightarrow \mathbb{R}$ is continuous, and $f_2 = \infty$ or $f_2 : R \rightarrow \mathbb{R}$ is continuous, and $f_1(x) < f_2(x)$ for every $x \in R$.

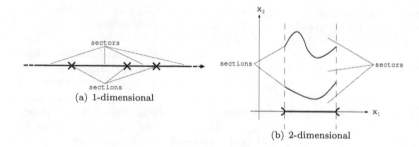

Figure 2.1: Sections and sectors in cylinders

Obviously, sections and sectors are cells. Figure 2.1 shows some sections and sectors of $\mathbb{R}^1$ in (a), and some sections and sectors of a cylinder over an interval in $\mathbb{R}^2$ in (b). The sections and sectors shown in Figure 2.1 also form stacks, as defined by the following definition.

Definition 2.43. Let $X \subseteq \mathbb{R}^n$. A *decomposition* of X is a finite collection of pairwise disjoint cells whose union is X. Let R be a cell, $r \in \mathbb{N}$, and $f_1, \ldots, f_r : R \to \mathbb{R}$ be continuous functions with $f_1(x) < f_2(x) < \cdots < f_r(x)$ for every $x \in R$. Then $(f_1, \ldots, f_r)$ defines a decomposition of $Z(R)$ consisting of the cells

- f_i-sections of $Z(R)$ for $1 \leq i \leq r$,

- (f_i, f_{i+1})-sectors of $Z(R)$ for $1 \leq i < r$,

- the $(-\infty, f_1)$-sector of $Z(R)$,

- the (f_r, ∞)-sector of $Z(R)$.

Such a decomposition is called a *stack over R* defined by $(f_1, \ldots, f_r)$. In the case of $r = 0$, the decomposition consists only of the $(-\infty, \infty)$-sector of $Z(R)$, i.e., the stack consists of the single cell $Z(R)$.

If the decomposition into stacks is made at every level, i.e., also for inner dimensions, the decomposition obtained is called cylindrical.

Definition 2.44. A decomposition D of $\mathbb{R}^n$ is called *cylindrical*, if either

(1) $n = 1$ and D is a stack over $\mathbb{R}^0$, or

(2) $n > 1$ and there is a cylindrical decomposition D' of $\mathbb{R}^{n-1}$ such that, for each cell R of D', D contains a stack over R.

Definition 2.45. A set $S \subseteq \mathbb{R}^n$ is called *semi-algebraic*, if it can be defined by a quantifier-free formula of polynomial equalities and inequalities.

A decomposition of $\mathbb{R}^n$ is called *algebraic* if each of its cells is a semi-algebraic set. A *cylindrical algebraic decomposition* (CAD) is a decomposition which is both cylindrical and algebraic.

---

[3]Square-free means that, for every $z \in \mathbb{R}$ with $f(z) = 0$, $(x - z)$ divides f in $\mathbb{R}[X]$, but $(x - z)^2$ does not. This implies that the sign of f changes at z.

Since the cells in a cylindrical algebraic decomposition can be defined by (in)equalities over polynomial expressions, the sectors are defined by root expressions (cf. Definition 2.40). A cylindrical algebraic decomposition is interesting when it exposes some properties w.r.t. a given formula φ. There exists a well-known family of algorithms to compute a cylindrical algebraic decomposition [ACM98] which is *sign-invariant* w.r.t. the polynomials ψ_i in φ (if every atomic formula is written in the form $\psi_i \, \rho \, 0$ where $\rho \in \{=, \geq, >, \leq, <, \neq\}$). That is, on every cell of the decomposition a given ψ_i has constant sign. This implies that the decomposition is also *truth-invariant* w.r.t. φ, i.e., the truth value of φ is constant on every cell of the decomposition. This class of algorithms consists of 3 phases. Let $x_1, \ldots, x_n$ be the variables and Ψ be the set of all polynomials in φ.

(1) Project the set $\Psi_n := \Psi$ of all polynomials to lower dimensions yielding $\Psi_{n-1}, \ldots, \Psi_1$ such that in every Ψ_i the highest variable is x_i.

(2) The roots of the univariate polynomials in Ψ_1 are the sections of a CAD of $\mathbb{R}$. The intervals between the roots (and to the left of the least root and to the right of the greatest root) form the sectors.

(3) Successively lift the CAD of $\mathbb{R}^{i-1}$ to $\mathbb{R}^i$ (for $2 \leq i \leq n$) until a CAD of $\mathbb{R}^n$ is reached. The sections of the CAD of $\mathbb{R}^i$ are defined by roots of polynomials in Ψ_i solved for x_i in dependence of $x_1, \ldots, x_{i-1}$.

The concrete algorithms [ACM98, Hon98, Bro01a] differ basically in how they perform the projections in the first step. Steps (1) and (2) are rather fast; most time is consumed in the lifting phase (3). The speed of the lifting depends heavily on the projections computed in (1).

In addition to the cylindrical decomposition itself, this procedure allows to compute so-called *test points* $t_S \in \mathbb{A}^n$ such that $t_S \in S$ for every cell S of the decomposition. By substituting t_S into φ one can test whether φ holds in S or not.

2.1.9 Quantifier Elimination

Quantifier elimination is a form of formula manipulation, namely computing a quantifier-free formula which is equivalent (in some structure) to a given formula with quantifiers.

Definition 2.46. Let $\varphi \in Fo(\mathcal{V})$ and $\psi \in Qf(fv(\varphi))$ and D a ring. ψ is called a *quantifier-free equivalent of φ in D* if $(\varphi \leftrightarrow \psi)$ holds in D.

An algorithm which computes quantifier-free equivalents for arbitrary formulas in a given structure is called a *quantifier elimination procedure*.

Note that the free variables in the quantifier-free equivalent ψ must also be free in φ, i.e., quantifier elimination must not introduce new variables.

Theorem 2.47. *There exists a quantifier elimination procedure in the rings $\mathbb{R}$ and $\mathbb{A}$. There exists no quantifier elimination procedure for the rings $\mathbb{Q}$ and $\mathbb{Z}$.*

Proof. The positive result for $\mathbb{R}$ was found by Tarski [Tar51]. The result holds for all real closed fields and, since $\mathbb{A}$ is a real closed field, also for $\mathbb{A}$. The negative result for $\mathbb{Q}$ and $\mathbb{Z}$ follows from the unsolvability of Hilbert's tenth problem [Dav73]. □

Today, efficient algorithms for quantifier elimination in the reals are known. Here, "efficient" means that the algorithm's complexity matches the known asymptotic lower bounds [DH88], i.e., they are doubly exponential in the number of quantifiers at worst. Cylindrical algebraic decomposition as introduced in Section 2.1.8 can be used to compute quantifier-free equivalents. The idea is that, for a given variable, one has to verify whether at least one cell (if x is existentially quantified) or all cells (if x is universally quantified) satisfy the formula by checking the test points of the cells in the respective stack.

Another efficient method which is applicable to formulas of low degree is based on virtual substitution [Wei88, LW93, Wei97]. We use mainly two tools to perform quantifier elimination: REDLOG[4] [DS97], which is a package for the REDUCE[5] [Hea68] computer algebra system, and QEPCAD[6] [Bro03]. In addition, we use the formula simplifier SLFQ[7], which is based on QEPCAD and [Bro01b], and our own implementation of cylindrical algebraic decomposition if we need access to the sections defining the cells (instead of a solution formula delivered by the quantifier elimination tools).

2.2   Parallel Programming

In this section, we introduce the polyhedron model, the model which we extend to allow some non-linearities in Chapter 5. Then, we give a short overview of one specific hardware architecture, graphics processors, which are nowadays being used to execute code which can be handled in the (extended) model.

2.2.1   The Polyhedron Model

Since parallel programming is inherently more difficult than sequential programming, methods to reduce the burden of parallelism in writing software have to be developed. Infusing parallelism automatically by applying a transformation to a given sequential program is one such approach. Earlier attempts of an automatic or semi-automatic parallelisation were text-based, i.e., the transformation was guided by textual characteristics of the source program. A more powerful approach is to use model-based transformation. Model-based automatic parallelisation relies on the ability to represent the operations performed by a given sequential code in an abstract representation. Parallelism or other desired properties like increased cache usage can be infused into the model of the program on the abstract level.

---

[4] Available at http://redlog.dolzmann.de/, visited 2009-05-29.
[5] Available at http://www.reduce-algebra.com/, visited 2009-05-29.
[6] Available at http://www.usna.edu/Users/cs/qepcad/B/QEPCAD.html, visited 2009-05-29.
[7] Available at http://www.usna.edu/Users/cs/qepcad/SLFQ/Home.html, visited 2009-05-29.

The polyhedron model (earlier called the polytope model) can represent loop nests with linear bounds and array accesses with linear subscripts in the body. Programs that can be modelled in it have been studied for several decades [KMW67, Lam74, Len93]. As the name suggests, polyhedra are used to describe the operations (i.e., loop iterations) of a given code. In addition, affine functions are used to model the data dependences between operations, i.e., the ordering of the operations which must be preserved during the transformation to retain the correctness of the program. Figure 2.2 gives an overview of the transformation process. In the first step, an abstract model of a given code is extracted. The model must retain all the properties of the code which are required for a correct execution, for example, its data dependences. In the second step, an optimising search for the best transformation which introduces the desired property into the code is performed. In the case of automatic parallelisation, this comprises computing two pieces of information, namely when (at what time) and where (on which processor) to execute each operation. The last step of the process is to generate code from the transformed model which can execute on the target platform. To facilitate the steps of the whole process, mainly computing

for $i := 0$ to n do
  for $j := 0$ to $i+2$ do
    $A(i,j) = A(i-1,j) + A(i,j-1)$;
  od
od

for $t := 0$ to $2n+2$ do
  forall $p := \max(0, t-n)$ to $\min(t, \lfloor t/2 \rfloor +1)$ do
    $A(t-p,p) = A(t-p-1,p) + A(t-p,p-1)$;
  od
od

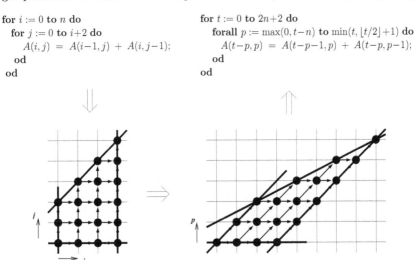

Figure 2.2: Overview over the automatic transformation process in the polyhedron model

dependences, performing an optimising search for the best transformation and generating target code, the class of programs which are manipulated must be constrained such that each of these tasks can be performed computationally. The main restriction in the polyhedron model is that the program must consist of **for** loops with statements with array accesses inside. Both the bounds of the loops and the subscripts of the arrays must be affine functions in the surrounding loop indices and structure parameters. This ensures that the index sets (cf. the next section) are polyhedra and the dependences can be described by affine expressions.

Let us now discuss the three phases of the transformation process in a bit more detail.

Dependence Analysis

The main purpose of a dependence analysis is to make the ordering on the operations of the program which is required to guarantee correct execution explicit. That is, dependence analysis determines, given two operations a and b of a program, whether a or b must be executed first, or that it does not matter which operation is performed first. Different granularities of the analysis are possible by choosing what is considered an "operation". In the context of the polyhedron model, we deal with loop programs and different iterations of a loop are considered different operations. To be precise, every execution of a statement in the body of the loop is an individual operation.

Definition 2.48. In a loop program, every statement S is surrounded by $depth(S) \in \mathbb{N}$ loops. $depth(S)$ is called the *nesting depth* (or level) of S. A statement S is said to *textually precede* a statement T, written $S \prec_t T$, if S occurs before T in the program text.

For two statements S and T, we denote the number of loops which surround both S and T by $surr(S,T)$.

To capture the notion of operations, we introduce the concept of index sets.

Definition 2.49. Let $\mathbf{p} \in \mathbb{Z}^k$ be the structure parameters and S a program statement. The parametric set $D_S(\mathbf{p}) \subseteq \mathbb{Z}^{depth(S)}$ of all values of the loop indices for which S is executed is called the *index set* of S. An *operation* is the execution of S for a value $\mathbf{i} \in D_S(\mathbf{p})$, written $\langle \mathbf{i}, S \rangle$. $\mathbf{i}$ is called the *iteration vector* of the respective operation.

In the polyhedron model, index sets of statements are described by affine inequalities. This implies that they are parametric polyhedra (in fact, parametric polytopes), or, more generally, parametric Z-polyhedra.

Next, we define a total ordering on operations which corresponds to the order of execution in the program.

Definition 2.50. Let $\langle \mathbf{i}, S \rangle$ and $\langle \mathbf{j}, T \rangle$ be two operations of a program. We say that $\langle \mathbf{i}, S \rangle$ *precedes* $\langle \mathbf{j}, T \rangle$, written $\langle \mathbf{i}, S \rangle \prec \langle \mathbf{j}, T \rangle$, if $\mathbf{i}_{|d} \prec \mathbf{j}_{|d}$ or ($\mathbf{i}_{|d} = \mathbf{j}_{|d}$ and $S \prec_t T$) where $d = surr(S,T)$.

Sometimes, we need to discern the individual memory read and write operations of an operation. These individual memory operations are called accesses.

Definition 2.51. Let S be a statement and $\langle \mathbf{i}, S \rangle$ an operation. Each construct a which accesses memory in S is called an *access*. An access is called a *write access* or a *read access*, if it writes to or reads from memory, respectively. A particular execution $\langle \mathbf{i}, a \rangle$ of a for an iteration vector $\mathbf{i}$ is called an *instance* of the access. The memory cell referred to by $\langle \mathbf{i}, a \rangle$ is denoted by $accelem(\langle \mathbf{i}, a \rangle)$.

Let us now discuss what it means that an operation q depends on an operation p. Since "depends" shall mean that q must be executed after p, there must be some effect of p which must be observed by q, or there must be an effect in q which must not be observed by p. The observable effects in programs are writes to memory cells.[8] This gives rise to the definition of the three classical types of dependence, in which at least one of the two operations performs a write access. In addition, we can also define one "dependence" type in which both operations only read from the memory cell.

Definition 2.52. Let p and q be operations of a program. q is said to *depend on* p, if $p \prec q$ and both operations access at least one common memory cell c. The dependence is called

- a *true* dependence, if p writes to c and q reads from c,

- a *anti* dependence, if p reads from c and q writes to c,

- an *output* dependence, if both p and q write to c,

- an *input* dependence, if both p and q read from c.

We write $p \rightarrow q$ to denote that q depends on p. If we want to specify the type of the dependence, we superset the type over the arrow as in $p \xrightarrow{\text{true}} q$.

We can extend the definition of a dependence to the access level by using access instances instead of operations.

Definition 2.53. Let a and b be access instances which access the same memory cell and let a and b be part of operations p and q, respectively. b is said to *depend on* a, written $a \rightarrow b$, if $p \prec q$ or ($p = q$ and a is executed before b in p). The type of dependence (true, anti, output, input) is defined as for dependences between operations (cf. Definition 2.52) and we write, e.g., $a \xrightarrow{\text{true}} b$ to denote a dependence of a certain type.

Note that, by the definitions given, an operation can never depend on itself, but there can be a dependence between different access instances of the same operation. Depending on the application, we require dependence information based on operations or on access instances.

Example 2.54. In the program shown in Figure 2.3, there is an output dependence from operation $\langle (0,3), S \rangle$ to $\langle (1,1), S \rangle$, as both operations write to $A[6]$. In addition, there is an anti dependence from access instances $\langle (0,3), A[2j] \rangle$ to $\langle (0,3), A[4i+2j] \rangle$ (anti because the read happens before the write), but there is no dependence from operation $\langle (0,3), S \rangle$ to itself.

Since programs usually depend on structure parameters, one cannot simply enumerate every dependent pair of operations or access instances. Instead, a

---

[8]On some hardware components, read accesses may have observable side effects like destroying the contents of a hardware register, but we only consider side effects of write accesses, here.

```
for (i=0; i<=1; i++)
  for (j=0; j<=3; j++)
S:         A[4*i+2*j] = A[2*j];
```

Figure 2.3: Example loop program with array access in statement S

general description of the dependences must be computed. In the polyhedron model, the subscripts of array accesses are restricted to affine expressions. A dependence between two accesses $A[f(\mathbf{i}, \mathbf{p})]$ and $A[g(\mathbf{i}, \mathbf{p})]$, where f and g are (possibly multi-dimensional) affine functions in the variables $\mathbf{i}$ and parameters $\mathbf{p}$, can only exist if the system of equalities

$$f(\mathbf{i}, \mathbf{p}) = g(\mathbf{i}', \mathbf{p})$$

holds for some values of $\mathbf{i}$, $\mathbf{i}'$, $\mathbf{p}$. Note that both accesses get a different set of variables ($\mathbf{i}$ vs. $\mathbf{i}'$), because the accesses to the same memory cell may be performed in different iterations. Since f and g are affine functions, the solutions for $\mathbf{i}$ and $\mathbf{i}'$ are affine functions (in the appropriate number of degrees of freedom), too. Section 5.1 describes dependence analysis in more details by means of the classical Banerjee method.

Transformation

In the transformation phase, the model of the given program whose dependences have been analysed is transformed such that desired properties are satisfied. Properties commonly desired are parallelism, efficient cache behaviour or low energy consumption (especially in embedded systems). The dependence information restricts the search space, because any legal transformation must respect the dependences. For example, when infusing parallelism, a dependence $p \rightarrow q$ for operations p, q means that, in the parallel program, p has to be executed before q, too, i.e., there must not be parallelism (or reversal of execution order) between p and q.

The most basic transformation in automatic parallelisation is to compute at what time to execute an operation and on which processor. These pieces of information are called schedule and placement.

Definition 2.55. A *schedule* for statements $S_1, \ldots, S_r$ with index sets $D_1(\mathbf{p}), \ldots, D_r(\mathbf{p})$ is a set of functions $\theta_a : D_a(\mathbf{p}) \rightarrow \mathbb{Z}^\tau$, $1 \le a \le r$, $\tau \in \mathbb{N}_+$ such that for any two dependent operations $\langle \mathbf{i}, S_u \rangle$ and $\langle \mathbf{i}', S_b \rangle$ $(1 \le a, b \le r)$ the following condition holds: $\theta_a(\mathbf{i}) \prec \theta_b(\mathbf{i}')$.

θ_a assigns to every operation of $\langle \mathbf{i}, S_a \rangle$ from $D_a(\mathbf{p})$ a point in time $\theta_a(\mathbf{i})$ at which it shall execute. The condition on the schedule functions of dependent operations ensures that the source of a dependence is executed before its target. We allow schedules to be multi-dimensional with lexicographic order (like hours, minutes, seconds on a clock) since it is often desirable to have more than one sequential dimension, e.g., to reduce the parallelism to fewer than all but one dimension. The schedule, as defined here, maps to integral points in time. We may also allow mappings to the rationals (or even reals) at first if we are careful to require a distance of at least 1 between dependent instances, i.e., the first non-zero entry in the vector $\theta_b(\mathbf{i}') - \theta_a(\mathbf{i})$ is at least 1. This allows to derive a schedule that maps to the integers by taking the componentwise floor $\theta'_a(\mathbf{i}) = \lfloor \theta_a(\mathbf{i}) \rfloor$, $\theta'_b(\mathbf{i}) = \lfloor \theta_a(\mathbf{i}') \rfloor$ of the rational schedules. Then, $\theta'_a(\mathbf{i})$ and $\theta'_b(\mathbf{i})$ are integral and satisfy $\theta'_a(\mathbf{i}) \prec \theta'_b(\mathbf{i}')$ (cf. [Fea92a, Theorem 6]). We exploit this relation, for example, in Section 5.2.2.

Parallelism is introduced into the model by the placement.

Definition 2.56. A *placement* (also called *allocation*) for statements $S_1, \ldots, S_r$ with index sets $D_1(\mathbf{p}), \ldots, D_r(\mathbf{p})$ is a set of functions $\pi_a : D_a(\mathbf{p}) \to \mathbb{Z}^\rho$, $1 \le a \le r$, $\rho \in \mathbb{N}_+$.

The placement determines the processor on which an operation executes. Note that this definition does not restrict placements in any respect. Any placement is valid, for example, taking $\pi_a(\mathbf{i}) = 0$ for all statements S_a is allowed. Of course, this all-zero placement does not exhibit any parallelism, since only one processor (namely processor 0) is used.

Schedule and placement together define a new coordinate system in which the transformed program executes in a parallel fashion. But before executable code is generated, one may want to apply other transformations that modify the coordinate system further. For example, tiling (cf. Section 5.3) is a technique to aggregate several operations, i.e., to coarsen the grain of the execution in order to improve the computation-to-communication ratio.

Code Generation

After the transformation phase, we have a model description of a program which gives, for every statement to be executed, the times and places of its intended execution in a multi-dimensional coordinate system. The target coordinate system is shared by all statements, i.e., the transformation phase equalises the dimensionality of all iteration domains through the transformation. To be able to execute the transformed program, executable code has to be constructed from the model. To this end, we have to create a loop nest which enumerates the points in the transformed domains in lexicographic order. For parallel dimensions, the order of enumeration is not important; usually, parallel loops (i.e., loops corresponding to a parallel dimension) will be marked to execute in parallel using constructs like the OMP pragma `#pragma omp parallel for`, or the parallel loop is really written as a conditional in the generated code which checks whether the thread reaching the respective location in the code is supposed to execute the inner dimensions. We present code generation in the polyhedral case and our method to perform an analogous operation in the non-linear case in Section 5.5.

2.2.2   Parallel Computing Hardware

In recent years, two developments in computing hardware have been exerting a seminal influence on parallel computing. On the one hand, clock frequencies of CPUs have not been increasing any further but have remained at approximately 3 GHz. Instead, chip manufacturers have been putting several cores, instead of one, onto a chip, starting the age of multicore computing with two to eight cores on a single chip, and the age of manycore computing with more than eight cores per chip. The other, related development has been the use of graphics processors for general-purpose computing. The computational power and increased flexibility (compared to earlier graphics processors) make such a use feasible. Both multicore/manycore CPUs and GPU computing pose their specific challenges. We introduce both concepts and discuss their peculiarities below.

Both developments, which make parallel computing increasingly mainstream, change the demands for parallel programs. Most notably, as almost every system will be a parallel system in the near future, programs must be flexible enough to use a statically not known number of processors/cores at run time. In the context of the polyhedron model, this requires a new parameter for the number of parallel threads, which more often than not leads to non-linearities in the model (cf. Section 5.3).

Multicore CPUs

From the programmer's point of view, multicore processors look very much like traditional SMP (symmetric multiprocessing) systems. But there are subtle differences. The cores of a physical processor unit share a single connection to main memory, i.e., if n cores try to access main memory at the same time, the effective bandwidth per core is $\frac{1}{n}$ of the total bandwidth. In addition, cores may share a second- or third-level cache, reducing the effective cache size of each core (if more than one core is actively using the cache). For both reasons, it is even more imperative—compared to multiprocessor systems—to reduce memory transfers and keep the memory footprint (i.e., the active cache size) small.

GPU Computing: NVIDIA's Compute-Unified Device Architecture

A new hardware platform for parallel computing is GPGPU (general-purpose graphics processing unit) computing. GPGPU computing employs powerful graphics processors and makes their computing power available for general-purpose applications instead of rendering graphics (their traditional function). When writing software for GPGPU computing, one has to account for the peculiar design of GPU processors owing to their graphics heritage. Two aspects of their design are of particular importance for achieving good performance. For one, graphics operations are often the same for many pixels; therefore, parallelism in GPU processors is only achieved when the same operation is applied to several operands. Secondly, graphics processors do not have a data cache.

Instead, they offer a so-called *scratchpad memory*, i.e., an explicitly address-able fast memory which is used as a replacement for the data cache. The main difference to a hardware-managed data cache is that scratchpad memory must be managed by software. We now present the SIMT programming model for GPGPU computing. This model is used by NVIDIA's Compute-Unified Device Architecture (CUDA) [NVI09], which we have used for our experiments.

The SIMT Programming Model The architecture of GPUs is derived from the classical *single instruction multiple data* (SIMD) architecture. In SIMD, there is one thread of execution per processor, but a processor has several arithmetic-logic units, i.e., a computational instruction can operate on several operands at the same time (as opposed to instructions dealing with control flow). For example, Intel's *Streaming SIMD Extensions* (SSE) [Int99] augments the x86 instruction set architecture with vector instructions for simultaneous operation on four single-precision floating point operands (among others). The control flow of a SIMD program remains single-threaded because only some arithmetic instructions deal with multiple operands in parallel.

The also classical *single program multiple data* (SPMD) programming model makes parallelism (e.g., multithreading) explicit for the programmer. There are several threads of execution in the program and each thread is free to take a different control path. This model is used by the well-known *Message Passing Interface* (MPI) library [Mes08] and the *Open Multi-Processing* (OpenMP) standard [Ope08]. SPMD is popular with distributed-memory parallel systems (using MPI) and SMP/multicore CPU systems (using MPI and/or OpenMP).

NVIDIA's *single instruction multiple threads* (SIMT) programming model is a combination of SIMD and SPMD which provides the programmer with an SPMD view of the parallelism, but has the SIMD restrictions for describing parallelism. There are several threads, each with its individual identifier and control flow. Different threads are allowed to follow different control flows. The difference to SPMD is that, when threads take different control paths, parallelism is lost and the processor alternates between the different control flow paths, i.e., the performance is essentially that of a sequential program. To achieve a parallel execution, threads must take the same path through the program and, hence, the execution is similar to SIMD, because the same instruction is applied to several data items at a time. Fortunately, not all threads are obliged to have the same control flow. In fact, only the threads in a so-called *warp* are subject to this restriction. The reason is the hardware architecture of GPUs, cf. Figure 2.4. A GPU device consists of several so-called *multiprocessors*. Each multiprocessor has several processors which execute instructions. Every processor has arithmetic and logic units but there is only one control unit per multiprocessor for instruction decoding and branching. Hence, the processors of a multiprocessor can only work on several data items at a time if they execute the same instruction. With current NVIDIA® graphics processor technologies, a multiprocessor consists of eight processors. In four clock cycles, the multiprocessor handles the instruction of 32 threads, provided that they all execute the same instruction. Accordingly, the *warp size* is 32, i.e., all threads with iden-

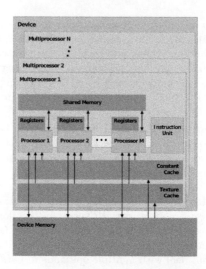

Figure 2.4: GPU architecture (image from [NVI09])

tifiers i such that $\lfloor \frac{i}{32} \rfloor$ has the same value must execute the same instruction or, otherwise, *divergence* occurs and the multiprocessor cannot execute all 32 threads of the warp simultaneously.

The code executing on a GPU, the so-called *kernel*, has to obey several restrictions. Most importantly, there is no run-time allocation, neither in the heap nor on the stack. This implies that GPU code cannot use recursion. The invocation of a kernel is organised in *blocks* (Figure 2.5). That is, the ID of a thread is given by a pair (b, t) where b is a one- or two-dimensional index of the thread's block and t a one-, two- or three-dimensional index within a block. Blocks execute independently, e.g., the run-time system may schedule the blocks among the multiprocessors of a GPU device. A single block always executes on a single multiprocessor. Therefore, the threads of a block have access to the scratchpad memory of the respective multiprocessor. We discuss scratchpad memory in the next paragraph.

Scratchpad Memory   The main memory of the GPU ("device memory" in NVIDIA's documents) is not fast enough to handle concurrent memory access requests by all the threads running on a multiprocessor; the latency may be several hundred clock cycles. The thread scheduler of a multiprocessor attempts to hide these latencies by scheduling some threads while others are waiting for data from memory, but this is not sufficient to exploit the full computing power of the device. One has to use the scratchpad memory of the multiprocessor (called "shared memory" in NVIDIA's documents), a much faster, but also much smaller, memory local to the multiprocessor which allows concurrent access without delay if certain alignment restrictions are being obeyed. The details of

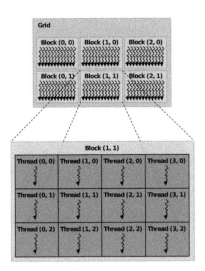

Figure 2.5: GPU architecture: blocks (image from [NVI09])

the restrictions depend on the hardware generation of the GPU; newer hardware
lifts some of the constraints imposed by earlier generations. The basic restriction
is as follows. The first and second half of a warp are each called a *half-warp*.
Suppose L, declared as `int L[]`, refers to the scratchpad memory (i.e., L points
to the beginning of the memory). Then the 16 threads of a half-warp can access
`L[f(i)]` (with i being the thread ID) simultaneously if

- $\lfloor \frac{f(i)}{16} \rfloor$ is the same on all threads of the half-warp, i.e., all threads of the
  half-warp access the same 64 byte memory bank (since `sizeof(int)` is 4
  in CUDA), and

- the expressions $f(i)$ mod 16 either evaluate equally in all threads, or they
  evaluate mutually differently.

These requirements imply that there are two access patterns which can be served
in one clock cycle. Either all 16 threads have to access the same memory cell,
or every thread must access a different 4-byte unit (e.g., an `int` or a `float`) at a
different offset (aligned on a 4 byte boundary), but all 16 accesses must address
the same 64-byte (= 16 units of 4 bytes) bank.

Due to this alignment restriction, it is desirable to organise simultaneous access to scratchpad memory such that adjacent threads access adjacent memory
cells.

Chapter 3

Related Work

3.1 Dependence Analysis

Dependence analysis for static control loop programs with affine bounds and affine array subscripts has been solved for quite some time [Fea91, PW92]. Subsequently, research has been focusing on more efficient algorithms and wider applicability. The aim of our work is clearly to achieve greater applicability. Extending the analysis to a bigger class of programs and maintaining its precision is difficult as it requires more powerful mathematical methods and faces undecidability problems. One way around this problem is to sacrifice precision of the analysis and handle "extended" constructs by heuristics or ask the user to state whether a condition arising during the analysis holds [PW92]. Our work clearly relates to work which uses more powerful mathematical tools.

Uninterpreted Function Symbols Uninterpreted function symbols for constructs which cannot be analysed were introduced by Pugh et al. [PW95]. By doing so, arbitrary non-linear (and non-polynomial) conditions can be handled, but the exact dependence information is only available at run time when the non-linear conditions can be evaluated. One strength of this approach is that the symbolic manipulation of the conditions remains possible.

Barthou's Approaches For exact dependence analysis, Barthou [Bar98] presents a modified Fourier-Motzkin elimination which handles equalities exactly by keeping track of the modulo conditions imposed by them. For example, when eliminating the variable j from a system with the equality $i + n \cdot j = k$ by substituting $j := \frac{k-i}{n}$ in the system, the condition $k - i \equiv_n 0$ must be satisfied since, otherwise, j is not integral. Barthou's algorithm can handle such non-linear parameters in some situations.

To handle a broader spectrum of non-linear (including non-polynomial) constraints, Barthou suggests to use resolution to derive linear conditions as consequences from the non-linear ones.

Interval Arithmetic   Recently, data dependence tests based on integer interval arithmetic have been proposed. The central concept of integer interval arithmetic is the integer interval equality, $f(\mathbf{x}) = [L(\mathbf{x}), U(\mathbf{x})]$, i.e., the question of whether $\mathbf{x} \in R$ (for some $R \subseteq \mathbb{Z}^n$) exists such that $L(\mathbf{x}) \leq f(\mathbf{x}) \leq U(\mathbf{x})$. To test for a dependence between two accesses $A[f(\mathbf{i})]$ and $A[g(\mathbf{i'})]$, the conflict equality $f(\mathbf{i}) = g(\mathbf{i'})$ is written as the integer interval equality

$$f(\mathbf{i}) - g(\mathbf{i'}) = [0, 0]$$

and is solved subject to the constraints

$$\mathbf{i} \in D_1, \qquad \mathbf{i'} \in D_2$$

where D_1 and D_2 are the iteration sets of the array accesses. Zhou and Zeng [ZZ08] present a method, called the polynomial variable interval (PVI) test, for detecting dependences when array subscripts are sums of powers of loop variables, like in $2 \cdot i + i^2 - 5 \cdot j^3$. Kyriakopoulos and Psarris [KP09] give an algorithm, called the non-linear variable interval (NLVI) test, to check for dependences in the presence of non-linearities and parameters. This algorithm also computes direction vector information. Both methods do not apply to arbitrary systems as so-called accuracy conditions have to be checked when a variable is eliminated. Only if the accuracy conditions hold, exact conditions for the feasibility of the conflict equalities are derived. Coupled array subscripts (i.e., systems of conflict equalities with equalities involving a common variable) cannot always be handled exactly. Our generalisation of Banerjee's dependence analysis is complementary as it handles one specific case (one non-linear parameter) of a system of conflict equalities with coupled equalities exactly.

Bernstein Expansion   Clauss and Tchoupaeva [CT04] propose to use Bernstein expansion for approximating polynomial functions. Bernstein polynomials form a basis for the ring of multivariate polynomials: any polynomial f can be written as a linear combination of Bernstein polynomials. The coefficients of the linear combination provide lower and upper bounds on the value of f on the box $[0, 1]^n$ and, by suitable substitutions, on any box, even parametric ones. The bounds are often exact; therefore, Bernstein expansion allows to perform range tests more accurately than with interval methods. Clauss and Tchoupaeva demonstrate that it can be used to disprove dependences in the presence of non-linear array subscripts, among other applications.

Chain of Recurrences   In the work by van Engelen et al. [vEBS+04], symbolic expressions are represented as chains of recurrences (CR). By applying CR algebra, this allows to handle some non-linear cases and perform the GCD test, the value range test and the extreme value test for detecting dependences, then.

3.2   Computing Schedules

Several methods for computing schedules have been suggested. Earlier methods relied on finding a hyperplane with a suitable orientation towards the uniform dependences of a program or recurrence equalities [KMW67, Lam74]. Darte and Robert [DR95] proposed asymptotically optimal solutions for parametric domains by considering a "limit problem" and the strongly connected cycles in the statement dependence graph. Feautrier presented a solution of the affine schedule problem using piecewise affine schedules for one-dimensional time [Fea92a] and also an extension to multidimensional time [Fea92b]. Feautrier's methods use integer linear programming for computing the schedule. An overview of scheduling techniques can be found in the book by Darte et al. [DRV00].

There has, by far, not been as much work with respect to non-linear schedules, presumably because no code generation method was available. Achtziger et al. [AZ00] used nonsmooth optimisation to compute linear and quadratic schedules and also discussed the synthesis of array processors from quadratic schedules.

3.3   Tiling

Tiling is a well-established technique of coarsening the grain of parallelism and increasing data locality in loop programs [XH97, Xue97b, GFL04]. The iteration space of the program is covered with (usually congruent) tiles, and the enumeration of the iteration points is changed so as to enumerate the tiles in the outer loops (i.e., dimensions) and the points in each tile in the inner loops.

To minimise communication startups and the volume of the data communicated, the shape and size of the tiles are usually chosen in dependence of the dependence vectors [Xue97a, ABRY01, GFL04], especially in the context of distributed-memory architectures. For shared-memory systems, the number of startups and the volume are less of a concern, as long as the transfer time of the data between cores stays small compared to the computation time for each tile. However, tiling remains an important technique for load balancing: tile shapes and sizes which distribute an equal amount of work across the cores must be chosen.

The foundations of tiling for supercomputers were described by Irigoin and Triolet [IT88]. Tiling as an optimising transformation to infuse parallelism, increase locality or reduce communications has been proposed as a partitioning-based approach [LL98] or, as presented here, as a transformation following space-time mapping [DV97, Gri04]. A novel approach, which derives the tiling and parallelism in an integrated fashion, has recently been proposed [BBK+08b]. All these approaches consider the dependences of the analysed program, which determine the legality of a tiling. Our analysis focuses on the parallel execution of tiled code, the necessary load balancing and the role of the index space bounds. Sequential execution efficiency (and code generation efficiency, which we have not studied) for parametrised tiles has been investigated recently [RKRS07].

3.4   Array Localisation

Improving data locality by transforming a loop nest to obtain temporal or spatial locality by reordering the loop iterations and/or changing the data layout has long been a subject of study [WL91, KRC97, BF03, BBK$^+$08b].

Earlier work relied on partitioning program data [PDN97]. Loop transformations have been used to simplify the reuse pattern [KRI$^+$01, KC02] in order to store the reused data compactly in scratchpad memory if such a transformation is permitted by the dependences. Later work [IBMD04] improves the situation by partitioning according to the coefficients of the array index expressions, thus, reducing the size of the blocks stored in scratchpad memory considerably. Chen et. al [CK08] present a method for minimising off-chip memory accesses by restructuring parallel code according to data tiles to create temporal locality across processors.

Ehrhart quasi-polynomials have been used to store compactly only the elements of an array used by the code after applying a transformation [CM00, LMC02] or to compute the number of accessed memory elements, cache misses, etc. [VSB$^+$04].

For our technique to be effective, locality improving transformations described in the previous work cited are desirable. Loechner et al. [LMC02] describe loop transformations which optimise data locality. They use Ehrhart quasi-polynomials for the precise and compact addressing of the array elements accessed by a loop nest. They focus on spatial and temporal reuse to enhance cache performance and TLB (translation lookaside buffer) effectiveness.

Baskaran et al. [BBK$^+$08a] execute tiled loop code on a graphics card with scratchpad memory. They approximate the local data of a tile by a rectangular superset, load the respective data into scratchpad memory before executing a tile and store it to global memory afterwards, but they do not compute the used data set precisely nor do they try to retain reused data in the scratchpad between tiles.

3.5   Code Generation

The problem of generating code from polyhedral descriptions has been studied for about two decades. Early work concentrated on code generation for a single statement [Iri88]. After seminal steps in this area [AI91], solutions were developed successively for the case with several statements and unions of polyhedra as iteration sets [CF93, Wet95, KPR95, QRW00, Bas04].

Code generation for a single statement has been solved for more general cases. In our own previous work [GGL04], we have shown that code can be generated for a polyhedral iteration set which may depend on non-linear parameters (i.e., the inequalities describing the index set may contain products between a variable and a polynomial in the parameters) using quantifier elimination in the reals.

Recently, an efficient method for generating code for a tiled index set of one statement with parametric parallelepiped tiles has been presented by Renganarayanan et al. [RKRS07]. They compute an approximation of the set of all tile origins (the so-called outset) to enumerate all non-empty tiles and, in a second step, generate code for the inner loops enumerating the points within the tiles. The method is efficient because computing the outset is linear in the number of constraints.

Chapter 4

Algorithms for Non-linearities

Efforts to extend the polyhedron model with non-linearities immediately lead to the question of whether the algorithms used frequently in the model can be modified to handle non-linear cases. The mathematical tools needed to do so are nontrivial (otherwise, the extensions would be part of the model already). In this chapter, we discuss three areas of non-linear mathematics, namely solving systems of equalities with one non-linear parameter, generalising Fourier-Motzkin elimination and the simplex algorithm to an arbitrary number of non-linear parameters, and using quantifier elimination in the reals to solve some non-linear problems. Chapter 5 applies the techniques and generalised algorithms described here to problems in the model-based transformation process built upon the polyhedron model. We are aware that the section on linear Diophantine equality systems with one non-linear parameter (Section 4.2) may be more challenging to some of the parallel programming audience. The algorithms presented here are meant to be implemented in a suitable library and used by parallelisation systems without the need to understand the details of the algorithms. Readers less interested in these details may want to go to the examples (Section 4.2.7) directly and skip the rest of Section 4.2 (we have to assume the reader has a basic familiarity with periodic numbers and quasi-polynomials in the examples, though).

4.1 The Generalised Model

In the classical polyhedron model for loop parallelisation, we deal with systems of equalities or inequalities with variables $x_1, \ldots, x_n$ and parameters $p_1, \ldots, p_k$ of the form

$$\sum_{i=1}^{n} c_i x_i + \sum_{i=1}^{k} d_i p_i + e \geq 0 \quad \text{or} \quad \sum_{i=1}^{n} c_i x_i + \sum_{i=1}^{k} d_i p_i + e = 0,$$

respectively, where $c_1, \ldots, c_n, p_1, \ldots, p_k, e \in \mathbb{Q}$, i.e., the (in)equalities are given by affine expressions (cf. Definition 2.11). The more general model which we aim at allows non-linearities. We distinguish two flavours of the non-linearity we allow:

1. A generalisation to allow non-linear parameters, i.e., the expressions are linear in the variables and the coefficients can be expressions in the parameters. The (in)equalities now take the form

$$\sum_{i=1}^{n} c_i x_i + d \geq 0 \quad \text{or} \quad \sum_{i=1}^{n} c_i x_i + d = 0,$$

respectively, where $c_1, \ldots, c_n, d \in D$ and D is a ring which contains expressions in the parameters. Depending on the application, we will choose the polynomials over the rationals (i.e., $\mathbb{Q}[p_1, \ldots, p_k]$), rational functions from $\mathbb{Q}(p_1, \ldots, p_k)$ or univariate quasi-polynomials (cf. Definition 2.27) for this ring D.

2. A generalisation with non-linear variables where we allow arbitrary polynomials in the variables and parameters as right-hand side, i.e.,

$$f \geq 0 \quad \text{or} \quad f = 0,$$

where $f \in \mathbb{Q}[x_1, \ldots, x_n, p_1 \ldots, p_k]$ or $f \in \mathbb{Q}(x_1, \ldots, x_n, p_1 \ldots, p_k)$ if we need to represent fractions.

The second case encompasses the first case, except when D is a ring of quasi-polynomials. Nonetheless, we distinguish the first case from the second as it exposes more structure (the equalities and inequalities are linear in the variables).

The polyhedron model has the appealing property that some algorithms (e.g., Fourier-Motzkin elimination) produce results without case distinctions on the parameters. This is due to the fact that the coefficients of the variables are constants. In our generalisation, this is no longer true and the corresponding computations must return results with case distinctions. The example $p \cdot x - 1 \geq 0$ illustrates this fact. If we assume nothing about parameter p, solving $p \cdot x - 1 \geq 0$ for $x \in \mathbb{Q}$ yields three different solutions:

- $x \geq \frac{1}{p}$ if $p > 0$,

- false if $p = 0$,

- $x < \frac{1}{p}$ if $p < 0$.

Therefore, algorithms for the model with non-linearities must produce results with case distinctions which are not necessary in the classical polyhedral case. We represent such case distinction as a decision tree. A leaf node of the tree carries a result for a specific case, and an inner node n represents some conditional. Each of the subtrees of n is applicable under a certain condition. We use the following definition for the decision tree data type, given as a prototypical Haskell data type:

data *Tree* α = *Leaf* α
         | *Cond   Condition* (*Tree* α) (*Tree* α)

The node types are:

- *Leaf   x*   represents a result with value x,

- *Cond φ $t_\top$ $t_\perp$*   represents a case distinction with an arbitrary quantifier-free logical formula φ as condition. $t_\top$ applies if φ holds, and $t_\perp$ applies if φ does not hold.

The result of solving $p \cdot x - 1 \geq 0$ for x can be represented as follows:

$$Cond \ p \neq 0 \ \left(Cond \ p < 0 \ \left(Leaf \ x \leq \tfrac{1}{p}\right) \left(Leaf \ x \geq \tfrac{1}{p}\right)\right) \ (Leaf \ \text{false})$$

4.2   Solving Systems of Linear Diophantine Equalities

Solving linear equality systems in the integers is the basis of dependence analysis (cf. Section 5.1). We start here by describing a basic technique to solve such systems and, then, discuss its extension to one non-linear parameter. Generalising this technique to a non-linear parameter has been the subject of a diploma thesis [Sch07] which laid the ground work and discovered the periodic behaviour of pointwise GCDs (cf. Lemma 4.3) and the possibility to use GCDs to test pointwise divisibility (cf. Theorem 4.13) in an ad-hoc formalism. In this work, we present the later reformulation and more precise rendering of the results [GS08] using quasi-polynomials together with the missing pieces (e.g., strong echelon form, Theorem 4.12) and a new proof for Lemma 4.3 which shows that GCDs can be computed by a pseudo-division.

4.2.1   Solving Systems of Linear Equalities

Let us look at the method to solve linear Diophantine equality systems used by Banerjee in his book on data dependence analysis [Ban93]. Given $x \cdot A = b$ with $A \in \mathbb{Z}^{m \times n}$, $b \in \mathbb{Z}^n$, the system can be solved for $x \in \mathbb{Z}^m$ by a well-known two-step procedure:

- First, $U \in \mathbb{Z}^{m \times m}$ and $S \in \mathbb{Z}^{m \times n}$ are computed such that U is unimodular, S is an echelon matrix and $U \cdot A = S$.

- Second, $t \cdot S = b$ is solved for $t \in \mathbb{Z}^m$ by computing a matrix $T \in \mathbb{Z}^{v \times m}$ (where $v \in \mathbb{N}$ is the number of degrees of freedom) and a vector $t_0 \in \mathbb{Z}^m$ such that the set of all solutions to $t \cdot S = b$ is given by $\{e \cdot T + t_0 \mid e \in \mathbb{Z}^v\}$, provided that $t \cdot S = b$ has solutions at all.

If $t \cdot S = b$ is feasible, the solutions of $x \cdot A = b$ are then given by

$$x \cdot A = b \iff x \in \{(e \cdot T + t_0) \cdot U \mid e \in \mathbb{Z}^v\}.$$

Example 4.1. Consider the following loop program:

```
for (i=0; i<=m; i++)
    for (j=0; j<=m; j++)
S:          A[3*i+2*j] = i+j;
```

To determine for which iterations there exists a dependence from $\langle(i,j),S\rangle$ to $\langle(i',j'),S\rangle$, we have to solve the equality system

$$3i + 2j = 3i' + 2j', \text{ i.e., } \begin{pmatrix} i & j & i' & j' \end{pmatrix} \cdot \begin{pmatrix} 3 \\ 2 \\ -3 \\ -2 \end{pmatrix} = 0.$$

To bring the coefficient matrix into echelon form, we subtract the second row from the first, i.e.,

$$U_1 \cdot \begin{pmatrix} 3 \\ 2 \\ -3 \\ -2 \end{pmatrix} = \begin{pmatrix} 1 \\ 2 \\ -3 \\ -2 \end{pmatrix} \quad \text{with} \quad U_1 = \begin{pmatrix} 1 & -1 & 0 & 0 \\ 0 & 1 & 0 & 0 \\ 0 & 0 & 1 & 0 \\ 0 & 0 & 0 & 1 \end{pmatrix}$$

and then subtract the new first row from the other rows in suitable multiples to make them vanish:

$$U_2 \cdot \begin{pmatrix} 1 \\ 2 \\ -3 \\ -2 \end{pmatrix} = \begin{pmatrix} 1 \\ 0 \\ 0 \\ 0 \end{pmatrix} \quad \text{with} \quad U_2 = \begin{pmatrix} 1 & 0 & 0 & 0 \\ -2 & 1 & 0 & 0 \\ 3 & 0 & 1 & 0 \\ 2 & 0 & 0 & 1 \end{pmatrix}$$

Hence, the matrices S and $U = U_2 \cdot U_1$ are:

$$S = \begin{pmatrix} 1 \\ 0 \\ 0 \\ 0 \end{pmatrix}, \quad U = \begin{pmatrix} 1 & -1 & 0 & 0 \\ -2 & 3 & 0 & 0 \\ 3 & -3 & 1 & 0 \\ 2 & -2 & 0 & 1 \end{pmatrix}$$

Solving $\begin{pmatrix} t_1 & t_2 & t_3 & t_4 \end{pmatrix} \cdot S = b = 0$ yields $t_1 = 0$, $t_2, t_3, t_4 \in \mathbb{Z}$. The overall solution is given by:

$$\begin{pmatrix} i & j & i' & j' \end{pmatrix} = t \cdot U = \begin{pmatrix} 0 & t_2 & t_3 & t_4 \end{pmatrix} \cdot \begin{pmatrix} 1 & -1 & 0 & 0 \\ -2 & 3 & 0 & 0 \\ 3 & -3 & 1 & 0 \\ 2 & -2 & 0 & 1 \end{pmatrix}$$

$$= \begin{pmatrix} -2t_2 + 3t_3 + 2t_4 & 3t_2 - 3t_3 - 2t_4 & t_3 & t_4 \end{pmatrix}$$

From this, we can see that the distance between the source and the target of a dependence

$$\begin{pmatrix} i - i' \\ j - j' \end{pmatrix} = \begin{pmatrix} -2t_2 + 3t_3 + 2t_4 - t_3 \\ 3t_2 - 3t_3 - 2t_4 - t_4 \end{pmatrix} = (-t_2 + t_3 + t_4) \begin{pmatrix} 2 \\ -3 \end{pmatrix}$$

is always a multiple of the vector $(2, -3)$.

It is well-known that the first step of the algorithm (computing U, S such that $U \cdot A = S$, U unimodular) is equivalent to computing extended greatest common divisors. A pivot is the GCD of the entries in the corresponding column and the cofactors needed to compute the pivot (i.e., the GCD) are exactly the cofactors of the extended GCD computation. In other words, this computation can be performed for $A \in D^{m \times n}$ where D is a Bézout ring (cf. Definition 2.8). But there is a catch with the required echelon form here; we discuss this problem and its solution for our application in Section 4.2.5.

The second step requires divisibility tests in the course of the forward substitution performed to solve $t \cdot S = b$. The question whether a divides b can also be answered by computing a GCD.

4.2.2 Pointwise Solutions

A natural way of modelling a generalisation of Banerjee's method by allowing one non-linear parameter is to take the entries of A and b not from $\mathbb{Z}$, but from $\mathbb{Z}[X]$ (or $\mathbb{Q}[X]$) with X playing the role of the parameter. Solving $x \cdot A = b$ now seems like solving for polynomials $x \in \mathbb{Z}[X]^m$ (or $x \in \mathbb{Q}[X]^m$) which satisfy the given equality. But it turns out that the polynomial solution of $x \cdot A = b$ is *not* what we need to describe the solutions of the equality system. Consider the following system:

$$\begin{pmatrix} i & j \end{pmatrix} \begin{pmatrix} X \\ 2 \end{pmatrix} = 1$$

For $i, j \in \mathbb{Z}[X]$, the system is infeasible because the constant term in the linear combination $i \cdot X + j \cdot 2$ is necessarily even and, hence, never equals 1. For $i, j \in \mathbb{Q}[X]$, there are infinitely many solutions, namely $i \in \mathbb{Q}[X]$, $j = \frac{1}{2}(1 - j \cdot X)$, but this does not represent the fact that $p \cdot i + 2 \cdot j = 1$ has solutions if and only if p is odd. Rather than in such polynomial solutions of the equality system, we are interested in *pointwise* solutions, i.e., we need to know for which $p \in \mathbb{Z}$ the system $x \cdot A(p) = b(p)$ is feasible and, for the feasible cases, which $x \in \mathbb{Z}$ solve the system (where x depends on p, of course). In the example, the solution is:

$$\begin{pmatrix} i & j \end{pmatrix} \begin{pmatrix} p \\ 2 \end{pmatrix} = 1 \quad \Longleftrightarrow \quad (i, j) \in \begin{cases} \varnothing & \text{if } p \equiv_2 0 \\ \left\{ \left(1 - 2t, \frac{1}{2}(1 - p - 2pt)\right) \mid t \in \mathbb{Z} \right\} & \text{if } p \equiv_2 1 \end{cases}$$

To capture the pointwise solutions, we have to compute a pointwise echelon form of matrix A, i.e., a matrix S such that $S(p)$ is the echelon form of $A(p)$ for every (but finitely many) $p \in \mathbb{Z}$. Similarly, we have to perform pointwise forward substitution in $t \cdot S(p) = b(p)$. We state our main result in its general form where the coefficients are allowed to be not only polynomials from $\mathbb{Z}[X]$ but entire quasi-polynomials from EQP in the following section. Then, we discuss computing extended GCDs in Section 4.2.4, followed by pointwise echelon form (Section 4.2.5) and forward substitution in Section 4.2.6.

4.2.3 Solving Systems of Linear Diophantine Equalities with One Non-linear Parameter

The solutions for x in $x \cdot A = b$ are functions in the unknown p of a certain structure, as the following theorem, our main theorem, states.

Theorem 4.2. *Let $A \in EQP^{m \times n}$ and $b \in EQP^m$. Then one can compute some finite set $M \subset \mathbb{Z}$, $l \in \mathbb{N}$ and $k \in \{0, \ldots, l\}$ different integers $n_1, \ldots, n_k$ with $0 \leq n_1 < \cdots < n_k < l$ such that $x \cdot A(p) = b(p)$ is feasible if, and only if, $p \in L$ with:*

$$L = M \cup L'$$
$$L' = (l\mathbb{Z} + n_1) \cup \cdots \cup (l\mathbb{Z} + n_k)$$

Furthermore, one can compute a matrix $U \in EQP^{m \times m}$ and, for $i \in \{1, \ldots, k\}$, $T_i \in EQP^{v_i \times m}$, $t_i \in EQP^m$ and $v_i \leq m$ such that for every $p \equiv_l n_i$, $p \notin M$

$$x \cdot A(p) = b(p) \;\Leftrightarrow\; x \in \big\{ (e \cdot T_i(p) + t_i(p)) \cdot U \mid e \in \mathbb{Z}^{v_i} \big\}$$

holds.

The theorem follows from the algorithms we give for the two phases of the solution procedure: Theorem 4.12, which states how to compute a pointwise echelon form S for A with $S = U \cdot A$, U unimodular, and Theorem 4.13, which states the feasibility of forward substitution in $t \cdot S = b$.

M represents special cases for p, i.e., the cases which deviate from the general, periodic behaviour of the solutions for $p \in L'$. The complete set of solutions for $x \cdot A = b$ in dependence of p is given by a case distinction which lists first the cases for $p \in M$, followed by the cases where $p \equiv_l n_i$. For each $p \in M$, the solutions are computed by solving the parameter-free system $x \cdot A(p) = b(p)$. The description of the solutions for the periodic cases is given in the theorem.

Our algorithms for computing M, U, l, k, the n_i, T_i, and t_i, stated as constructive proofs of the propositions made, are presented in the following. First, we look at the computation of the pointwise extended GCD. Second, we extend the GCD computation to compute a pointwise echelon form of a given matrix. Third, we look at forward substitution within the echelon matrix by divisibility tests.

4.2.4 Extended Greatest Common Divisor Computation

The aim of this section is to show that the pointwise GCD of two polynomials is always an entire quasi-polynomial. For example, the pointwise GCD of $f = X$ and $g = 2$ is the entire quasi-polynomial $[2, 1]$, as $\gcd(f(p), g(p))$ is 2 for even p and 1 for odd p. In addition, one can always find entire quasi-polynomials v and w such that the Bézout identity $\gcd(f(p), g(p)) \sim v(p) \cdot f(p) + w(p) \cdot g(p)$ holds. In the following lemma, this is stated formally (using the formulation with a unimodular matrix U for the Bézout identity) and the proof gives a procedure to compute the GCD and U.

Lemma 4.3. *Let* $f, g \in \mathbb{Z}[X]$. *Then one can compute* $U \in EQP^{2 \times 2}$ *and* $d \in EQP$ *such that*

$$d \sim \gcd_{EQP}(f, g)$$
$$d(p) \sim \gcd_{\mathbb{Z}}\big(f(p), g(p)\big)$$
$$\det\big(U(p)\big) \sim 1$$
$$\binom{d}{0} = U \cdot \binom{f}{g}$$

for all $p \in \mathbb{Z}$.

In our own previous work, we have shown that the GCD and the unimodular matrix U can be computed by an ad-hoc introduction of a certain number of case distinctions and appropriate substitutions for X for each case [GS08]. Here, we give another proof based on a pseudo-division.

Lemma 4.4. *Let* $f \in \mathbb{Q}[X]$ *and* $l \in \mathbb{N}_+$ *such that* $l \cdot f \in \mathbb{Z}[X]$. *Then the quasi-polynomial denoted by* $\lfloor f \rfloor$ *and defined by*

$$\lfloor f \rfloor := f - \big[\mathrm{frac}\big(f(0)\big), \ldots, \mathrm{frac}\big(f(l-1)\big)\big],$$

has the following properties:

$$\lfloor f \rfloor \in EQP, \quad \big(\forall p : p \in \mathbb{Z} : \lfloor f \rfloor(p) = \lfloor f(p) \rfloor\big).$$

Proof. For any monomial $m = aX^n$ with $n \geq 1$ of f, we have the following equality: $m(lp + i) = a \sum_{j=0}^{n} \binom{n}{j}(lp)^j i^{n-j} = ai^n + al \sum_{j=1}^{n} \binom{n}{j} l^{j-1} p^j i^{n-j}$. Since $al \in \mathbb{Z}$ by hypothesis, $\mathrm{frac}\big(m(lp+i)\big) = \mathrm{frac}(ai^n)$, i.e., the fractional part of any monomial depends only on i (and not p or l); hence, $\mathrm{frac}(f)$ has a period of l (where l need not be minimal). $\qquad\square$

We can deduce from the proof that the condition on l can be relaxed such that l need not be a multiple of the denominator of every coefficient (i.e., $l \cdot f \in \mathbb{Z}[X]$), because l need not be a multiple of the denominator of the constant coefficient, since the fractional part of the constant coefficient is constant anyway.

Definition 4.5. *Let* $f, g, \tilde{q}, \tilde{r} \in \mathbb{Q}[X]$, $g \neq 0$ *and* $f = \tilde{q} \cdot g + \tilde{r}$ *with* $\deg(\tilde{r}) < \deg(g)$. *We then call* $\mathrm{pquot}(f, g) := \lfloor \tilde{q} \rfloor \in EQP$ *the pseudo-quotient of* f *divided by* g *and* $\mathrm{prem}(f, g) := f - \mathrm{pquot}(f, g) \cdot g \in \mathcal{P}[X]$ *the pseudo-remainder of* f *modulo* g.

pquot is well-defined, since there is only one choice for $\tilde{q}, \tilde{r} \in \mathbb{Q}[X]$ with the stated properties; this is a well-known fact from the properties of polynomial division in $\mathbb{Q}[X]$. Note that $\mathrm{pquot}(f, g) \in EQP$, but $\mathrm{prem}(f, g) \in \mathcal{P}[X]$ in the general case. But for two polynomials $f, g \in \mathbb{Z}[X]$, the remainder is integer-valued, too.

Lemma 4.6. *Let* $f, g \in \mathbb{Z}[X]$, $g \neq 0$. *Then* $\mathrm{prem}(f, g) \in EQP$.

Proof. Obvious from Definition 4.5. □

Lemma 4.7. *Let* $f, g \in \mathbb{Z}[X]$ *with* $f, g \neq 0$ *and* $\deg(f) = \deg(g)$ *and let* $r := \mathrm{prem}(f, g)$. *Then* $\mathrm{pquot}(f, g) \in \mathbb{Z}$, $r \in \mathbb{Z}[X]$ *and* $\deg(r) \leq \deg(g)$ *holds. If* $\deg(r) = \deg(g)$, *then* $|\mathrm{HC}(r)| < |\mathrm{HC}(g)|$.

Proof. Let f, g be as stated. Then $\tilde{q}$ (from Definition 4.5) is from $\mathbb{Q}$; hence, $\lfloor \tilde{q} \rfloor \in \mathbb{Z}$. This implies $\mathrm{prem}(f, g) \in \mathbb{Z}[X]$ and $\deg(r) \leq \deg(g)$. If $\deg(r) = \deg(g)$, then $\mathrm{HC}(r) = (\tilde{q} - \lfloor \tilde{q} \rfloor) \cdot \mathrm{HC}(g)$, and since $|\tilde{q} - \lfloor \tilde{q} \rfloor| < 1$, it follows that $|\mathrm{HC}(r)| < |\mathrm{HC}(g)|$. □

Lemma 4.8. *Let* $f, g \in \mathbb{Q}[X]$, $g \neq 0$, $q = \mathrm{pquot}(f, g)$, $r = \mathrm{prem}(f, g)$. *Then* $f = q \cdot g + r$ *and* $\deg(r) \leq \deg(g)$.

Proof. Let f, g, p, q as stated and $\tilde{q}, \tilde{r}$ as in Definition 4.5. $f = q \cdot g + r$ is obvious from the definition (Definition 4.5). Since q and $\tilde{q}$ only differ in the constant coefficient (cf. Lemma 4.4), r and $\tilde{r}$ differ only in terms with degree less than or equal to $\deg(g)$. Hence, $\deg(r) \leq \deg(g)$ follows from $\deg(\tilde{r}) < \deg(g)$. □

The stated properties allow to compute a pointwise GCD of $f, g \in \mathbb{Z}[X]$ in EQP by repeated remainder operations. The reason is that, by taking remainders repeatedly, in each step either the degree is reduced (if $\deg(f) > \deg(g)$ or $\deg(f) = \deg(g)$ and $\mathrm{HC}(g)$ divides $\mathrm{HC}(f)$) or the absolute value of the leading coefficient (if $\deg(f) = \deg(g)$ and $\mathrm{HC}(g)$ does not divide $\mathrm{HC}(f)$), ensuring progress in the computation.

Note that we could define remainders differently as they are not uniquely determined. For example, for $f = 4X$ and $g = 3X$, our choice is a quotient of 1 and a remainder of X, but we could also use a quotient of 2 and a remainder of $-2X$. This is due to the fact that, instead of the "floor" of the quotient in $\mathbb{Q}[X]$, one could also choose the "ceiling" for $\mathrm{pquot}(f, g)$. In the example, $1 = \lfloor \frac{4}{3} \rfloor$ and $2 = \lceil \frac{4}{3} \rceil$. As stated in Definition 4.5, we decide to use the *floor* variant; the following algorithms work equally well with the *ceiling* variant.

Proof of Lemma 4.3. Let $f, g \in \mathbb{Z}[X]$. Assume w.l.o.g. that $\deg(f) \geq \deg(g)$. We show that one can construct a finite remainder sequence for f and g. If $g = 0$, then f is the only element in the remainder sequence. Otherwise, let $r := \mathrm{prem}(f, g)$, $q := \mathrm{pquot}(f, g)$.

1. If $\deg(f) = \deg(g)$, the computation continues with (g, r).

2. If $\deg(f) > \deg(g)$, then we compute $l := \mathrm{lp}(r)$ remainder sequences for (g, r_i) for $0 \leq i < l$ and $r_i := \mathrm{con}_l(r, i)$. These sequences can be combined into one sequence for f and g by combining the components again. The sequences can have different lengths, but they can be made equal by enlarging the shorter sequences by replacing the last division

$$g_{n-1} = q_n \cdot g_n$$

by

$$g_{n-1} = (q_n - 1) \cdot g_n + g_n$$
$$g_n = 0 \cdot g_n + g_n$$
$$\vdots$$
$$g_n = 1 \cdot g_n$$

to replicate the last remainder as often as needed. Hence, the sequences can be combined into one sequence.

The termination follows due to Lemma 4.7 and Lemma 4.8. In the second recursive case, $\deg(g)$ decreases in the recursion. In the first recursive case, $\deg(g)$ may decrease (if $HC(g)$ divides $HC(f)$) or stay the same, but, then, $|HC(g)|$ (which is a natural number) decreases. By Lemma 2.9, the existence of a terminating remainder sequence implies that the last remainder is a GCD in EQP of f and g. And a matrix U can be extracted from the remainder sequence with the properties stated in the lemma. This completes the proof of the existence of GCDs in EQP.

The uniqueness of GCDs in EQP (and the justification for the notation $d \sim \gcd_{EQP}(f, g)$) follows from Lemma 2.9, too, but we can also prove it explicitly. Assume that $d, d' \in EQP$ are both GCDs of $f, g \in EQP$. This implies that there exist $u, v \in EQP$ such that $d = u \cdot d'$ and $d' = v \cdot d$ and, hence, $d = u \cdot v \cdot d$. In the pointwise view, this means that, for every $p \in \mathbb{Z}$, $d(p) = u(p) \cdot v(p) \cdot d(p)$. This implies $u(p) \cdot v(p) = 1$ and $u(p), v(p) \in \{-1, 1\}$. Therefore, u and v are units in EQP and $d \sim d'$.

In addition, since $f = q \cdot g + r$ implies $f(p) = q(p) \cdot g(p) + r(p)$ for every $p \in \mathbb{Z}$, we have a remainder sequences in $\mathbb{Z}$, for the function values, too, and $d \sim \gcd_{EQP}(f, g)$ implies $d(p) \sim \gcd_{\mathbb{Z}}(f(p), g(p))$.   □

This proof, especially the argumentation that $d(p) \sim \gcd_{\mathbb{Z}}(f(p), g(p))$ is implied by $d \sim \gcd_{EQP}(f, g)$, may raise the question of why the same line of argumentation cannot be used in $\mathbb{Z}[X]$ or $\mathbb{Q}[X]$. Obviously, in $\mathbb{Z}[X]$ we cannot compute remainder sequences, because the equality $f = q \cdot g + r$ cannot be satisfied for, e.g., $f = X^2$, $g = 2X$. In $\mathbb{Q}[X]$, the same arguments apply, but then $d \sim \gcd_{\mathbb{Q}[X]}(f, g)$ implies $d(p) \sim \gcd_{\mathbb{Q}}(f(p), g(p))$, i.e., d is a pointwise GCD in $\mathbb{Q}$. But since $\mathbb{Q}$ is a field, all elements except zero are associated, i.e., for all $a, b, c \in \mathbb{Q} - \{0\}$, we have $\gcd_{\mathbb{Q}}(a, b) \sim c$, i.e., the consequence is a trivial statement. Only in EQP, the consequence for pointwise GCDs is nontrivial.

A corollary to Lemma 4.3 is that the proposition remains valid when f and g are allowed to be chosen from EQP instead of $\mathbb{Z}[X]$.

Corollary 4.9. *Lemma 4.3 holds even for $f, g \in EQP$.*

Proof. Let $l \in \mathbb{N}_+$ be a common period of all coefficients of f and g. Then the polynomials $f_i := \mathrm{con}_l(f, i)$ and $g_i := \mathrm{con}_l(g, i)$ for $0 \leq i < l$ are elements of $\mathbb{Z}[X]$ by Lemma 2.29. We can compute remainder sequences for (f_i, g_i) as in the proof of Lemma 4.3. By componentwise combination of these remainder sequences (as in the second case in the proof of Lemma 4.3), we obtain a remainder sequence for (f, g) and, hence, the proposition follows due to the same reasons as Lemma 4.3. $\square$

Another way of expressing that EQP allows to compute pointwise GCDs is to say that evaluation is a homomorphism w.r.t. computing GCDs.

Corollary 4.10. *Substitution of an element $p \in \mathbb{Z}$ for the unknown X, i.e., the function $\sigma_p : EQP \to \mathbb{Z}$ defined by $\sigma_p(f) = f(p)$ is a homomorphism from $(EQP, \gcd_{EQP})$ to $(\mathbb{Z}, \gcd_{\mathbb{Z}})$.*

Proof. Follows directly from the preceding corollary. $\square$

Since we are able to compute pointwise GCDs and unimodular matrices which describe the row operations of the GCD computation, we can, in the well-known manner described by Banerjee for the non-parametric case, use this computation of GCDs for computing echelon forms of matrices.

Corollary 4.11. *Let $A \in EQP^{m \times n}$. Then one can compute $U \in EQP^{m \times m}$ and $S \in EQP^{m \times n}$ such that S is echelon, $S = U \cdot A$ and $\det(U) \sim 1$.*

4.2.5   Pointwise Echelon Form

It is important to observe that, for S computed by repeated GCD computations, S is in echelon form, but $S(p)$ is *not* necessarily in echelon form for every $p \in \mathbb{Z}$. For example,

$$S = \begin{pmatrix} [1,0] \cdot X & 1 \\ 0 & 1 \end{pmatrix}$$

is clearly echelon, but $S(p)$ is not echelon for $p = 0$ and every odd p, since the upper left entry vanishes at these points. We need a stronger, pointwise echelon form. A pointwise echelon form for the example is the matrix

$$S' = \begin{pmatrix} [1,0] \cdot X & 1 \\ 0 & [1,0] \end{pmatrix}$$

which is obtained from S by one additional row operation, namely subtracting $[0,1]$ multiplied by the first row from the second row. Note that this leaves the zero in the lower left corner intact. Now $S'(p)$ is echelon for all $p \neq 0$. There is no way to compute an S' from S (by row operations) which is echelon for all p. But, as the following theorem shows, the set of exceptions (the values of p for which the computed matrix is not echelon) can always be kept finite.

Theorem 4.12. *Let $A \in EQP^{m \times n}$. Then one can compute a finite set $M \subset \mathbb{Z}$ and matrices $U \in EQP^{m \times m}$ and $S \in EQP^{m \times n}$ such that S is echelon, $S = U \cdot A$, $\det(U) \sim 1$ and $S(p)$ is echelon for every $p \in \mathbb{Z} - M$.*

Proof. Compute S_0 and U_0 from A as by Corollary 4.11. Let us describe a procedure which recursively transforms S_0 to pointwise echelon form. The idea is that, if a pivot vanishes periodically because some constituents are zero, we apply some additional elementary row operations to matrix S_0 in the respective constituents to obtain a pointwise echelon form in these constituents (as in the simple example above). Note that this does not change the constituents in which the pivot does not vanish periodically.

If there is no pivot in S_0, we are finished. Else, let $d \in EQP$ be the pivot element of the first row of S_0 and W be the submatrix of S_0 consisting of the columns to the right of this pivot, i.e.,

$$S_0 = \begin{pmatrix} 0 & \begin{pmatrix} d \\ 0 \\ \vdots \\ 0 \end{pmatrix} & W \end{pmatrix}.$$

Compute the zeros of d, i.e., by Lemma 2.34, the set M_0 of non-periodic roots, and $l, k, n_1, \ldots, n_k$ as in the lemma. For each $i \in \{1, \ldots, k\}$, let $W_i := \mathrm{con}_l(W, n_i)$. Note that, in general, $W_i \in EQP^{m \times e}$ (for some $e \in \mathbb{N}$) as l need not be a period of W. Compute, by applying the procedure we develop here recursively to the W_i, the matrices $\bar{W}_i$ which are in strong echelon form, sets M_i such that $\bar{W}_i(p)$ is only non-echelon if $p \in M_i$ and matrices U_i which describe the row operations performed on W_i to obtain $\bar{W}_i$. Let $M' := M_0 \cup (lM_1 + n_1) \cup \cdots \cup (lM_k + n_k)$ and let $\bar{S}$ be the matrix obtained by replacing every constituent n_i of W in S_0 by the entries of $\bar{W}_i$ for every $i \in \{1, \ldots, k\}$. The handling of the pivot d is now finished, but the procedure must be applied to any further pivots. Let S' be the submatrix of $\bar{S}$ to the right and below the pivot d (not including the pivot row and column). By applying the procedure we develop here recursively to S', we get S'', U'' and M''. Obtain the final matrix S by replacing S' in $\bar{S}$ by S'' and set $M := M' \cup M''$. Compute the final matrix U from the matrices U_0, the U_i, and U'':

$$U := \begin{pmatrix} 1 & 0 \\ 0 & U'' \end{pmatrix} \cdot V \cdot U_0$$

where V describes the additional pivoting steps made in W described by the matrices U_i, i.e.,

$$V := \mathrm{comb}(V_0, \ldots, V_{l-1}) \quad \text{with} \quad V_j := \begin{cases} U_j & \text{if } j \in \{n_1, \ldots, n_k\} \\ I_m & \text{otherwise} \end{cases}$$

for $0 \le j < l$. □

The columns in which the pivots for the different cases on p are found can be computed, together with the computation of the pointwise echelon form, as the zeros of the (possible) pivots indicate when the respective matrix entry is not a pivot in the pointwise echelon form.

4.2.6   Forward Substitution

After computing a pointwise echelon form S of A, the next step of solving $x \cdot A = b$ is to perform forward substitution in the system $t \cdot S = b$. This is done by testing the divisibility of the entries in b by corresponding pivot elements of S and solving (by substitution) for the entries of t. In the parametric case, care has to be taken as to where to find the pivots. As noted in the previous section, in pointwise echelon form, the pivots of $S(p)$ are not necessarily found at the same positions as in S. By applying the procedure given in the proof of Theorem 4.12, one finds, for each case ($=$ a congruence class of p modulo l), the correct location of the pivot.

What remains to be done to obtain a complete solution algorithm is to give an algorithmic divisibility test (which also computes the quotient in the case of divisibility). This last step is formalised in the following theorem.

Theorem 4.13. *Let $f, g \in EQP$ and let $D(f \mid g) \subseteq \mathbb{Z}$ denote the set of integers p with $f(p) \mid g(p)$. Then one can compute some $l \in \mathbb{N}$, some finite set $M \subset \mathbb{Z}$ and $k \in \{0, \ldots, l\}$ different integers $0 \le n_1 < \cdots < n_k < l$ such that*

$$D(f \mid g) = M \cup (l\mathbb{Z} + n_1) \cup \cdots \cup (l\mathbb{Z} + n_k).$$

Moreover, we can compute $q \in EQP$ such that $q(p) = \frac{g(p)}{f(p)}$ holds for all $p \in D(f \mid g) - M$, $f(p) \ne 0$.

Proof. Let $h \in EQP$ be a pointwise GCD of f and g. Since $f(p) \mid g(p)$ iff $\gcd_{\mathbb{Z}}\big(f(p), g(p)\big) \sim f(p)$, we have $D(f \mid g) = R(h - f) \cup R(h + f)$ and this proves the claimed structure of $D(f \mid g)$ and gives an algorithm for computing M, l, and $n_1, \ldots, n_k$ due to Lemma 2.34 and Corollary 4.9. q is then computed as an entire quasi-polynomial with $\mathrm{con}_{l'}(q, i) \cdot \mathrm{con}_{l'}(f, i) = \mathrm{con}_{l'}(g, i)$ for a common period $l' := \mathrm{lcm}\big(\mathrm{lp}(f), \mathrm{lp}(g), l\big)$ and all $0 \le i < l'$ with $i \equiv_l n_j$, $1 \le j \le k$ by polynomial division for each i and with arbitrary other components. Note that $\mathrm{con}_{l'}(f, i), \mathrm{con}_{l'}(g, i) \in \mathbb{Z}[X]$ and that $\mathrm{con}_{l'}(f, i)(p) \mid \mathrm{con}_{l'}(g, i)(p)$ for all $p \in \mathbb{Z}$ and $i \equiv_l n_j$. $\square$

Putting the location of the pivots, the divisibility test just described and the general forward substitution method together, we can algorithmically determine the cases for which $t \cdot S(p) = b(p)$ has a solution and obtain the matrices T_i and vectors t_i (cf. Theorem 4.2) for each case; the technical details are straightforward.

4.2.7   Examples

Let us now present a few examples for the solutions of linear Diophantine equality systems with one non-linear parameter. We start with the initial mini-example and consider the system $p \cdot i + 2 \cdot j = 1$. From the coefficients p and 2 it is clear that the system is feasible if, and only if, p is odd. The polynomial formulation (with X for p) is:

$$\begin{pmatrix} i & j \end{pmatrix} \cdot \begin{pmatrix} X \\ 2 \end{pmatrix} = 1$$

To solve the system, we perform echelon reduction on the coefficient matrix as the first step. Reducing the column is equivalent to finding the GCD of X and 2. Since the pseudo-quotient $\mathrm{pquot}(X, 2)$ is $\frac{1}{2}X + [0, -\frac{1}{2}]$ and, hence, the pseudo-remainder $\mathrm{prem}(X, 2)$ is $[0, 1]$, i.e., the equality

$$X = 2 \cdot (\frac{1}{2}X + [0, -\frac{1}{2}]) + [0, 1]$$

holds. Since the remainder $[0, 1]$ vanishes in the first constituent (i.e., for $p \equiv_2 0$), we continue only for the second constituent and divide 2 by 1 with a remainder of 0. By looking at the modified remainder sequence (note that we added $[-1, 0]$ to $\mathrm{pquot}(X, 2)$ to make the lengths equal, see also the proof of Lemma 4.3)

$$X = 2 \cdot (\frac{1}{2}X + [-1, -\frac{1}{2}]) + [2, 1]$$
$$2 = [2, 1] \cdot [1, 2] + 0$$

we find that the GCD is $[2, 1]$ because it is the last non-zero remainder in the modified sequence. A matrix U describing the GCD computation can be extracted from the remainder sequence according to Lemma 2.9:

$$U = \begin{pmatrix} 0 & 1 \\ 1 & -[1, 2] \end{pmatrix} \cdot \begin{pmatrix} 0 & 1 \\ 1 & -(\frac{1}{2}X + [-1, -\frac{1}{2}]) \end{pmatrix} = \begin{pmatrix} 1 & -\frac{1}{2}X + [1, \frac{1}{2}] \\ -[1, 2] & [\frac{1}{2}, 1]X \end{pmatrix}$$

The matrix S (the echelon form of the original coefficient matrix) is given by:

$$S = U \cdot \begin{pmatrix} X \\ 2 \end{pmatrix} = \begin{pmatrix} [2, 1] \\ 0 \end{pmatrix}$$

The next step in solving the equality system is to solve $\begin{pmatrix} t_1 & t_2 \end{pmatrix} \cdot S = 1$ for $t_1, t_2 \in \mathbb{Z}$. Obviously,

$$\begin{pmatrix} t_1 & t_2 \end{pmatrix} \cdot \begin{pmatrix} [2, 1] \\ 0 \end{pmatrix} = 1$$

is only feasible for $p \equiv_2 1$ because 2 does not divide 1:

$$(t_1, t_2) \in \begin{cases} \varnothing & \text{if } p \equiv_2 0 \\ \{(1, t) \mid t \in \mathbb{Z}\} & \text{if } p \equiv_2 1 \end{cases}$$

Transforming back the solutions to the original problem by computing $(t_1 \; t_2) \cdot U$, we obtain the solutions for the original problem:

$$\begin{pmatrix} i & j \end{pmatrix} \cdot \begin{pmatrix} p \\ 2 \end{pmatrix} = 1 \iff (i, j) \in \begin{cases} \varnothing & \text{if } p \equiv_2 0 \\ \{(1 - 2t, \frac{1}{2}(1 - p - 2pt)) \mid t \in \mathbb{Z}\} & \text{if } p \equiv_2 1 \end{cases}$$

As an example which shows that the degrees of freedom in the solution can depend on the residue class of p, let us consider the system $x \cdot A(p) = b(p)$ with

$$A = \begin{pmatrix} [0,1,2]X & X \\ [0,1,1]X & X \end{pmatrix}, \qquad b = \begin{pmatrix} X & X \end{pmatrix}.$$

Note that the first column of A vanishes for $p \equiv_3 0$ and for $p \equiv_3 1$ the columns are linearly dependent. A weak echelon form for A (as computed by our implementation) is

$$S_w = \begin{pmatrix} [-1,-1,0]X & [-1,-1,1]X \\ 0 & [-1,0,1]X \end{pmatrix}.$$

The upper left entry vanishes for $p = 0$ and if $p \equiv_3 2$. For $p \equiv_3 2$, $S_w(p)$ is clearly not echelon. The strong echelon form computed by our implementation (and the respective matrix U) is

$$S = \begin{pmatrix} [-1,-1,0]X & -X \\ 0 & [-1,0,0]X \end{pmatrix}, \qquad U = \begin{pmatrix} 0 & -1 \\ 1 & [-2,-1,-1] \end{pmatrix}$$

which is obtained from S_w by subtracting the first row from the second row in the third component (note that this leaves the zero in the lower left column intact) and a not strictly necessary multiplication of the third component with -1; our implementation computes echelon forms such that the determinant of the matrix U is always $+1$. In addition to S itself, our implementation computes that the pivots of $S(p)$ are in the first and second column if $p \equiv_3 0$, in the first column only if $p \equiv_3 1$, in the second column only if $p \equiv_3 2$ and that $p = 0$ is an exceptional case (it deviates from the other $p \equiv_3 0$ cases). The equality system is then solved by solving the exceptional case separately (the system $x \cdot A(0) = b(0)$ is parameter-free and can be solved by the well-known method) and performing forward substitution for the three cases of $(t_1 \ t_2) \cdot S_i = (\mathrm{con}_3(X,i) \ \mathrm{con}_3(X,i))$ where S_i for $i \in \{0,1,2\}$ is the restriction of S to the respective constituents. For example, in the case $i = 1$ we have to solve

$$\begin{pmatrix} t_1 & t_2 \end{pmatrix} \begin{pmatrix} -3X & -3X \\ 0 & 0 \end{pmatrix} = \begin{pmatrix} 3X & 3X \end{pmatrix}.$$

Since $-3p'$ divides $3p'$ for every $p' \in \mathbb{Z}$, we get $t_1 = -1$, $t_2 \in \mathbb{Z}$ for every $p' \in \mathbb{Z}$ (and $p = 3p' + 1$). Multiplying $(t_1 \ t_2)$ with U yields the solutions for x. The complete solution of $x \cdot A(p) = b(p)$ for all cases of p is computed as:

$$x \in \begin{cases} \{(t_1, t_2) \mid t_1, t_2 \in \mathbb{Z}\} & \text{if } p = 0 \\ \{(0,1)\} & \text{if } p \equiv_3 0,\ p \neq 0 \\ \{(t_2, 1 - t_2) \mid t_2 \in \mathbb{Z}\} & \text{if } p \equiv_3 1 \\ \emptyset & \text{if } p \equiv_3 2 \end{cases}$$

4.2.8 Floor and Modulo Operations

Let us briefly note that the technique can be applied to input systems with floor and modulo operations. To the automatic parallelisation community, these operations may be of more interest than quasi-polynomials themselves. The floor expression $\lfloor \frac{p}{d} \rfloor$ for a parameter p and $d \in \mathbb{N}_+$ can be expressed by a quasi-polynomial (cf. Lemma 4.4)

$$\left\lfloor \frac{p}{d} \right\rfloor = \frac{1}{d}p - [0, \frac{1}{d}, \ldots, \frac{d-1}{d}]$$

and the modulo expression $p \bmod d$ can be trivially written as $[0, 1, \ldots, d-1]$. Therefore, the operations floor, ceiling and modulo on the parameter can be expressed in a way that make our techniques applicable.

4.2.9 Beyond a Single Parameter

The techniques presented in Section 4.2.3 cannot be generalised to systems with more than one non-linear parameter. This follows from the fact that the number of operations (with $+$, $-$, $\cdot$, $\lfloor \div \rfloor$, and mod as elementary operations) for computing $\gcd(p_1, p_2)$ in dependence of $p_1, p_2 \in \mathbb{Z}$ is unbounded; more precisely, for infinitely many $p_1, p_2 \in \mathbb{Z}$, the number of operations is in $\Omega(p_1 + p_2)$ [vdD03]. Although there is no hope for the general case with the techniques presented, special cases can be solved. To perform echelon reduction it is sufficient for the entries whose GCD is to be computed (i.e., a lower part of a column) to be uni-parametric. Therefore, if it is possible to make the respective entries uni-parameteric by permuting columns and/or rows, echelon reduction can be performed.

The result of forward substitution can be represented by a finite case distinction because only finitely many divisibility tests are required in any case. In other words, forward substitution can be performed in much more general settings than presented here because representing all cases in the result is only an overhead in both space and run-time requirements since all the conditionals have to be stored and evaluated at run time. Our method of performing forward substitution for the single parameter case (cf. Section 4.2.6) computes explicit results for the different residue classes modulo p and, therefore, greatly reduces the number of cases, although this is not strictly necessary for a complete procedure.

4.3 Using Quantifier Elimination to Solve Problems in the Generalised Model

In the previous section, the main obstacle was that integral solutions of the examined equality systems were required. In some cases, integrality is not required for correctness, i.e., we can apply algorithms which compute solutions in the real numbers and the real solutions are sufficient to achieve the desired transformation. We encounter this situation when computing schedules (cf. Section 5.2), performing tiling (cf. Section 5.3) and at generating code (cf. Section 5.5).

Quantifier elimination can be used to do two things:

- compute a quantifier-free formula which is equivalent to a given formula with quantifiers,

- compute solutions (i.e., values) for the quantified variables that validate the given formula by quantifier elimination with answer.

Both can be used to solve problems in the generalised model.

To be able to apply quantifier elimination to a problem, we have to express the problem as a first-order logical formula with the operators $+$, $-$, $\cdot$, and the usual equality and ordering relations of the real numbers. A given polyhedron (which may depend on possibly non-linear parameters) can be described by a finite set of inequalities S in the variables $x_1, \ldots, x_n$. We assume that the inequalities in S are denominator-free (this can always be achieved by multiplying every inequality with the common denominator d of its coefficients, or d^2 when the sign of d is not known) because the logical language has no division symbol (cf. Definition 2.20).

4.3.1 Equivalent Formulas

As an example where computing an equivalent formula is useful, let us consider one typical operation on polyhedra: projecting out one dimension. This is usually performed with methods like Fourier-Motzkin elimination or dual description methods. Consider the following formula describing a two-dimensional polyhedron in the dimensions x and y with a non-linear parameter n:

$$\varphi = (0 \leq x \leq n \wedge x \leq n \cdot y \leq 2 \cdot x)$$

Since the formula has the term $n \cdot y$, it can only be treated in the generalised model. Projecting onto the x-dimension is simple in this case, yielding

$$\varphi_x = (0 \leq x \leq n),$$

but the projection onto y is not obvious. Both projections can be described using quantifiers, since the projection results φ_x and φ_y are equivalent to formulas with existential quantifiers:

$$\varphi_x \leftrightarrow \exists y\,(\varphi)$$
$$\varphi_y \leftrightarrow \exists x\,(\varphi)$$

Computing the quantifier-free equivalent φ_x with QEPCAD yields, in effect, the formula $0 \leq x \leq n$ shown above. Unfortunately, using REDUCE yields

$$\varphi_x = \big((n \cdot x \geq 0 \wedge n \neq 0 \wedge x \geq 0) \vee (n - x \geq 0 \wedge x = 0 \wedge x = 0)\big),$$

which has the same logical meaning, but is less suitable for further processing as it does not exhibit the fact that φ_x can be written as a single conjunction. For φ_y, the situation is even worse. QEPCAD computes

$$\varphi_y = \Big(n \geq 0 \wedge \big(n = 0 \vee (y \geq 0 \wedge y \leq 2)\big)\Big)$$

and REDUCE's answer is

$$\varphi_y = \big((n \cdot y - n \le 0 \wedge n \cdot y \ge 0) \vee (n \cdot y - n \ge 0 \wedge n \cdot y - 2 \cdot n \le 0 \wedge n \ge 0)\big).$$

From QEPCAD's answer we learn that there is a difference between $n = 0$ and $n > 0$, as the projection is $y \in \mathbb{R}$ for $n = 0$ and $0 \le y \le 2$ for $n > 0$. The formula we desire for φ_y is

$$\varphi_y = \big(n = 0 \ \dot{\vee} \ (n > 0 \wedge 0 \le y \le 2)\big),$$

(where $\dot{\vee}$ denotes exclusive or) which exhibits the fact that $n = 0$ and $n > 0$ are disjoint cases. Such a formula can be represented as a decision tree. Let us discuss how we can obtain a representation of a projection result as a decision tree with finitely many cases and a conjunctive formula at each leaf. The following theorem about Algorithm 4.1 and its proof show how to compute a suitable case distinction on the parameters. The formula simplification in the algorithm makes sure that we do not output superfluous bounds and, if the simplifier detects infeasible formulas, that no infeasible cases are reported in the result (which would be harmless but is usually undesirable).

Theorem 4.14. *Let* $\varphi \in Qf(\{v_1, \ldots, v_n\} \cup \{p_1, \ldots, p_k\})$ *be a quantifier-free formula linear in* $v_1, \ldots, v_n$ *such that* $\varphi(\cdot, \mathbf{p})$ *is equivalent to a conjunction for any value of the parameters* $\mathbf{p}$. *Then one can compute* $l \in \mathbb{N}$, *conjunctions* $\varphi_1, \ldots, \varphi_l \in Qf(\{v_1, \ldots, v_n\} \cup \{p_1, \ldots, p_k\})$ *linear in* $v_1, \ldots, v_n$ *and formulas* $\psi_1, \ldots, \psi_l \in Qf(\{p_1, \ldots, p_k\})$ *such that*

$$\varphi \leftrightarrow \bigvee_{i=1}^{l} (\psi_i \wedge \varphi_i)$$

$$\psi_i \rightarrow \exists v_1 \cdots \exists v_n \, (\varphi_i) \qquad \qquad \text{for } 1 \le i \le l$$

$$\neg(\psi_i \wedge \psi_j) \qquad \qquad \text{for } 1 \le i < j \le l$$

hold in $\mathbb{R}$ *according to Algorithm 4.1.*

Proof. Let φ be ,as stated. The algorithm checks for which $\mathbf{p}$ each atomic formula α_i in φ^+ forms a bound of the polyhedron described by φ. α_i is a bound of the polyhedron if, and only if, κ_i holds (this follows from Lemma 2.23 because, by assumption, φ describes a polyhedron for every choice of the parameters, i.e., all relevant bounds are weak inequalities of the form $f \ge 0$ or $f \le 0$). The formulas κ'_A describe all possible combinations in the parameters w.r.t. the κ_i, i.e., if $\kappa_A(\mathbf{p})$ holds for a given assignment of the parameters, then the bounds of the polyhedron are given by exactly the α_i with $i \in A$. Hence, the polyhedron is defined by ρ'_A if $\kappa_A(\mathbf{p})$ holds. To make sure that we output only non-empty polyhedra, the formulas η_A check whether ρ'_A is satisfiable in the variables for a given $\mathbf{p}$. The final case distinction on the parameters is given by the simplifications of all feasible $\kappa'_A \wedge \eta_A$ (as κ_A) and the respective formula defining the polyhedron ρ_A, which is a simplification of ρ'_A under κ_A. $\square$

Input: φ is a quantifier-free formula linear in the variables $v_1, \ldots, v_n$ but not necessarily linear in the parameters $\mathbf{p}$; $\varphi(\cdot, \mathbf{p})$ is equivalent to a polyhedron for any assignment of the parameters $\mathbf{p}$.

Output: $\{(\psi_1, \varphi_1), \ldots, (\psi_l, \varphi_l)\}$ such that $\psi_1, \ldots, \psi_l$ are formulas in the parameters only, $\varphi_1, \ldots, \varphi_l$ are conjunctions linear in the variables, $\varphi \leftrightarrow \bigvee_{i=1}^{l}(\psi_i \wedge \varphi_i)$, $\psi_i \rightarrow \exists v_1 \cdots \exists v_n \, (\varphi_i)$ for $1 \leq i \leq l$ and $\neg(\psi_i \wedge \psi_j)$ for $1 \leq i < j \leq l$.

a) Let, for some suitable $m \in \mathbb{N}$, $\alpha_1, \ldots, \alpha_m \in At(\{v_1, \ldots, v_n\} \cup \{p_1, \ldots, p_k\})$ be the atomic formulas in φ^+.

b) Let κ_i be a quantifier-free equivalent of $\forall v_1 \cdots \forall v_n \, (\varphi \rightarrow \alpha_i)$ for $1 \leq i \leq m$.

c) Let $M = \{1, \ldots, m\}$. For every $\varnothing \not\subseteq A \subseteq M$, construct:

$$\kappa'_A := \bigwedge_{i \in A} \kappa_i \wedge \bigwedge_{i \in M-A} \neg\kappa_i$$

$$\rho'_A := \bigwedge_{i \in A} \alpha_i$$

d) Let η_A be a quantifier-free equivalent of $\exists v_1 \cdots \exists v_n \, (\rho'_A)$.

e) Let κ_A be the result of simplifying $\kappa'_A \wedge \eta_A$.

f) Let ρ_A be the result of simplifying ρ'_A under κ_A.

g) The final result is given by all (κ_A, ρ_A)-pairs which describe feasible conditions on the parameters and a feasible polyhedron, respectively:

$$R := \{(\kappa_A, \rho_A) \mid \varnothing \not\subseteq A \subseteq M, \rho_A \neq \text{false}, \kappa_A \neq \text{false}\}$$

h) return R.

Algorithm 4.1: Computing an explicit representation for a non-linearly parametrised polyhedron by quantifier elimination

The algorithm has, as shown, a complexity exponential in the number m of atomic formulas in φ because all subsets of $M = \{1, \ldots, m\}$ are considered. In an implementation, care should be taken to save computations by exploiting the fact that, if $\bigwedge_{i \in A} \kappa'_i$ is infeasible, then $\kappa'_{A'}$ for any $A' \supseteq A$ is infeasible, too.

An immediate consequence of Theorem 4.14 is that we can handle projections of non-linearly parametrised polyhedra, since the projection $\exists v_n (\varphi)$ is, for every assignment of the parameters, equivalent to a polyhedron.

Corollary 4.15. *Let* $\varphi \in Qf(\{v_1, \ldots, v_n\} \cup \{p_1, \ldots, p_k\})$ *be a conjunction of atomic formulas linear in the variables* $v_1, \ldots, v_n$. *Then, one can compute* $l \in \mathbb{N}$, *conjunctions* $\varphi_1, \ldots, \varphi_l \in Qf(\{v_1, \ldots, v_n\} \cup \{p_1, \ldots, p_k\})$ *linear in the variables* $v_1, \ldots, v_n$ *and* $\psi_1, \ldots, \psi_l \in Qf(\{p_1, \ldots, p_k\})$ *such that the following formulas hold in* $\mathbb{R}$:

$$\exists v_n(\varphi) \leftrightarrow \bigvee_{i=1}^{l} (\psi_i \wedge \varphi_i)$$

$$\psi_i \rightarrow \exists v_1 \cdots \exists v_{n-1}(\varphi_i) \qquad \text{for } 1 \leq i \leq l$$

$$\neg(\psi_i \wedge \psi_j) \qquad \text{for } 1 \leq i < j \leq l$$

To continue the previous example, REDUCE's answer to the quantifier elimination question $\exists x (\varphi)$ with $\varphi = (0 \leq x \leq n \wedge x \leq n \cdot y \leq 2 \cdot x)$ is

$$\varphi_y = \big((n \cdot y - n \leq 0 \wedge n \cdot y \geq 0) \vee (n \cdot y - n \geq 0 \wedge n \cdot y - 2 \cdot n \leq 0 \wedge n \geq 0)\big).$$

The atomic formulas of this disjunctive normal form are:

$$\alpha_1 = (n \cdot y - n \leq 0)$$
$$\alpha_2 = (n \cdot y \geq 0)$$
$$\alpha_3 = (n \cdot y - n \geq 0)$$
$$\alpha_4 = (n \cdot y - 2 \cdot n \leq 0)$$
$$\alpha_5 = (n \geq 0)$$

This yields the following κ_i formulas, the quantifier-free equivalents of $\forall y (\varphi_y \rightarrow \alpha_i)$:

$$\kappa_1 = \kappa_3 = (n \leq 0), \qquad \kappa_2 = \kappa_4 = \kappa_5 = (\text{true})$$

The formulas κ'_A which are not equivalent to false and the respective formulas ρ'_A and η_A are given by:

$\kappa'_{\{2,4,5\}} = (n > 0)$
$\rho'_{\{2,4,5\}} = (n \cdot y \geq 0 \wedge n \cdot y - 2 \cdot n \leq 0 \wedge n \geq 0)$
$\eta_{\{2,4,5\}} = (n \geq 0)$

$\kappa'_{\{1,2,3,4,5\}} = (n \leq 0)$
$\rho'_{\{1,2,3,4,5\}} = (n \cdot y - n \leq 0 \wedge n \cdot y \geq 0 \wedge n \cdot y - n \geq 0 \wedge n \cdot y - 2 \cdot n \leq 0 \wedge n \geq 0)$
$\eta_{\{1,2,3,4,5\}} = (n \geq 0)$

Simplifying $\kappa'_A \wedge \eta_A$ (obtaining κ_A) and simplifying ρ'_A w.r.t. κ_A (obtaining ρ_A) using SLFQ yields:

$$\kappa_{\{2,4,5\}} = (n > 0), \qquad\qquad \rho_{\{2,4,5\}} = (0 \leq y \leq 2)$$
$$\kappa_{\{1,2,3,4,5\}} = (n = 0), \qquad\qquad \rho_{\{1,2,3,4,5\}} = (\text{true})$$

This represents the final result $\{(n = 0, \text{true}), (n > 0, 0 \leq y \leq 2)\}$, the projection of the original formula onto y with a case distinction on n and a conjunctive formula for each of the two cases.

4.3.2 Quantifier Elimination with Answer

As an example of a question which can be expressed by quantifier elimination with answer, we consider the lexicographic minimum of a polyhedron. Since the logical language used does not contain a notion of lexicographic ordering, we have to define the lexicographic "less-than or equal to" relation $\preceq$ based on the standard ordering $<$ on the real numbers, see Definition 2.1. To find a formula describing the lexicographic minimality of a finite point $(x_1, \ldots, x_n)$, we translate the following property L into a logical formula:

> The point $(x_1, \ldots, x_n)$ is the lexicographic minimum of the given polyhedron if it lies inside the polyhedron and it is lexicographically less than or equal to every other point $(y_1, \ldots, y_n)$ which also lies inside the polyhedron.

To express this property for a polyhedron in the variables $(x_1, \ldots, x_n)$ defined by φ, we define $\psi := \varphi[x_1 := y_1, \ldots, x_n := y_n]$ for some new variables $y_1, \ldots, y_n$ (i.e., ψ is the same as φ with y_i instead of x_i). Then property L can be expressed by the formula μ:

$$\mu := \varphi \wedge \forall y_1 \ldots \forall y_n \left(\psi \rightarrow (x_1, \ldots, x_n) \preceq (y_1, \ldots, y_n) \right)$$

The existence of a lexicographic minimum $(x_1, \ldots, x_n)$ is expressed by the formula:

$$\exists x_1 \cdots \exists x_n (\mu)$$

Some quantifier elimination tools can "solve" this problem by finding conditions under which values for $x_1, \ldots, x_n$ exist such that μ becomes true, and calculate such values for the variables $x_1, \ldots, x_n$. That is, the answer given by the quantifier elimination procedure is a set

$$\{(\gamma_i, [x_1 := t_{i,1}, \ldots, x_n := t_{i,n}]) \mid 1 \leq i \leq l\}$$

for some $l \in \mathbb{N}$, where γ_i is a quantifier-free logical formula in the parameters and $t_{i,1}, \ldots, t_{i,n}$ are expressions in the parameters describing the lexicographic minimum under the condition γ_i. This procedure is called "quantifier elimination with answer".

Example 4.16. Consider the system

$$q \leq x_2 \leq p \cdot x_1$$

in the variables x_1, x_2 and the parameters p, q. The formula μ for this system is:

$$\mu := (q \leq x_2 \land x_2 \leq p \cdot x_1) \quad \land$$
$$\forall y_1 \forall y_2 \left(q \leq y_2 \land y_2 \leq p \cdot y_1 \rightarrow x_1 < y_1 \lor (x_1 = y_1 \land x_2 \leq y_2) \right)$$

REDLOG's answer to the question $\exists x_1 \exists x_2 \, (\mu)$ is:

$$\{ (p > 0, [x_1 := \frac{q}{p}, x_2 := q]) \}$$

This means that, in the case of $p > 0$, there is a finite lexicographic minimum, namely at $(\frac{q}{p}, q)$. Otherwise (i.e., for $p \leq 0$) there is no finite lexicographic minimum, since the polyhedron is either empty or unbounded.

4.4 Obtaining Generalised Algorithms via Program Transformation

In this section, we explore ways to derive algorithms for the generalised polyhedron model from existing algorithms for the classical polyhedron model. We give an informal description of program transformation rules which generalise an existing algorithm. Then, we look at Fourier-Motzkin elimination and the simplex algorithm. This is a summary of our previous work [Grö03, GGL04]. Finally, we present a special case for Fourier-Motzkin elimination in which decision tree simplification can be avoided.

4.4.1 New Algorithms by Program Transformation

Some algorithms (e.g., Fourier-Motzkin elimination and the simplex algorithm) contain case distinctions on the signs of intermediate values (computed from the input values, i.e., the coefficients of the input inequalities). The general structure of such a case distinction is

> **if** $f \geq 0$ **then**
> $\quad t_+$
> **else**
> $\quad t_-$

where f is an expression derived from the input values of the algorithm by arithmetic operations. If the input inequalities contain non-linear parameters, f is not a rational number but an expression in the parameters, e.g., $f = \frac{f_1}{f_2}$ for $f_1, f_2 \in \mathbb{Q}[p_1, \ldots, p_m]$, $f_2 \neq 0$. It is generally impossible to decide which sign f has (since it depends on the values of the parameters, in general), so we modify the algorithm such that the above case distinction in the algorithm's *code* is

replaced by a case distinction in the resulting *data structure*. We rewrite the
above code to

$$Cond \ (f \geq 0) \ t_+ \ t_-$$

In addition to this transformation of case distinctions, we have to make some
other changes in the algorithm:

- We have to replace an expression e which constructs a final result by
  Leaf e.

- If some function $f :: \alpha \rightarrow \beta$ is applied to an expression e which changes its
  type from α to *Tree* α during the generalisation, we have to map f over
  the whole tree e, i.e., apply f to every leaf of e, by using some suitable
  combinator. The choice of the combinator depends on whether f has to
  be generalised to have the new type $\alpha \rightarrow$ *Tree* β, or not [Grö03].

We do not formally apply this informally defined set of transformation rules
to existing implementations of algorithms. Implementing the transformation
system seems more difficult than implementing generalised versions of existing
algorithms following the ideas of this transformation system. In addition, it
may be desirable to deviate from strictly applying the transformation rules. In
Fourier-Motzkin elimination, for example, we optimise the sets of lower and upper bounds by checking whether, for two bounds b_1 and b_2, one of the relations
$b_1 \leq b_2$ or $b_1 \geq b_2$ holds and remove the irrelevant bound. In the generalised
Fourier-Motzkin elimination, this may depend on parameters, so the transformation system would generate a case distinction. But usually we do not want
a case distinction in this case since, if neither $b_1 \leq b_2$ nor $b_1 \geq b_2$ holds, we
simply keep both bounds b_1 and b_2 in the set of lower or upper bounds.

Tree Simplification

The main challenge arising from the transformation system just given is to
simplify the decision trees constructed by generalised algorithms. We use a
top-down simplification procedure. The simplification starts at the root node
of the decision tree with a *context* C which contains all the assumptions on
the parameters, e.g., $C = \{p_1 \geq 0, p_2 > 4\}$. We illustrate the simplification
procedure by looking at the node $n = Cond \ (f \geq 0) \ t_+ \ t_-$. When the simplifier
reaches this node, it checks whether the context implies one of the conditions
$f \geq 0$ or $f < 0$. If so, node n is replaced by the respective subtree of n and
the simplification continues on that subtree. If not, the node n is retained and
the simplifier is applied recursively to the two subtrees t_+ and t_-. For each
of the subtrees, the context is modified to contain the condition which makes
the respective subtree applicable. For t_+, the new context is $C \cup \{f \geq 0\}$ and
for t_- the simplification continues with $C \cup \{f < 0\}$. The full simplification
procedure we use [Grö03] is more sophisticated and handles a richer decision
tree data type which can represent other case distinctions than the discussed
Cond constructor.

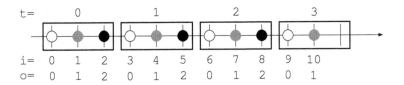

Figure 4.1: A tiled iteration domain

Checking whether context C implies a certain condition is done by deciding, for example, the logical formula $\forall p_1 \cdots \forall p_k \left(\bigwedge C \to f < 0 \right)$.

4.4.2 Fourier-Motzkin Elimination and Simplex

Two algorithms which occur frequently in the context of the polyhedron model are Fourier-Motzkin elimination and the simplex algorithm. Both algorithms operate in the real domain, i.e., they do not give any guarantees on the integrality of their results. In some situations, e.g., when generating code using Fourier-Motzkin elimination or estimating communication volumes, this is sufficient, because a slight "overestimate" of the domains in the reals does not hurt. In other situations, like dependence analyses, integrality is required and we must use generalised algorithms which guarantee the integrality of the solutions computed.

Let us present an introductory example of the need for parametric Fourier-Motzkin elimination, which uses a parametric tiling, i.e., a tiling whose tile size is not fixed at compile time. To describe such a parametric tiling (and other problems which require parameters as coefficients of variables), we have to use a generalised version of the polyhedron model in which the coefficients of variables may depend on parameters.

A Parametric Tiling Example

As an example of a problem expressed in the generalised model, take a very simple one-dimensional tiling. Consider the index set defined by the following inequality system in the variable i for $n \geq 0$:

$$0 \leq i \leq n \tag{4.1}$$

We desire a tiling of this index set into tiles of size p (for $p \geq 1$), i.e., p adjacent points of the index set shall be contained in the same tile. This can be described by the following inequality system:

$$\begin{aligned} 0 \leq o \leq p - 1 \\ i = p \cdot t + o \end{aligned} \tag{4.2}$$

where variable t denotes the number of a tile and variable o is the offset of a point within its tile (in this case, from the left end of the tile). Figure 4.1

illustrates the tiled index set for $n = 10$ and $p = 3$. Obviously, p is a non-linear parameter in the inequality system formed by systems (4.1) and (4.2) since it appears as coefficient of variable t. To obtain an enumeration (using Fourier-Motzkin) of the tiled index space with a loop for the tile numbers t, and inside that loop another loop for the coordinate i, we have to eliminate the variables in the order o, i, t. We first solve $i = p \cdot t + o$ for o and eliminate o by substituting into the two inequalities. Then, we solve the system for i:

$$
\begin{aligned}
0 &\leq i \\
p \cdot t &\leq i \\
i &\leq n \\
i &\leq p \cdot t + p - 1
\end{aligned}
$$

We eliminate i from this system by comparing lower bounds against upper bounds. This yields (after dropping two superfluous inequalities to simplify the calculation):

$$
\begin{aligned}
1 - p &\leq p \cdot t \\
p \cdot t &\leq n
\end{aligned}
$$

To solve the system for t, we have to divide by coefficient p. In general, this would require a case distinction on the sign of p, since, for $p < 0$, the relation symbols must be changed when dividing by p, and if $p = 0$ we cannot solve for t at all. A naïve implementation of Fourier-Motzkin would produce the following two-fold case distinction (since there are two inequalities with p as coefficient of t):

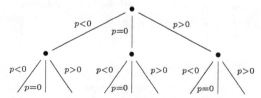

An implementation of an algorithm for the generalised polyhedron model should avoid such superfluous cases. Quantifier elimination allows to check whether $\forall p \, (p \geq 1 \rightarrow p > 0)$ holds. The formula $p \geq 1$ is the precondition on p stated above and $p > 0$ is one of the possible cases in the above case distinction. Here, quantifier elimination establishes that the formula is true. Therefore, we arrive at the following projection of the original system onto t and i:

$$
\frac{1}{p} - 1 \leq t \leq \frac{n}{p}
$$
$$
\max(0, p \cdot t) \leq i \leq \min(n, p \cdot t + p - 1)
$$

In our own previous work [Grö03], we have shown that Fourier-Motzkin elimination in the reals can be performed in the presence of arbitrary many non-linear parameters, since the number of case distinctions required is bounded by the number of inequalities and variables, i.e., it does not depend on the values of the parameters. Quantifier elimination in the reals is used to reduce the number of case distinctions. In Section 4.4.3, we illustrate a special case, related to code generation for tiled program models, which does not require quantifier elimination.

We now discuss generalising the simplex algorithm for non-linear parameters. In contrast to Fourier-Motzkin elimination, the simplex algorithm does not guarantee, at first, that the number of case distinctions made at maximum is independent of the values of the coefficients. So, termination, i.e., the finiteness of the constructed decision tree, has to be shown explicitly, as there are algorithms which produce infinite decision trees even with the best possible top-down tree simplification.

Example 4.17 (An algorithm that cannot be generalised syntactically). Applying the generalisation by program transformation to the following function

$$\text{pos} : \mathbb{Q} \to \mathbb{Q}$$
$$\text{pos}(x) = \begin{cases} x & \text{if } x \geq 0 \\ \text{pos}(x+1) & \text{if } x < 0 \end{cases}$$

yields the following generalised version:

$$\text{pos}^g : \mathbb{Q}[p_1, \dots, p_k] \to \text{Tree } \mathbb{Q}[p_1, \dots, p_k]$$
$$\text{pos}^g(f) = \text{Cond } (f \geq 0) \ (\text{Leaf } f) \ \big(\text{pos}^g(f+1)\big)$$

This generalised function produces, for some input f, an infinite decision tree:

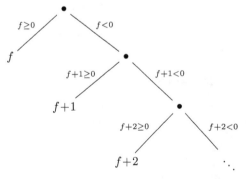

Unfortunately, the conditions on every finite prefix of the infinite branch are consistent. So algorithm pos cannot be generalised by a purely syntactic program transformation, even with tree simplification.

Termination (i.e., the construction of a finite decision tree) is guaranteed if every infinite branch has a finite prefix which is inconsistent. This condition ensures that searching top-down for contradictions and cutting off branches with infeasible conditions eliminates the infinite branch. Note that it does not suffice to use, for any given values of the parameters, only a finite prefix of the tree. In pos^g, this is the case, yet the tree cannot be made finite. The following lemma states that a generalised simplex always terminates if one adheres to a certain rule to choose the pivots.

Lemma 4.18. *The primal simplex algorithm together with Bland's minimal index rule [Bla77], which always chooses a pivot column with minimal index and a pivot row with minimal index in the pivot column, produces only decision trees which can be reduced to finite trees by a top-down decision tree simplification procedure which detects inconsistent conditions on the constructed branches.*

Proof. Let S be an inequality system of k inequalities in n variables. Each pivoting step requires $n + k$ case distinctions to find the pivoting column in the tableau, and at most $\frac{1}{2}(k + 1)k$ case distinctions to find the pivoting row. Therefore, a single pivoting step can only give rise to a finite number of case distinctions (at most $\frac{1}{2}(n + k)(k + 1)k$). If the context (the conditions in the decision tree above the current position) implies that all the coefficients of the objective function are non-positive, the optimum has been found and the tree construction stops. If, on the other hand, this is not the case, then there exist parameter values which satisfy the context and do not make the coefficients of the objective function all non-positive; the computation (and tree construction) continues for that case with an appropriate pivoting step.

Assume that this procedure returns a decision tree which contains an infinite branch. The branch must describe a computation with infinitely many pivoting operations. Since simplex can only make $\binom{n+k}{k}$ pivoting steps before it finds the optimum, and non-termination is only possible by cycling (c.f. [Chv83, Theorem 3.1]), the branch must describe a sequence of pivoting steps which cycle. On the other hand, the selection of the pivots follows Bland's rule by premise, which guarantees that no cycling can occur. This is a contradiction and, hence, the assumption that an infinite branch exists after top-down simplifying the decision tree is false.   □

4.4.3   Fourier-Motzkin Special Case

Quantifier elimination can be the dominating factor of the overall computation time when applying a generalised algorithm. Therefore, it is desirable to find special cases in which no need for quantifier elimination arises. Although some elimination algorithms take advantage of some properties of the formula, like the linearity of the formula in the variable to be eliminated [Wei88], we are not aware of a procedure which exploits stronger structural guarantees, like that the handled domain is a polyhedron.

We present here briefly one special case of Fourier-Motzkin elimination which can be exploited when generating loop nests which describe the tiling of an index space. In the case that the coefficient matrix of the system can be written as the product of a matrix with constant entries and a (parametric) lower triangular matrix with non-negative entries on the diagonal, case distinctions are never required.

Lemma 4.19. *Let $A \cdot \mathbf{x} + \mathbf{a} \geq 0$ with $A \in \mathbb{Q}(p_1, \ldots, p_k)^{m \times n}$, $\mathbf{a} \in \mathbb{Q}(p_1, \ldots, p_k)^n$ be an inequality system in the variables $\mathbf{x} = (x_1, \ldots, x_n)$ and the parameters $p_1, \ldots, p_k$. When the coefficient matrix A can be written as a product $A = K \cdot L$, where $K \in \mathbb{Q}^{m \times n}$ is a constant matrix and $L \in \mathbb{Q}(p_1, \ldots, p_k)^{n \times n}$ is a lower triangular matrix (possibly containing parameters) such that the assumptions on the parameters imply that the diagonal entries of L are positive, then Fourier-Motzkin elimination of $A \cdot \mathbf{x} + \mathbf{a} \geq 0$ does not lead to any case distinctions.*

Proof. Let $A, K, L, \mathbf{a}$ be as stated. For the following, we need a convention how a result of Fourier-Motzkin elimination is represented in matrix notation. Given $E \cdot \mathbf{x} + \mathbf{e} \geq 0$ with $\mathbf{x} = (x_1, \ldots, x_n)$, we assume that variables are eliminated in the order $x_n, \ldots, x_1$ and the result is $F \cdot \mathbf{x} + \mathbf{f} \geq 0$ such that every row $(r_1, \ldots, r_n)$ of F describes a bound for a variable x_j where $j = (\max i : 1 \leq i \leq n : r_i \neq 0)$ and $r_j \in \{-1, 1\}$.

We can now state a procedure that performs Fourier-Motzkin elimination on the system $A \cdot \mathbf{x} + \mathbf{a} \geq 0$ and yields a system $T \cdot \mathbf{x} + \mathbf{t} \geq 0$ representing the result in the representation just introduced:

(1) Perform Fourier-Motzkin elimination on $K \cdot \mathbf{y} + \mathbf{a} \geq 0$, yielding $S \cdot \mathbf{y} + \mathbf{s} \geq 0$ as the result.

(2) For every inequality in $S \cdot L \cdot \mathbf{x} + \mathbf{s} \geq 0$ do: if x_i is the leftmost variable with a non-zero coefficient, divide the inequality by the entry at (i, i) in L (this is the absolute value of the leftmost non-zero coefficient). This yields the equivalent system $T \cdot \mathbf{x} + \mathbf{t} \geq 0$.

We claim that $T \cdot \mathbf{x} + \mathbf{t} \geq 0$ is one of the possible results of Fourier-Motzkin elimination on $A \cdot \mathbf{x} + \mathbf{a} \geq 0$. The correctness of this procedure follows from the fact that L is a lower triangular matrix with positive entries. For every row $\mathbf{r} = (r_1, \ldots, r_j, 0, \ldots, 0)$ with $r_j \neq 0$ of S, $\mathbf{r} \cdot L$ is a row $(l_1, \ldots, l_n)$ such that $l_{j+1} = \ldots = l_n = 0$ and l_j is $\pm$ the diagonal entry of L at (j, j) (because $r_j = \pm 1$), so the entry corresponding to l_j in T is ± 1.

Let $j \in \{1, \ldots, n\}$ and $\mathbf{w} \in \mathbb{R}^j$ such that $(S \cdot L)_j \cdot \mathbf{w} + \mathbf{s}_j \geq 0$ holds. The matrix $(S \cdot L)_j$ and the vector $\mathbf{s}_j$ are obtained from $S \cdot L$ and $\mathbf{s}$ by removing all rows and columns from the system $(S \cdot L) \cdot \mathbf{x} + \mathbf{s} \geq 0$ that describe bounds on x_i with $i > j$. Then, $\mathbf{z} := L_j \cdot \mathbf{w}$ (with L_j being the submatrix of L consisting of the first j rows and columns) satisfies $S_j \cdot \mathbf{z} + \mathbf{s}_j \geq 0$ because L is lower triangular with positive entries on the diagonal. Hence, there exists $\mathbf{y} \in \mathbb{R}^n$ such that $S \cdot \mathbf{y} + \mathbf{s} \geq 0$ and $\mathbf{y}_{|j} = \mathbf{z}$ since S is obtained from K by Fourier-Motzkin elimination. Because L is non-singular and lower triangular, this implies that $\mathbf{x} \in \mathbb{R}^n$ exists such that $(S \cdot L) \cdot \mathbf{x} + \mathbf{s} \geq 0$ and $\mathbf{x}_{|j} = \mathbf{w}$.

This proves that the system $(S \cdot L) \cdot \mathbf{x} + \mathbf{s} \geq 0$ contains descriptions of the projections to lower dimensionality (because for every point $\mathbf{w}$ that satisfies the constraints in "outer" variables, there exists a point $\mathbf{x}$ with full dimensionality which satisfies all constraints). In addition, $(S \cdot L) \cdot \mathbf{x} + \mathbf{s} \geq 0$ (and, hence, $T \cdot \mathbf{x} + \mathbf{s} \geq 0$) is equivalent to $A \cdot \mathbf{x} + \mathbf{a} \geq 0$ by construction.

The system $T \cdot \mathbf{x} + \mathbf{s} \geq 0$ can be computed without case distinctions because case distinctions are necessary neither in (1), since K is a constant matrix, nor in (2), since all the division operations are by positive entries of L. □

The challenge Lemma 4.19 poses is how to find suitable K, L for a given A, if such K and L exist at all. We do not solve this problem here, but note that one case (constants and products of parameters as coefficients) can be handled easily. We make use of the following corollary, which states this case formally, when generating tiled code for a single statement (because this can be done by Fourier-Motzkin elimination, cf. Section 5.3).

Corollary 4.20. *If* $p_1, \ldots, p_k > 0$ *is assumed and* A *is of the form*

$$A = \begin{pmatrix} \mathbf{v}_1 q_1 & \cdots & \mathbf{v}_n q_n \end{pmatrix}$$

where $\mathbf{v}_1, \ldots, \mathbf{v}_n \in \mathbb{Q}^m$, $q_i = \prod_{j=1}^{k} p_j^{e_{i,j}}$ *for* $1 \leq i \leq n$ *and* $e_{i,j} \in \mathbb{Z}$ *for* $0 \leq i \leq n$, $1 \leq j \leq k$, *then Fourier-Motzkin elimination can be applied to* $A \cdot \mathbf{x} + \mathbf{a} \geq 0$ *without making case distinctions.*

Using the following matrices K and L, the corollary follows from Lemma 4.19:

$$K = \begin{pmatrix} \mathbf{v}_1 & \cdots & \mathbf{v}_n \end{pmatrix}, \quad L = \begin{pmatrix} q_1 & 0 & \cdots & 0 \\ 0 & \ddots & \ddots & \vdots \\ \vdots & \ddots & \ddots & 0 \\ 0 & \cdots & 0 & q_n \end{pmatrix}$$

K is a constant matrix, L is a lower triangular matrix with positive entries on the diagonal since $p_1, \ldots, p_k > 0$ implies $q_1, \ldots, q_n > 0$, and $A = K \cdot L$.

Chapter 5

Application of Algorithms for Non-linearities to the Polyhedron Model

5.1 Dependence Analysis

As a first algorithm which we generalise to non-linear input, let us look at data dependence analysis according to Banerjee [Ban93]. We first present the basics of Banerjee's algorithm before we describe our generalisation (using the algorithms presented in Chapter 4) and, for comparison, quantifier elimination with answer in the integers.

Banerjee's Algorithm

For two accesses in a loop program

$$S_1 : \quad \ldots A[f(\mathbf{i_1})] \ldots$$
$$S_2 : \quad \ldots A[g(\mathbf{i_2})] \ldots$$

a necessary condition for the existence of a dependence between the operations $\langle \mathbf{i_1}, S_1 \rangle$ and $\langle \mathbf{i_2}, S_2 \rangle$ (due to the accesses to A) is that the equality system

$$f(\mathbf{i_1}) = g(\mathbf{i_2})$$

has a solution in $\mathbb{Z}$ (cf. Section 2.2.1). In Banerjee's terminology, this is called the *conflict equality system*. In the example program in Figure 5.1, the equality describing the conflict between $\langle (i_1, j_1), S_1 \rangle$ and $\langle (i_2, j_2), S_2 \rangle$ is

$$p \cdot i_1 + 2 \cdot j_1 = p \cdot i_2 + 2 \cdot j_2$$

Note that both operations have different index vectors ((i_1, j_1) and (i_2, j_2), respectively) since the accesses to the same memory cell may happen in different iterations of the loops. The conflict equality system describes the set of all possible shared memory accesses. But not all of the solutions correspond to

```
for (i=0; i<=m; i++)
    for (j=0; j<=m; j++)
S:          A[p*i+2*j] = i+j;
```

Figure 5.1: Example loop program with a non-linear parameter in the array subscript in statement S

operations in the program. The index vectors have to be restricted to the iteration space of the respective statements, i.e., in the example, the conditions $0 \leq i_1, j_1, i_2, j_2 \leq m$ (derived from the loop bounds) have to hold. These restrictions are called the *existence inequalities*.

A third group of restrictions is the set of equalities and inequalities describing the *order* of the execution. To express that $\langle (i_1, j_1), S \rangle$ is executed before $\langle (i_2, j_2), S \rangle$, we have to add the constraint $i_2 > i_1 \vee (i_2 = i_1 \wedge j_2 \geq j_1)$, i.e., the index vectors are ordered lexicographically.

Banerjee's data dependence analysis takes a two phase approach:

1. In the first phase, the conflict equality system is solved in $\mathbb{Z}$.

2. In the second phase, the solution of the conflict equality system is combined with the existence inequalities and the order constraints. Fourier-Motzkin elimination (in the reals) is used to project the system to the index variables. This elimination has to be performed for every disjunct in the order constraint, since Fourier-Motzkin cannot handle disjunctions (only conjunctions) of constraints.

Due to the use of Fourier-Motzkin elimination, Banerjee's analysis is not exact in the general case: the feasibility of the existence inequalities and the order constraints in the integers (to be precise: in the lattice described by the conflict equality system) is not tested. For practical program analysis, this is a minor problem since it occurs only for very "narrow" iteration spaces. Hence, solving the conflict equality system exactly is the central part of the analysis. Even the infeasibility of this equality system is a very valuable information: no dependences can exist and there is, for example, a maximal degree of parallelism possible. Solving the conflict equalities in the reals (using Groebner bases etc.) is not a viable option, because systems infeasible in the integers may be feasible in the reals and far too many solutions (all the non-integral solutions) would not correspond to operations in the program and describe false dependences which limit the amount of potential parallelism.

5.1.1   Generalisation to One Non-linear Parameter

Generalising Banerjee's analysis to one non-linear parameter is straight forward. The first phase, solving the conflict equality system, can be performed using the generalised solution procedure for linear Diophantine equality systems, which we have presented in Section 4.2. For the second phase, we have our generalised

Fourier-Motzkin procedure of Section 4.3 which can handle one or several non-linear parameters.

5.1.2 Using Weak Quantifier Elimination in the Integers

Our technique for computing the solutions of linear equality systems with one non-linear parameter can be viewed as a special case of weak quantifier elimination in the integers. Therefore, one can also try to compute dependence information by expressing the dependence relation as a formula. For two given array accesses $A[f(\mathbf{i})]$ in a statement S and $A[g(\mathbf{j})]$ in a statement T, there exists a dependence from $\langle \mathbf{i}, S \rangle$ to $\langle \mathbf{j}, T \rangle$ (assuming S precedes T textually) if, and only if, the formula $\exists \mathbf{i}\, \exists \mathbf{j}\, (\delta)$ holds, where

$$\delta = \big(\mathbf{i} \in D_S \wedge \mathbf{j} \in D_T \wedge \mathbf{i} \preceq \mathbf{j} \wedge f(\mathbf{i}) = g(\mathbf{j})\big)$$

and D_S and D_T are the iteration domains of the statements S and T, respectively. If S does not textually precede T, one has to replace $\mathbf{i} \preceq \mathbf{j}$ by $\mathbf{i} \prec \mathbf{j}$. Eliminating $\exists \mathbf{i}\, \exists \mathbf{j}\, (\delta)$ yields the condition (in the parameters) for which dependences exist. To yield a description of the dependences itself, we have to perform quantifier elimination with answer, but we have to ask a question which has only one answer (or none if it cannot be solved) as quantifier elimination with answer gives us only one example of all possible answers. For dependences, it is most useful to ask for the lexicographically greatest (i.e., in the execution latest) source of a given target. To obtain this information, we eliminate the formula

$$\exists \mathbf{i} \left(\delta \wedge \forall \mathbf{i}'\, \big(\delta[\mathbf{i} := \mathbf{i}'] \to \mathbf{i}' \preceq \mathbf{i}\big)\right)$$

which expresses that $\mathbf{i}$ is the lexicographically greatest vector that satisfies δ. Quantifier elimination with answer yields a case distinction with solutions for $\mathbf{i}$ in dependence of $\mathbf{j}$ and the parameters.

5.1.3 Example

We have implemented our procedure for solving linear Diophantine equality systems in one non-linear parameter in the LooPo loop restructuring system [GL97]. Let us now analyse the data dependences for the example program from Figure 5.1.

The program and its dependences for $p = 3$ and $p = 4$ are depicted in Figure 5.2. This example is a prototype of program codes that use strided access to arrays. For example, to enable the use of a row, a column, or a diagonal of a matrix as an argument to a function which expects a vector, some linear algebra libraries take, for every vector V, an additional stride argument p. By accessing every p^{th} element, i.e., like in $V[p \cdot i]$, matrix rows, columns, and diagonals can be selected by using the respective distance between neighbouring elements as stride (e.g., 1, the width of the matrix, and the width of the matrix plus 1, respectively, for arrays stored in row-major order).

```
for (i=0; i<=m; i++)
    for (j=0; j<=m; j++)
S:          A[p*i+2*j] = i+j;
```

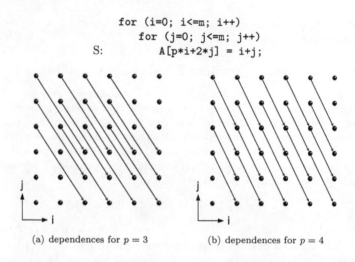

(a) dependences for $p = 3$ (b) dependences for $p = 4$

Figure 5.2: Example program and its data dependences for $m = 5$

To establish which iterations (i_1, j_1) and (i_2, j_2) in the example program write to the same memory location, we have to consider the conflict equality

$$p \cdot i_1 + 2 \cdot j_1 = p \cdot i_2 + 2 \cdot j_2.$$

To find the integral solutions for (i_1, j_1, i_2, j_2) in dependence of p, we apply the algorithm given in Section 4.2, i.e., we replace p by X and solve the system $(i_1 \ j_1 \ i_2 \ j_2) \cdot A = 0$ for $i_1, j_1, i_2, j_2 \in EQP$ where

$$A = \begin{pmatrix} X \\ 2 \\ -X \\ -2 \end{pmatrix}.$$

The echelon reduction on A starts by computing the pointwise GCD of $f = X$ and $g = 2$. This computation, which yields $[2, 1]$, and the computation of a suitable matrix U have been presented in Section 4.2.7 already. The third and fourth row do not add any further constraints on the GCD, so the GCD of all four rows is $[2, 1]$ and we omit these computations. The overall result are matrices S and U such that $S = U \cdot A$ and $\det U \sim 1$. Our implementation computes the following values for S and U:

$$S = \begin{pmatrix} [2, 1] \\ 0 \\ 0 \\ 0 \end{pmatrix}, \quad U = \begin{pmatrix} 0 & 0 & [0, -1] & [0, \frac{1}{2}]X + [-1, -\frac{1}{2}] \\ [1, -1] & 0 & [0, -1]X & [0, \frac{1}{2}]X^2 + [\frac{1}{2}, -\frac{1}{2}]X \\ 0 & [1, -1] & [0, -2] & [0, 1]X + [1, -1] \\ 0 & 0 & [1, 2] & [-\frac{1}{2}, -1]X \end{pmatrix}$$

Since the pivot element $[2,1]$ of S is not a zero-divisor in EQP, S is in pointwise echelon form, i.e., $S(p)$ is echelon for all but finitely many $p \in \mathbb{Z}$. Since the quasi-polynomial $[2,1]$ has no zeros at all, $S(p)$ is echelon for all $p \in \mathbb{Z}$. Performing forward substitution in $(t_1 \; t_2 \; t_3 \; t_4) \cdot S = 0$ yields $t_1 = 0$, $t_2, t_3, t_4 \in \mathbb{Z}$; in this example, there is no case distinction on p necessary to represent the solutions for t. The solutions for i_1, j_1, i_2, j_2 are then given by $t \cdot U = (0 \; t_2 \; t_3 \; t_4) \cdot U$ and this yields for $p \equiv_2 0$:

$$i_1 = t_2$$
$$j_1 = t_3$$
$$i_2 = t_4$$
$$j_2 = \tfrac{1}{2}p \cdot t_2 + t_3 - \tfrac{1}{2}p \cdot t_4$$

and for $p \equiv_2 1$:

$$i_1 = -t_2$$
$$j_1 = -t_3$$
$$i_2 = -p \cdot t_2 - 2 \cdot t_3 + 2 \cdot t_4$$
$$j_2 = (\tfrac{1}{2}p^2 - \tfrac{1}{2}p) \cdot t_2 + (p-1) \cdot t_3 - p \cdot t_4$$

These solutions to the conflict equality system reveal the difference in the dependence structure of the program for even versus odd p when we take the order of execution into account (cf. Figure 5.2). For $\langle (i_1, j_1), S \rangle$ to precede $\langle (i_2, j_2), S \rangle$, either $i_1 < i_2$ or $i_1 = i_2 \wedge j_1 < j_2$ must hold. In both cases for p, $i_1 = i_2$ implies $j_1 = j_2$ and, hence, there is no dependence with $i_1 = i_2$. If we assume $i_1 < i_2$, it is easy to see that, for $p \equiv_2 0$, the minimal i_2 which solves the system is $i_2 = i_1 + 1$, which implies $j_2 = j_1 - \tfrac{1}{2}p$. On the other hand, for $p \equiv_2 1$, $i_2 - i_1 = (1-p)t_2 - 2t_3 + 2t_4$ must be even since p is odd; therefore, the minimal solution for i_2 is $i_2 = i_1 + 2$ and $j_2 = j_1 - p$. From this, the conditions on m for dependences to exist can be computed using the existence inequalities $0 \leq i_1, j_1, i_2, j_2 \leq m$. This completes the dependence analysis of the program (the set of *all* dependences is the transitive closure of the given dependences):

$$\langle (i,j), S \rangle \to \langle (i+1, j - \tfrac{p}{2}), S \rangle \quad \text{if} \quad \begin{cases} p \equiv_2 0, m \geq 1, -2m \leq p \leq 2m, \\ 0 \leq i \leq m-1, \\ \max(0, \tfrac{p}{2}) \leq j \leq \min(m, m+\tfrac{p}{2}) \end{cases}$$

$$\langle (i,j), S \rangle \to \langle (i+2, j - p), S \rangle \quad \text{if} \quad \begin{cases} p \equiv_2 1, m \geq 2, -m \leq p \leq m, \\ 0 \leq i \leq m-2, \\ \max(0, p) \leq j \leq \min(m, m+p) \end{cases}$$

Using Redlog

As an alternative to our generalisation of the classical Banerjee analysis, we have also tried to compute the dependences using weak quantifier elimination in the

```
        for (i=0; i<=m; i++)
    S:      A[i+n] = f(A[i]);
```
(a) Original program

```
      for (i=0; i<=⌊ m/n ⌋; i++)
        parfor (j=0; j<=min(n-1,m-n*i); j++)
    S:      A[n*i+j+n] = f(A[n*i+j]);
```
(b) Parallel version after modulo transformation

Figure 5.3: Example program for non-linear schedule

integers. The existence, conflict and ordering restrictions can be expressed by the formula δ:

$$\delta = \Big(0 \le i_1, j_1, i_2, j_2 \le m \wedge p \cdot i_1 + 2 \cdot j_1 = p \cdot i_2 + 2 \cdot j_2 \wedge$$
$$\big(i_1 < i_2 \vee (i_1 = i_2 \wedge j_1 < j_2)\big)\Big)$$

We compute first the quantifier-free equivalent μ of

$$\forall i_3 \forall j_3 \, \big(\delta[i_1 := i_3, j_1 := j_3] \rightarrow i_3 < i_1 \vee (i_3 = i_1 \wedge j_3 \le j_1)\big),$$

which expresses that (i_1, j_1) is the lexicographically maximal source of the dependence. Then, we ask for solutions of i_1, j_1 in

$$\exists i_1 \exists j_1 \, (\delta \wedge \mu)$$

by quantifier elimination with answer. The computation takes about 55 seconds on an Intel® Core™2 Duo 6600 processor with 2.4 GHz with REDLOG (using one core). The result is a case distinction with solutions for each case that is about 200,000 lines long (in REDUCE's standard output format) and contains many bounded quantifiers and congruences, some of them modulo the parameter. All in all, this result seems rather unsuitable for further processing.

5.2   Computing Schedules

As a simple example of finding a non-linear schedule which is superior to linear schedules, let us look at the code shown in Figure 5.3(a). Obviously, n successive iterations of the loop on i can be executed in parallel as the only dependence is $\langle i, S \rangle \rightarrow \langle i+n, S \rangle$. But this cannot be expressed by a linear schedule of the form $\theta(i) = a \cdot i + b$ for $a, b \in \mathbb{Q}$. The only way in which a linear schedule can express this is by applying a modulo transformation first, i.e., transforming to a two-dimensional iteration domain where the inner loop (on a new loop variable j) enumerates the n successive operations (except, possibly, in the last iteration of the loop on i). But this transformation introduces non-linearities in the loop bounds: $\frac{0}{n}$ and $\frac{m}{n}$ in the loop on i and $n \cdot i$ in the loop on j and, additionally, $n \cdot i$ in the body of the loop (cf. Figure 5.3(b)). So this transformation is outside the classical polyhedron model and generates non-linearities to be handled in the code generation phase.

We present two methods to compute non-linear schedules. The first is a direct generalisation of the classical Feautrier method, the second an application of quantifier elimination with answer. A resulting parallel version of the code, which is similar to the result of modulo transformation, is given in Section 5.2.3.

5.2.1 Schedule by Simplex

Minimising a target function over a polyhedron or computing the lexicographic minimum of a polyhedron has been used as the foundation for computing schedules [Fea92a]. With a generalised simplex available, we can extend the basic algorithms to the case with non-linear parameters. We only discuss one-dimensional scheduling here; the extension to multidimensional schedules is analogous to the classical case [Fea92b]. A prototype of a one-dimensional schedule for a statement S is the function

$$\theta_S(\mathbf{i}) = \mathbf{a_S} \cdot \mathbf{i} + b_S$$

where $a_S \in \mathbb{Q}(p_1, \ldots, p_k)^n$, $b_S \in \mathbb{Q}(p_1, \ldots, p_k)$ $(n, k \in \mathbb{N})$ are the coefficients of the schedule to be determined in the parameters $\mathbf{p} = (p_1, \ldots, p_k)$ and $\mathbf{i} \in \mathbb{Z}^n$ denotes an iteration vector. A usual requirement on the schedule is that it never assigns negative execution times, i.e.,

$$\theta_S(\mathbf{i}) \geq 0 \quad \Leftrightarrow \quad \mathbf{a}_S \mathbf{i} + b_S \geq 0 \qquad \text{for } \mathbf{i} \in D_S(\mathbf{p})$$

where $D_S(\mathbf{p})$ is the (parametric) iteration domain of S. A schedule is valid w.r.t. to a dependence between statements S and T

$$\langle \mathbf{si} + s_0, S \rangle \longrightarrow \langle \mathbf{tj} + t_0, T \rangle \qquad \text{for } (\mathbf{i}, \mathbf{j}) \in D(\mathbf{p})$$

where $s \in \mathbb{Q}(\mathbf{p})^n$, $t \in \mathbb{Q}(\mathbf{p})^m$, $s_0, t_0 \in \mathbb{Q}(\mathbf{p})$ and $D(\mathbf{p}) \subseteq \mathbb{Z}^{n+m}$ $(m \in \mathbb{N})$, if

$$\big(\forall \mathbf{i}, \mathbf{j} : (\mathbf{i}, \mathbf{j}) \in D(p) : \theta_T(\mathbf{tj} + t_0) - \theta_S(\mathbf{si} + s_0) \geq 1 \big).$$

This condition together with the non-negativity constraint for the schedules yields the system to solve:

$$\mathbf{a}_T(\mathbf{tj} + t_0) + b_T - \mathbf{a}_S(\mathbf{si} + s_0) - b_S - 1 \geq 0 \qquad \forall (\mathbf{i}, \mathbf{j}) \in D(\mathbf{p})$$
$$\mathbf{a}_S \mathbf{i} + b_S \geq 0 \qquad \forall \mathbf{i} \in D_S(\mathbf{p})$$
$$\mathbf{a}_T \mathbf{i} + b_T \geq 0 \qquad \forall \mathbf{i} \in D_T(\mathbf{p})$$

This is not a linear system in the schedule coefficients $\mathbf{a}_T$ and $\mathbf{a}_S$ as they occur in products with the loop indices $\mathbf{i}$ and $\mathbf{j}$. But we can apply Farkas' lemma as is done in the linearly parametric case. By equating coefficients, the system is transformed into one which is linear in $\mathbf{a}_S$ and $\mathbf{a}_T$ and can be solved for these coefficients.

If the dependence is, in fact, a uniform dependence (i.e., the distance between the source and the target of the dependence is constant), the computation is simplified since the ordering condition does not give rise to products between unknowns (since $\mathbf{a}_T = \mathbf{a}_S$) as illustrated by example in Figure 5.3(a). The dependences are given by $i \rightarrow i + n$ for $0 \leq i \leq m - n$, i.e., $s = t = 1$, $s_0 = 0$, $t_0 = n$. Since there is only one statement, we have $S = T$ and, hence, only one schedule prototype as $a_T = a_S$, $b_T = b_S$:

$$\theta_S(i) = a_S \cdot i + b_S$$

This yields the following ordering condition according to the above formula:

$$a_T(ti + t_0) + b_T - a_S(si + s_0) - b_S - 1 \geq 0$$
$$\Leftrightarrow \quad a_S \cdot n - 1 \geq 0$$

From this, the minimal solution $a_S = \frac{1}{n}$ is obvious. For examples with more than one loop index, we still have to perform the full procedure as for two variables, there is no guarantee that the solutions for $\mathbf{a_S}$ are bounded. Therefore, the non-negativity of the schedule can easily be violated.

Example 5.1 (Example 2.2 in [AZ00]). Let us consider the following iteration domain D:

$$2 \leq x \leq n$$
$$4 \leq y \leq n$$
$$n - x \leq y$$

and dependences:

$$(x - 1, x) \rightarrow (x, y)$$
$$(x, y - 1) \rightarrow (x, y)$$

To find a legal schedule $\theta(x, y) = ax + by + c$ with $a, b, c \in \mathbb{Q}(n)$, the following conditions must hold:

$$\big(\forall x, y : (x, y) \in D : \theta(x, y) \geq 0\big)$$
$$\big(\forall x, y : (x, y) \in D \wedge x \geq 3 : \theta(x, y) - \theta(x - 1, x) \geq 1\big)$$
$$\big(\forall x, y : (x, y) \in D \wedge y \geq 5 : \theta(x, y) - \theta(x, y - 1) \geq 1\big)$$

The additional restrictions $y \geq 5$ and $x \geq 3$ constrain the conditions to those (x, y) where the respective dependence exists. Substituting $\theta(x, y)$ by its definition yields:

$$\big(\forall x, y : (x, y) \in D : ax + by + c \geq 0\big)$$
$$\big(\forall x, y : (x, y) \in D \wedge x \geq 3 : -bx + by + a - 1 \geq 0\big)$$
$$\big(\forall x, y : (x, y) \in D \wedge y \geq 5 : b - 1 \geq 0\big)$$

The second condition $(b-1 \geq 0)$ needs no further processing (it does not mention the iteration set variables because it is derived from a uniform dependence). The other two conditions are transformed using Farkas' lemma:

$$
\begin{aligned}
ax + by + c &= \delta_1(x-2) + \delta_2(n-x) + \delta_3(y-4) \\
&\quad + \delta_4(x+y-n) + \delta_5(n-y) + \delta_0 \\
-bx + by + a - 1 &= \lambda_1(x-3) + \lambda_2(n-x) + \lambda_3(y-4) + \lambda_4(x+y-n) \\
&\quad + \lambda_5(n-y) + \lambda_0 \\
\delta_0, \ldots, \delta_5, \lambda_0, \ldots, \lambda_5 &\geq 0 \\
b - 1 &\geq 0
\end{aligned}
$$

The δ_i and λ_i are multiplied with the affine expressions defining the respective domain. By equating coefficients in the equalities, we obtain the final system:

$$
\begin{aligned}
a &= \delta_1 - \delta_2 + \delta_4 \\
b &= \delta_3 + \delta_4 - \delta_5 \\
c &= -2\delta_1 + n\delta_2 - 4\delta_3 - n\delta_4 + n\delta_5 + \delta_0 \\
-b &= \lambda_1 - \lambda_2 + \lambda_4 \\
b &= \lambda_3 + \lambda_4 - \lambda_5 \\
a - 1 &= -3\lambda_1 + n\lambda_2 - 4\lambda_3 - n\lambda_4 + n\lambda_5 + \lambda_0 \\
\delta_0, \ldots, \delta_5, \lambda_0, \ldots, \lambda_5 &\geq 0 \\
b - 1 &\geq 0
\end{aligned}
$$

Our generalised simplex implementation computes the solution $a = n-3$, $b = 1$, $c = -n$ as the lexicographic minimum for (a, b, c) in about 4.8 seconds on an Intel® Core™ 2 Duo 6600 processor with 2.4 GHz. The schedule obtained $\theta(x, y) = (n-3) \cdot x + y - n$ is in accordance with the optimal schedule linear in x and y computed by Achtziger et al. [AZ00].

5.2.2   Schedule by Quantifier Elimination

The existence of a schedule can be expressed as a logical formula; hence, one can try to use quantifier elimination to find the coefficients of a suitable schedule. A schedule $\theta(i) = a \cdot i + b$ is valid if it respects the dependences. For the example in Figure 5.3(a), this is expressed by the formulas $\nu(t)$ and $\tau(t)$:

$$\nu(\theta) = \forall i \, \big(0 \leq i \leq m \rightarrow \theta(i) \geq 0\big),$$
$$\tau(\theta) = \forall i_1 \forall i_2 \, \big(0 \leq i_1, i_2 \leq m \wedge i_1 + n = i_2 \rightarrow \theta(i_1) \geq 0 \wedge \theta(i_1) + 1 \leq \theta(i_2)\big).$$

$\nu(\theta)$ requires $\theta(i) \geq 0$ to allow only schedules with non-negative time steps. To find a schedule, we could try to ask for solutions of a and b in $\exists a \exists b \, \big(\nu(\theta) \wedge \tau(\theta)\big)$. Unfortunately, this allows an answer (and, in fact, REDLOG delivers this answer) of

$$\big(\text{true}, [a := +\infty_1, b := +\infty_2]\big)$$

(under the assumption that $n > 0$), because the fact that sufficiently large a and b exist to make the formula true (expressed by $a = +\infty_1$ and $b = +\infty_2$) is a proof of its validity. We must further constrain the possible choices for the coefficients of the schedule. What can be expressed easily is the requirement for the schedule to assign the least execution time among all schedules of the same form, i.e., for every other schedule $\theta'(i)$ of the form $a'i + b'$, $\theta'(i) \geq \theta(i)$, for all i from the iteration domain, holds:

$$\sigma(\theta) := \nu(\theta) \wedge \tau(\theta) \wedge$$
$$\forall a' \, \forall b' \left(\nu(a'i + b') \wedge \tau(a'i + b') \rightarrow \forall i \, (0 \leq i \leq m \rightarrow \theta(i) \leq a'i + b') \right).$$

Asking REDLOG for a and b in $\exists a \exists b \left(\sigma(a \cdot i + b) \right)$ under the assumption $m, n > 0$ yields[1]

$$\left\{ \left(m < n, [a := 0, b := 0] \right), \left(m \geq n, [a := \frac{1}{n}, b := 0] \right) \right\}$$

after about 2.7 seconds of computation on a 2.4 GHz Intel® Core™2 Duo 6600 processor. By flooring the resulting rational schedule, we obtain the desired integral schedule $\theta(i) = \lfloor \frac{i}{n} \rfloor$ for $m \geq n$. It the case $m < n$, the solution is $\theta(i) = 0$, since all iterations of the loop on i can be executed in parallel. We also tried Example 2.2 from [AZ00], for which we computed a linear schedule in Example 5.1 using our generalised simplex, but we did not succeed in getting an answer from REDLOG in a reasonable time (several hours).

5.2.3   Code Generation Considerations

A non-linear, fractional, floored schedule like $\theta(i) = \lfloor \frac{i}{n} \rfloor$ raises the question how we can generate code which executes according to such a schedule. In Section 5.5, we present a procedure to generate code for iteration sets which are bounded by arbitrary polynomials. It is possible to express the given schedule by polynomial bounds. Let t be the time coordinate, i.e., the loop iterator to enumerate $\theta(i)$. Then, we can write $t = \theta(i)$ equivalently using polynomials only by the system

$$n \cdot t + r = i$$
$$0 \leq r \leq n - 1$$

which exploits the fact that $i \bmod n$ must be between 0 and $n - 1$ (bounds included), assuming $n \geq 1$. Together with the iteration set bounds of the original program

$$0 \leq i \leq m$$

we can generate code and obtain

---

[1] Actually, REDLOG computes the condition $m \cdot n > 0 \wedge m - n \geq 0$ for the second case; obviously, REDLOG's simplifier does not derive that $m \cdot n$ is positive from the context $m, n > 0$.

```
for (t=⌈1-n/n⌉; t<=⌊m/n⌋; i++) {
    parfor (i=max(n*t,0); i<=min(n*t+n-1,m); i++) {
        r = i-n*t;
        A[i+n] = f(A[i]);
    }
}
```

as parallel code (cf. Section 5.5.9).

5.3 Tiling

The main objective in tiling is to coarsen the grain of the execution, i.e., to group several operations together and treat them as a unit of work. In automatic parallelism, tiling is applied to reduce the number of communications, i.e., data exchange and synchronisation is only performed once per tile instead of after every operation or time step, respectively. In this section, we show that the bounds of tiles need not be parallel to bounds of the index space and that the code generated by tiling, although it has complex loop bounds, can be executed efficiently because, with optimising compilers, the innermost loop will still consist of only a few instructions. In addition, tiling with parametric tile sizes (which leads to non-linearities) generates only slightly more complicated code, and the execution times and cache behaviour are almost indistinguishable from code for fixed tilings.

5.3.1 Tiling with Parallelepiped Tiles

Tiling is simplest when opposite bounds of the index space are geometrically parallel. As an example, let us consider a popular iterative matrix algorithm from scientific computing: one-dimensional successive over-relaxation (1d-SOR). Here is the sequential loop nest:

```
for (k=1; k<=m; k++)
    for (i=2; i<=n-1; i++)
        A[i] = (A[i-1] + A[i+1]) * 0.5;
```

Parameter n refers to the size of the array being processed, and m is the number of sweeps across the array. A valid space-time mapping has to satisfy the criterion that, in the transformed program, the dependences must point forward in time (i.e., every computation depends only on computations in the past). Additionally, since we apply tiling after space-time mapping, we must ensure that it does not generate cyclic communication dependences (which can happen when several communications are being aggregated); this is achieved by requiring that communications are directed to processors with the same or a higher number than the sender's number [GFG05].

Our polyhedral loop paralleliser LooPo performs an optimising search over affine space-time mappings, i.e., it chooses an affine time coordinate $\theta(k, i)$ and an affine space coordinate $\pi(k, i)$ which satisfy the given constraints, minimise the number of required time steps and do not waste virtual processors. The

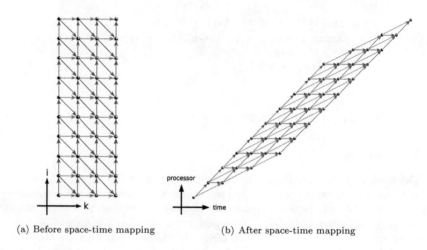

(a) Before space-time mapping   (b) After space-time mapping

Figure 5.4: 1d-SOR: Index space with dependences

details of the theory can be found elsewhere [Gri04]. In the case of the 1d-SOR example, LooPo chooses the space-time mapping which maps loop step (k, i) to the execution time $\theta(k, i) = 2 \cdot k + i - 4$ and to the virtual processor $\pi(k, i) = k + i - 3$. Figure 5.4 shows the index space of 1d-SOR before and after space-time mapping.

Next, the space-time mapped model is being tiled. A tiling leads to a doubling of the number of dimensions. Each index point is described by a coordinate in the space of tiles, and an offset within the tile. The usual choice of tile shape in the space-time mapping community is rectangular since, intuitively, time and space are orthogonal after space-time mapping. But, since the bounds of the index space are geometrically parallel, an obvious choice of tile shape is a parallelogram which has two bounds parallel to the bounds of the index space. Figure 5.5 shows a part of the space-time mapped index space with rectangular and parallelogram tiles.

Care has to be taken as to which tiles can be executed in parallel. Before tiling, all index points (k, i) with the same time coordinate $\theta(k, i)$ are executed in parallel. Afterwards, tiles with the same time coordinate in the tile space *must not* be executed in parallel, since the tiles span, in general, more than one time coordinate of the index space and, hence, dependences between tiles can exist. A so-called *skewing* [GFL04] has to be performed and tiles whose time coordinate t_T and processor coordinate p_T have a common sum $t_T + p_T$ can be executed in parallel. This applies equally to rectangular and parallelogram tiles. The result for rectangular tiles is depicted in Figure 5.6.

Due to the skewing, the number of tiles which can be executed in parallel is not determined by the height of the tiles, but by their width (in the case of the parallelogram tiles) or their width and height together (in the case of rectangular tiles). To achieve a balanced load of the processors, the size of the

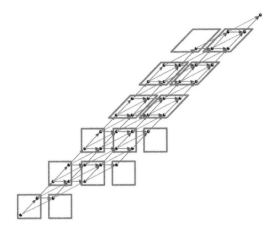

Figure 5.5: 1d-SOR: Space-time mapped index space with rectangular and parallelogram tiles

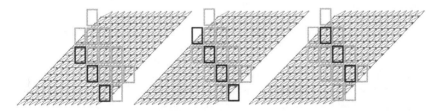

Figure 5.6: Skewing: Tiles which can be executed in parallel (highlighted) in successive time steps

tiles depends on the number NC of available cores. The relations of height and width are given by

$$\text{width} = \frac{m}{f \cdot \text{NC}}, \quad \text{height} \geq 1 \qquad \text{(parallelograms)}$$

$$\text{width} = \frac{m}{f \cdot \text{NC}} - \text{height}, \quad 1 \leq \text{height} < \frac{m}{f \cdot \text{NC}} \qquad \text{(rectangles)}$$

where $f \geq 1$ is an arbitrary integral factor denoting the number of tiles to be assigned to one core. It may seem that a rectangular tiling cannot lead to a balanced load because there are incomplete tiles along the borders of the index space. But, by closer inspection (cf. Figure 5.6), it becomes clear that, with the given choice of the tile width and height, there are either NC complete tiles in parallel, or NC + 1 tiles of which the first and the last (the tiles crossing the borders of the index space) are partially empty and which together form one complete tile (regarding the number of computations). Therefore, if we distribute one such diagonal of tiles cyclically across the cores, each core will execute one complete tile (in terms of the number of operations performed).

5.3.2   Intermezzo: Triangular Index Space

A slightly more complicated case than an index space with parallel bounds is an index space of triangular shape. An example is the backward substitution phase of Gaussian elimination:

```
for (i=1; i<=n-1; i++)
   for (k=0; k<=i-1; k++)
      B[i] = B[i] - A[i][k]*B[k];
```

The index space after space-time mapping with $\theta(i,k) = k$ and $\pi(i,k) = i - 1$ is shown in Figure 5.7. To achieve load balancing, one would have to choose "growing" tiles, but this is illegal because it would generate tiles with cyclic dependences. Due to the dependences, which are of the form $\langle (t,p), S \rangle \rightarrow \langle (t+1, p+a), S \rangle$ for $a \geq 0$, only a rectangular tiling[2] is legal and easy to describe.

A rectangular tiling poses two problems. Only on one border, the covering tiles are incomplete, such that they cannot match with another tile to form a complete tile, and the number of parallel tiles is not constant in time. The space-time mapping suggests that the program can start with a high degree of parallelism which shrinks progressively. But, due to the skewing required by tiling, the parallelism has a growing phase first, followed by the shrinking phase. To address the problem of incomplete tiles, we would have to use a tiling with two different tile shapes, namely two triangles, one with the same orientation as the index space and the other such that both triangles together form a rectangle. With suitably chosen tile sizes, the first triangles will line up with the diagonal border of the index space and no point inside the tiles will be

---

[2]Or another parallelepiped tiling with an angle of at least $\frac{\pi}{2}$ between the spanning vectors, but this does not improve the situation.

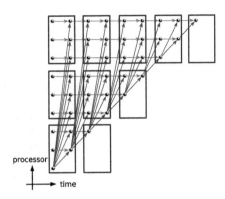

Figure 5.7: Backward substitution: Index space after space-time mapping with rectangular tiles

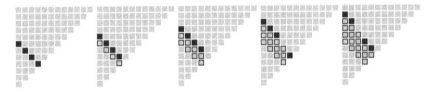

Figure 5.8: Cyclic parallel execution: Highlighted tiles are executed in parallel, bordered tiles are completed in preceding time steps.

wasted. This approach leads to complex target code, and we have not pursued it any further.

To handle the varying number of parallel tiles, we suggest to use an inter-diagonal mapping of tiles to cores. Figures 5.8 shows the aspired distribution of tiles for a part of the execution. Executing tiles on different diagonals in parallel, as shown in the figure, is legal for diagonals with at least NC tiles, since there are no data dependences between the tiles executed in parallel. In the beginning and the end of the execution, the number of parallel tiles is less than NC and we cannot utilise all cores, but the biggest part of the index space (provided that NC is small compared to the number of tiles) can be executed using all cores.

A simple model for estimating the performance of this inter-diagonal tiling and comparing it with the standard execution, is to count the number of index points within each tile (as an estimate for its execution time) and computing the execution time of the whole program from this, taking delays imposed by synchronisation into account. This simple model predicts the following speedups:

NC	2	4	8
speedup standard	1.83	3.08	4.62
speedup inter-diagonal	1.83	3.41	5.22

Due to the incomplete tiles along one of the borders and the smaller degree of parallelism in the beginning and the end, the expected speedups are sub-linear and, for two cores, almost identical. Only with four or more cores a noticeable difference is predicted. Currently, there is no tool support to generate code for the inter-diagonal tile mapping. We have performed a few experiments with hand-written code; unfortunately, it turns out that managing the inter-diagonal mapping requires more overhead to manage the execution of the tiles and, hence, the overall execution time is almost the same as for the standard time mapping. At the moment, we are not pursuing this approach any further.

5.3.3   Computing the Tiling

To describe the tiling of an index space, we need the following information [AI91]:

- an index space described by an inequality system $S \cdot (x_1 \cdots x_n)^{\mathrm{T}} + s \geq 0$ in the variables $x_1, \ldots, x_n$,

- a tile shape described by an inequality system $T \cdot (o_1 \cdots o_n)^{\mathrm{T}} + t \geq 0$ in the variables $o_1, \ldots, o_n$, and

- vectors $l_1, \ldots, l_n$ which describe the translation between the base tile and other tiles; the matrix $A = (l_1 \cdots l_n)$ is called the *lattice*.

The tiling is described by the following system:

$$
S \cdot \begin{pmatrix} x_1 \\ \vdots \\ x_n \end{pmatrix} + s \geq 0, \quad T \cdot \begin{pmatrix} o_1 \\ \vdots \\ o_n \end{pmatrix} + t \geq 0, \quad \begin{pmatrix} x_1 \\ \vdots \\ x_n \end{pmatrix} = A \cdot \begin{pmatrix} t_1 \\ \vdots \\ t_n \end{pmatrix} + \begin{pmatrix} o_1 \\ \vdots \\ o_n \end{pmatrix} \quad (5.1)
$$

where $(t_1, \ldots, t_n)$ are the coordinates of a tile in the tile space. In the classical polyhedron model, the lattice cannot contain parameters, since these would appear non-linearly in system (5.1). In our generalised model, this is no problem. To obtain a tiling whose tiles are parallelepipeds (i.e., opposite sides are parallel) whose size depends on parameters, we choose linearly independent vectors $v_1, \ldots, v_n \in \mathbb{Q}^n$ which span the (unscaled) tile and use a lattice defined by

$$
A = K \cdot \begin{pmatrix} p_1 \\ \vdots \\ p_n \end{pmatrix} \quad (5.2)
$$

where $K = (v_1 \cdots v_n)$. The tile shape is defined by:

$$
K^{-1} \cdot \begin{pmatrix} o_1 \\ \vdots \\ o_n \end{pmatrix} \geq 0, \quad -K^{-1} \cdot \begin{pmatrix} o_1 \\ \vdots \\ o_n \end{pmatrix} + K^{-1} \begin{pmatrix} p_1 - 1 \\ \vdots \\ p_n - 1 \end{pmatrix} \geq 0
$$

```
#define S1(i, k) { A[i]=(A[i-1]+A[i+1])*0.5; }

int upperBound1 = floord(5*m+3*n-14,1500);
for (glT1=-1; glT1 <= upperBound1; glT1++) {
  int lowerBound2 = max(ceild(375*glT1-1499,1875),
        max(ceild(750*glT1-m-1498,2250),max(ceild(750*glT1-2*m-n+5,750),0)));
  int upperBound2 = min(floord(1500*glT1+2*n+1493,7500), min(floord(m+n-4,1500),
        min(floord(1500*glT1+1499,4500),floord(1500*glT1+1499,1500))));
  #pragma omp parallel for schedule(static,1) private(vT1,vP1)
  for (rp1=lowerBound2; rp1 <= upperBound2; rp1++) {
    int lowerBonud3 = max(750*glT1-750*rp1,max(3000*rp1-n+3,max(1500*rp1,0)));
    int upperBound3 = min(floord(1500*glT11500*rp1+1499,2), min(3000*rp1+2998,
        min(1500*rp1+m+1498,2*m+n-5)));
    for (vT1=lowerBound3; vT1 <= upperBound3; vT1++) {
      int upperBound4 = min(1500*rp1+1499,min(floord(vT1+n-3,2),vT1));
      for (vP1=max(1500*rp1,max(ceild(vT1,2),vT1-m+1)); vP1 <= upperBound4; vP1++) {
        S1(vT1-vP1+1, -vT1+2*vP1+2);
      }
    }
  }
}
```

Figure 5.9: 1d-SOR: generated target code for parallelepiped 2250×1500 tiling

Looking at the definition of A in equation (5.2), it is easy to see that A satisfies the preconditions of Lemma 4.19. From that, one can deduce that tiling with parallelepiped tiles never leads to case distinctions and, hence, the loops generated for the parametrically tiled iteration domain (by applying our generalised Fourier-Motzkin elimination) will not be much more complicated than the code generated for a fixed tiling. Of course, the parametric tiling gives rise to a few more bounds; see the next section for a comparison.

5.3.4   Generated Code

The program transformation and code generation are fully automatic. We use the tools of LooPo for dependence analysis, computing and applying space-time mappings, and tiling in the model. CLooG [Bas04] generates sequential loops in the fixed tiling case and our generalised Fourier-Motzkin is used for the parametric tiling. A postprocessing phase (developed by LooPo team members) annotates the generated loops with OpenMP pragmas and inserts the transformed loop bodies into the rest of the code. The only manual part in the whole process is to select spanning vectors of the tiles, by which the tile shape and (in the case of a fixed tiling) size are determined.

For the 1d-SOR example, the generated code for a 2250×1500 parallelogram tiling is shown in Figure 5.9, and Figure 5.10 shows the code for a parametric $w \times h$ tiling with parameters w and h. Note that there are four for loops: the outer two enumerating the tiles, the inner two enumerating the points within the respective tile. The second loop is marked omp parallel for, since it enumerates the parallel tiles. The body of the loop has become more complex compared to the original program, because the original loop indices i and k, in which the statement is expressed, have to be reconstructed from the new

```
#define S1(i, k) { A[i]=(A[i-1]+A[i+1])*0.5; }

int upperBound1 = floord(w*n+(w+h)*m-4*w-h,h*w)
for (glT1=ceild((-2*h+1)*w+h,h*w); glT1<=upperBound1; glT1++) {
  int lowerBound2 = max(max(max(ceild(-w+1,w),ceild(h*glT1-n-m+4,h)),
   ceild(h*glT1-n-w+4,w+h)),ceild(h*glT1-n-2*w+5,2*w+h)),ceild(-h*glT1+n+2*m-5,w-h));
  int upperBound2 = min(min(min(min(floord(m-1,w),floord(h*glT1+h-1,h)),
   floord(-h*glT1-w-h+2,w-h)),floord(h*glT1+h-1,w+h)),floord(h*glT1+m+h-2,2*w+h));
  for (rp1=lowerBound2; rp1<=upperBound2; rp1++) {
    int lowerBound3 = max(max(max(max(0,2*w*rp1),2*h*glT1-2*h*rp1-n+3),
        h*glT1-h*rp1),h*glT1+(w-h)*rp1);
    int upperBound3 = min(min(min(min(2*h*glT1-2*h*rp1+2*h-2,n+2*m-5),
        h*glT1-h*rp1+n+m-2),2*w*rp1+n+2*w-5),h*glT1+(w-h)*rp1+w+h-2);
    for (vT1=lowerBound2; vT1<=upperBonud3; vT1++) {
      int lowerBound4 = max(max(max(ceild(vT1,2),vT1-m+1),h*glT1-h*rp1),
        -w*rp1+vT1-w+1);
      int upperBound4 = min(min(min(floord(vT1+n-3,2),vT1),h*glT1-h*rp1+h-1),
        -w*rp1+vT1);
      for (vP1=lowerBound4; vP1<=upperBound4; vP1++) {
        S1(vT1-vP1+1, -vT1+2*vP1+2);
      }
    }
  }
}
```

Figure 5.10: 1d-SOR: generated target code for parametric parallelepiped $w \times h$ tiling

indices. Note that the parametric version has some more loop bounds than the fixed tiling version.

A fast execution of the program may seem unlikely due to the complex bounds of the loops and the necessary reconstruction of the original indices in the body. But it turns out that i is an induction variable even after the transformation and, hence, the addresses of $A[i-1]$, $A[i]$, $A[i+1]$ are computed by simple additions. GCC 4.2.1 generates the following x86 assembly code for the body of the innermost loop (in both versions):

```
.L87:
        fldl    (%eax)
        addl    $1, %edx
        faddl   -16(%eax)
        fmul    %st(1), %st
        fstpl   -8(%eax)
        addl    $16, %eax
        cmpl    %edx, %ecx
        jge     .L87
```

The computation $A[i] = (A[i+1] + A[i-1]) * 0.5$ is performed by the four floating-point instructions (`fldl`, `faddl`, `fmul`, `fstpl`) and the other four instructions deal with the loop counter and update `%eax`, which holds the address of $A[i+1]$. This implies that the loop bounds are only computed rarely compared to the execution of the body, provided that the innermost loop has a sufficient number of iterations.

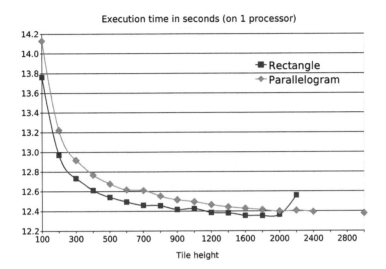

Figure 5.11: Tiling overhead in 1d-SOR for $n = 10^6, m = 9,000$ (x-axis non-linear)

We ran our experiments on a machine with four cores, consisting of two Dualcore AMD Opteron^{TM} 275 processors with 2.2 GHz and 2 GB of RAM. Since this is a NUMA (non-uniform memory access) architecture, we have to take care not to spoil the benchmarks with local vs. remote memory effects. As it turns out, memory locality does not play a significant role in 1d-SOR because of its cache behaviour; see below.

The complex loop bounds and the reconstruction of the original loop indices still permit the innermost loop to be small. Let us now discuss the question of how many iterations the innermost loop must have to make the effort of computing the complex loop bounds negligible. Figure 5.11 shows the execution times for $n = 10^6$, $m = 9000$ and varying tile heights (the innermost loop enumerates the height dimension of the tile) for fixed tilings. The tile width has been chosen according to the formulas presented above with $f = 1$. The execution time converges towards about 12.38 seconds. We observe that the parallelogram tiling has a slightly higher overhead (the loop bounds are more complex). With the rectangular tiling, the tile height can only be increased up to about 2000, since the tile width has to be set to $\frac{m}{NC}$ − height, i.e., 2250 − height in our case. Therefore, the tiles become very narrow for heights greater than 2000 and, accordingly, the second innermost loop has only a few iterations which causes noticeable overhead for heights greater than 2000. The parallelogram tiling does not suffer from such a restriction; the height can be increased arbitrarily, since the width is fixed, in this example, to 2250. On the other hand, we have to note that the run-time evaluation of the loop bounds can suffer integer overflows, e.g., the program does not execute correctly for tile heights of 2400

Instructions	Reads Total	Misses	Writes Total	Misses	
18k	16k	2			for glT1=
102k	88k				for rp1=
42,235k	21,099k	18k			for vT1=
36,056,066k	14,035k				for vP1=
35,999,928k	17,999,964k	3,973k	8,999,982k	0	A[i]=...

Table 5.1: 1d-SOR: cache misses (L1 and L2 combined) for rectangular tiling with tile size 1500×750

	Rectangular Tiling			Parallelogram Tiling		
Cores	1	2	4	1	2	4
	Width=850, Height=1400					
Time in secs	12.38	6.33	3.23			
speedup	1.00	1.95	3.82			
Efficiency	99.76%	97.55%	95.59%			
	Width=650, Height=1600			Width=2250, Height=3000		
Time in secs	12.35	6.32	3.26	12.38	6.28	3.17
speedup	1.00	1.95	3.79	1.00	1.97	3.90
Efficiency	100.00%	97.71%	94.71%	99.76%	98.33%	97.40%

Table 5.2: 1d-SOR: speedups (efficiency relative to best execution)

and 2600 (which are missing in the diagram for this reason). We do not provide separate run-time measurements for the parametric tiling, since the run times we observed for the parametric version were at most 1% worse than the run time of the corresponding fixed version code. This underlines that run-time efficiency correlates strongly with the non-overhead of executing the body of the innermost loop.

The 1d-SOR example also demonstrates that space-time mapping and tiling can reduce the execution time by enhancing the cache behaviour. Compared to the original execution, the tiled program is a vast improvement. The original program takes 75.4 seconds to execute. With space-time mapping, but without tiling, the execution time is still 23.6 seconds. Only after tiling, the time reduces to about 12.4 seconds. Analysis using the Cachegrind tool of the Valgrind suite [NS07] shows that almost no cache misses occur (Table 5.1). For the backward substitution example, Cachegrind reports a cache miss rate of about 8.5% for both the standard parallel and the inter-diagonal parallel execution.

For 1d-SOR, Table 5.2 shows some of the best speedup and efficiency values (efficiency relative to the best observed execution). The rectangular tiling with the best execution time on four cores achieves 95.59% efficiency using a 850 × 1400 tiling. The best parallelogram tiling is 2250 × 300 with an efficiency of 99.76% on one core and 97.40% on four cores. The parallelogram tiling shows a slightly better scaling behaviour, so it overtakes the rectangular tiling which has a slightly better execution time on one core.

5.4 Array Localisation

The success of parallelising an algorithm depends on two factors. First, the computations must be arranged suitably to exploit the available computational power efficiently. Second, data transport between the computing entities must not spoil the efficiency of the execution by consuming a considerable amount of the total execution time. With current architectures, several levels of data storage are available: registers, caches, CPU-local main memory, main memory of remote CPUs, remote network storage. Due to the dramatic difference in their performance, which is, for technical and economic reasons, reflected in the smaller sizes of faster storage, the data accessed often must be kept in the fastest memory. Program transformations which increase locality have been studied widely (cf. Section 3). On special-purpose architectures, like embedded systems and graphics processors, fast cache memory is not managed automatically by hardware but has to be managed explicitly by software. We aim at an automatic explicit management of so-called scratchpad memories present in such architectures.

Since we aim at full automation, the techniques are not applicable to arbitrary programs. They must be loop nests with bounds linear in the surrounding loops and structure parameters containing bodies with array accesses with affine subscripts, i.e., we are working with programs that are studied in the context of the polyhedron model (cf. Section 2.2.1). Our presentation here is an extended version of our previous work [Grö09].

As an example of the desired transformation, let us look at the example program in Figure 5.12(a). It consists of an outer sequential time loop and an inner parallel loop. Each iteration (t, p) updates an array element $A[t+p+1]$. Since every time step t accesses array elements $A[t+1], \ldots, A[t+n+1]$, there is considerable overlap in the array elements used in successive time steps, namely n elements. For example, the first time step $t = 0$ accesses the elements $A[1], \ldots, A[n+1]$, the second time step $t = 1$ accesses $A[2], \ldots, A[n+2]$ and uses $A[2], \ldots, A[n+1]$ again. If the accesses to array A have high latency, i.e., it is not stored in the fastest available memory, the execution of the program can be accelerated by keeping the relevant parts of A in a faster memory. One possible way to achieve this localisation is shown in Figure 5.12(b). Array L is assumed to be stored in fast memory. In every iteration of the loop on t, element $A[t+n+1]$ of A, which has not been accessed in the previous iteration, is brought into L at $L[n]$. After the computation, $L[0]$ is exported to $A[t+1]$, because it is not needed in the next iteration, and the elements of L are shifted inside L to bring them into the appropriate position for the next iteration. In addition, elements are moved to/from L before and after the loop on t, respectively. Having to move all (but one) elements of L can be costly depending on the architecture. With memory local to the computing cores (which may require only one cycle per memory access) the overall positive effect of the transformation outweighs this additional cost. As the `syncparfor` statements in the code shown suggest, this reorganisation can be executed synchronously in parallel, i.e., as a simultaneous assignment.

```
                                    for (x=0; x<=n-1; x++)
                                      L[x] = A[x+1];
                                    for (t=0; t<=n; t++) {
                                      L[n] = A[t+n+1];
for (t=0; t<=n; t++)                  parfor (p=0; p<=n; p++)
   parfor (p=0; p<=n; p++)              L[p] = f(L[p]);
     A[t+p+1] = f(A[t+p+1]);          A[t+1] = L[0];
                                      syncparfor (x=1; x<=n; x++)
        (a) original program           L[x-1] = L[x];
                                    }
                                    parfor (x=0; x<=n-1; x++)
                                      A[n+x+2] = L[x];
```

                                                (b) localised version

Figure 5.12: Locality-improving transformation on a simple parallel program

We propose a way of computing the array elements which have to be moved into L before each time step, exported from L and reorganised in L after each time step. The reorganisation step requires particular attention because, as can be seen in the above example, it overwrites elements of L. Therefore, an in-situ reuse of the same L requires an ordering of the overwriting operations that does not destroy data elements before they have been copied.

5.4.1   Prerequisites

We require dependence information on the level of access instances which is precise, i.e., there must not be dependences which follow from other dependences by transitivity. This is different from the more usual, statement-based definition. With this definition, there are two dependences in the statement

   A[i] = A[i] + A[i] ,

namely an input dependence from one of the read accesses to the other (the choice of the direction is arbitrary) and an anti dependence from the later read access to the write access. With the usual definition, there are no dependences inside one statement instance. We require this finer granularity of dependences to capture that, in this example, all three accesses in the above statement refer to the same memory cell and, hence, it is sufficient to fetch $A[i]$ once from global memory for both read accesses and that $A[i]$ is immediately overwritten again, so the fetched value must not be cached for following statements.

5.4.2   Locality Transformation

We consider codes of the form shown in Figure 5.13, i.e., there is one outer sequential loop on t enumerating the *time steps* of the program and there are zero, one, or several sequential and/or parallel loops on i inside (which need not be perfectly nested, even though the code fragment shown in the figure is).

```
for (t ∈ T) {
    (par)for (i ∈ D(t)) { body with A[f₁(i, t)], ..., A[fₙ(i, t)] }
}
```

Figure 5.13: Program to be transformed with one outer sequential time loop

The computation statements inside the loops on $\mathbf{i}$ contain accesses $A[f_j(\mathbf{i}, t)]$ $(1 \leq j \leq n)$ to an array A. The transformation can be applied successively for several different arrays, but we restrict our presentation to the case of a single array.

Each array access $A[f_j(\mathbf{i}, t)]$ is part of a statement with an index set $D_j(t)$, which depends on the point t in time, i.e., the access is executed for every $\mathbf{i} \in D_j(t)$ for given t. To make our technique applicable, $D_j(t)$ must be a (parametric) Z-polyhedron. For the ease of notation, we omit the dependence on the parameters $\mathbf{p}$ of the index sets and other sets and functions. For example, we write $D_j(t)$ instead of the more elaborate $D_j(t, \mathbf{p})$. The aim of the proposed transformation is to achieve that some or all array elements accessed at time t are loaded into the local memory L of the compute node before the execution of the operations at time t. This requires answers to three questions:

1. Where (at which index) do we place elements to be stored in L?

2. Which elements are present at time t and which elements are loaded into and which are removed from L before/during/after time t?

3. What happens to the elements in L between time t and $t+1$?

Answers to these questions are given in the following sections. In Section 5.4.3, we present how we map elements from A to L, assuming that we know already which elements from A are to be mapped to L. Sections 5.4.4 and 5.4.5 present two answers to the second question. Finally, we discuss answers to the third question (applicable to both previous answers to Question 2) in Section 5.4.6.

5.4.3 The New Location of Array Elements

The local storage caches some elements of A at a given time to accelerate their access. Let $C(t)$ be the indices of the elements of A to be cached in L at time t, i.e., $\mathbf{x} \in C(t)$ means that $A[\mathbf{x}]$ is available in L. We require $C(t)$ to be a Z-polyhedron.

We map the elements of A, which are present in L at a given time to L such that $L[0], L[1], \ldots$ contain the cached elements of A in ascending order, i.e., if $A[\mathbf{x}_1]$ and $A[\mathbf{x}_2]$ are mapped to $L[y_1]$ and $L[y_2]$, respectively, then $\mathbf{x}_1 \prec \mathbf{x}_2$ implies $y_1 < y_2$. This way, we can determine the index of an element $A[\mathbf{x}]$ in L by the number of elements $\mathbf{z} \in C(t)$ which precede $\mathbf{x}$ in lexicographic order. To this end, we consider the parametric set defined by

$$A_{\prec}(\mathbf{x}, t) = \{\mathbf{z} \mid \mathbf{z} \in C(t) \wedge \mathbf{z} \prec \mathbf{x}\}.$$

Note that $A_{\prec}(\mathbf{x}, t)$ is a union of parametric Z-polyhedra because the lexico-graphic order $\prec$ corresponds to a disjunction of affine conditions. The number of integral points in $A_{\prec}(\mathbf{x}, t)$ is the number of array indices in $C(t)$ up to, but not including, $\mathbf{x}$ (at time t). Computing the number of integral points in $A_{\prec}(\mathbf{x}, t)$ (cf. Section 2.1.4) yields a set $\{(c_1, \rho_1), \ldots, (c_q, \rho_q)\}$ of conditions c_j on the parameters (including $\mathbf{x}$ and t) and quasi-polynomials ρ_j, where $\rho_j(\mathbf{x}, t)$ evaluates to the number of integral points in $A_{\prec}(\mathbf{x}, t)$ if $c_j(\mathbf{x}, t)$ holds. If we combine the c_j and ρ_j to a conditional expression ρ, which evaluates to ρ_j if c_j holds, then the location of an element $A[\mathbf{x}]$ in the local storage at time t is given by $L[\rho(\mathbf{x}, t)]$ (provided that $\mathbf{x} \in C(t)$).

By construction, we have the ordering property stated in the following lemma.

Lemma 5.2. *Let $t \in \mathbb{Z}$ and $\mathbf{x}_1, \mathbf{x}_2 \in C(t)$. Then $\mathbf{x}_1 \prec \mathbf{x}_2 \Leftrightarrow \rho(\mathbf{x}_1, t) < \rho(\mathbf{x}_2, t)$.*

The total amount of local storage needed can be computed by counting $C(t)$ and maximising w.r.t. to t. For each of its constituents, one can maximise $|C(t)|$, e.g., by quantifier elimination in the reals (cf. Section 4.3.2) or maybe Bernstein expansion [CT04]. The overall maximum is then the maximum of the maxima of the distinct cases, of course.

If $|C(t)|$ exceeds the available storage for at least one value of $t \in T$, we cannot localise w.r.t. the loop on t. We must find an inner sequential loop or create one with the right granularity (i.e., memory footprint) by applying tiling on one of the inner dimensions to create a suitable time loop, cf. Section 5.4.7.

5.4.4 Localisation Based on Access Instances

Localisation can be achieved without dependence information if we perform it based on access instances only. The set of array elements accessed by $A[f_j(\mathbf{i}, t)]$, with iteration domain $D_j(t)$ at time t, is given by the parametric Z-polyhedron $C_j(t) = \{f_j(\mathbf{i}, t) \mid \mathbf{i} \in D_j(t)\}$. The set of all array elements accessed at time t is given by the union of the $C_j(t)$. The most obvious choice of $C(t)$ to be stored in L is the set of exactly the elements accessed at a given time step but, since any superset represents a correct transformation, it is worthwhile to add another degree of freedom. Often, we encounter algorithms which have an alternating access pattern, for example, at even time steps one part of the data is accessed and at odd time steps a different part of the data. With the obvious choice of $C(t)$, we would transform the program such that the contents of L is replaced completely at every time step. Such situations are remedied by introducing a *localisation window*, i.e., by permitting the scope of elements kept in L to be larger than the current point in time. We describe the localisation window by its width w ($w \geq 1$) which denotes the number of successive time steps considered to be part of the window. We now define $C(t)$ by

$$C(t) = \bigcup_{j=1}^{n} \bigcup_{\tau=0}^{w-1} C_j(t + \tau).$$

Note that $w = 1$ is the case in which $C(t)$ contains only the elements accessed at the current time t. From $C(t)$, one can compute $\rho(\mathbf{x}, t)$ as described in Section 5.4.3. Let us now address the question of data movement, i.e., which elements to move in/out and around (within L) at a given time step. There are three parts involved:

1. a "move in" phase which loads data not present in local storage before the computation of the current time step,

2. a "move out" phase which removes data not needed at the next time step from local storage and puts it to global memory,

3. a "reorganisation" phase between two successive time steps, in which the data in local storage are retained in local storage but moved to the the correct location for the next computation.

The array elements relevant for each of these three phases are given by the following sets:

$$I(t) := C(t) - C(t-1), \quad O(t) := C(t) - C(t+1), \quad G(t) := C(t) \cap C(t+1).$$

$I(t)$ contains the indices of elements used at t but not at $t-1$, i.e., the elements to be moved to local storage for step t; $O(t)$ contains the indices of elements used only at t but not at $t+1$, i.e., the elements to be moved out after step t; and $G(t)$ contains the elements used at both t and $t+1$, i.e., the elements which must remain in local storage and have to be reorganised between t and $t+1$. Each of these three sets is a union of Z-polyhedra.

It is tempting to try to optimise the move-in and move-out sets by, for example, moving out only the elements in $O(t)$ that have actually been overwritten at time t. But this "optimisation" is incorrect, since an element may have been overwritten several time steps before it is moved out (and may only have been read in between). A correct and exact optimisation of data move in and out requires dependence analysis techniques and is presented in Section 5.4.5.

During the reorganisation phase, care has to be taken not to overwrite data which must still be moved before the next time step begins. A simple way to avoid this problem is to use a second local storage to which the reorganised data is written and swap the two storage areas after reorganisation. Using pointer exchange for efficiency, this approach has little run-time overhead, but uses twice as much local storage. This may be sufficient, but the amount of local storage is often limited, e.g., in embedded devices. We present techniques for remedying this drawback in Section 5.4.6.

A sketch of the code after the localising transformation is shown in Figure 5.14. The array accesses $A[f_j(\mathbf{i}, t)]$ in the body (cf. Figure 5.13) have been replaced by $L_1[\rho(f_j(\mathbf{i}, t), t)]$. Local storage spaces L_1 and L_2 are exchanged (by swapping pointers) after reorganisation and before the move-in phase of the next time step. Another way to look at this reorganisation is to view it as a big simultaneous assignment, i.e., the elements which remain in L move to their new locations simultaneously without overwriting each other. If there is

```
for (t ∈ T) {
    parfor (x ∈ I(t)) L₁[ρ(x,t)] = A[x];              // move in
    (par)for (i ∈ D(t)) {
        body with L₁[ρ(fⱼ(i,t),t)] instead of A[fⱼ(i,t)]
    }
    parfor (x ∈ O(t)) A[x] = L₁[ρ(x,t)];              // move out
    parfor (x ∈ G(t)) L₂[ρ(x,t+1)] = L₁[ρ(x,t)];      // reorganisation
    swap(L₁, L₂);
}
```

Figure 5.14: Preliminary localised code based on access instances with two local storages

enough room in the register space of the parallel processor, the reorganisation can be performed within a single local storage by letting every parallel thread read a certain number of elements from L, performing a barrier synchronisation between the threads, and letting every thread write its elements back to L in their new positions. But this requires double the amount of space, too, since we have to have enough room in the register space of the parallel processors. In Section 5.4.6, we show why a single area of local storage is sufficient and why we only need a constant amount of register space.

5.4.5   Localisation Based on Dependences

The access-based localisation of memory accesses presented in Section 5.4.4 is simple in the sense that no dependence information is required by the localising transformation. On the other hand, this simplicity leads to overhead in the data movement, for example, by loading elements into local storage which are never read but only written. A dependence-based approach can remedy this situation. Provided that an exact dependence analysis of the loop nest is available, we can mark each access as global or local. Whether to access global or local memory depends on whether the desired value is present in local storage or not. This way, there are no separate move-in and move-out statements which precede and succeed the computation statements, respectively. Instead, they are integrated into (or next to) the computations themselves.

Let $\mathcal{R}$ be the set of read access instances and $\mathcal{W}$ be the set of write access instances of the program. We write $time(a)$ to denote the time step in which an access instance a is executed; $win(a_1, a_2)$ denotes that an access instance a_2 is inside the localisation window starting at a_1: $0 \leq time(a_2) - time(a_1) \leq w$, i.e., a_2 happens at most w time steps after a_1. We define global writes $\mathcal{W}_g$ and local writes $\mathcal{W}_l$ as follows:

$$\mathcal{W}_g = \{w \in \mathcal{W} \mid \neg(\exists w' : w' \in \mathcal{W} : w \xrightarrow{\text{out}} w' \wedge win(w, w'))\}$$

$$\mathcal{W}_l = \{w \in \mathcal{W} \mid (\exists r : r \in \mathcal{R} : w \xrightarrow{\text{flow}} r \wedge win(w, r))\}$$

A write is global if the value is not overwritten inside the localisation window. A write is local if the value is read later inside the localisation window. Note that, by this definition, there can be writes that are both global and local. This happens when the value is not overwritten in the localisation window and, therefore, has to be written to global memory at some point (and we choose to do immediately), but it is read again later, so we also keep the value in local memory. It is also possible for a write to be neither global nor local; this means that the value will be overwritten and not read inbetween and, hence, we can drop the write entirely.

Reads have to be partitioned into three groups. A read is local ($\mathcal{R}_l$) if the value accessed is present in local storage because it has been read or written earlier in the localisation window. A read is global ($\mathcal{R}_g$) if no prior access in the localisation window has been made and no later read access will be made. A read is from global memory with a successive store to local memory ($\mathcal{R}_{gl}$) if no prior access has been made but, later in the localisation window, the value will be read again.

$$\mathcal{R}_l = \{r \in \mathcal{R} \mid \left(\exists w : w \in \mathcal{W} : w \xrightarrow{\text{flow}} r \wedge win(w,r)\right) \vee$$
$$\left(\exists r' : r' \in \mathcal{R} : r' \xrightarrow{\text{in}} r \wedge win(r',r)\right)\}$$
$$\mathcal{R}_g = \{r \in \mathcal{R} \mid \neg\left(\exists r' : r' \in \mathcal{R} : r \xrightarrow{\text{in}} r' \wedge win(r,r')\right)\} - \mathcal{R}_l$$
$$\mathcal{R}_{gl} = \{r \in \mathcal{R} \mid \left(\exists r' : r' \in \mathcal{R} : r \xrightarrow{\text{in}} r' \wedge win(r,r')\right)\} - \mathcal{R}_l$$

The elements that are present in local storage are given by

$$C(t) = \{accelem(a) \mid a \in \mathcal{R}_l \cup \mathcal{R}_{gl} \cup \mathcal{W}_l, t \leq time(a) < t + w\}.$$

From $C(t)$, we can again compute $\rho(\mathbf{x}, t)$ (cf. Section 5.4.3), which gives the location of an element $A[\mathbf{x}]$ in L at a given time t. The reorganisation of L between time steps is described by the set $G(t) = C(t) \cap C(t+1)$ as in Section 5.4.4.

There is one detail which we have to consider with this approach. Scheduling a parallel program usually does not impose restrictions on input dependences. It is allowed that an input dependence $r_1 \xrightarrow{\text{in}} r_2$ with $r_1 \in \mathcal{R}_{gl}$ is not carried by a sequential loop and r_1 and r_2 reside on different processors. In this case, it is possible that the read from global memory and the following write to the local memory cell for r_1 are, in fact, executed *after* r_2, which is supposed to read the same value as r_1 from local memory, because the ordering of the operations between the two involved processors is not determined. To guarantee a correct execution of the transformed programs, we have either to require that input dependences respect the same restrictions as the other dependence types or to emit a barrier synchronisation statement which makes sure that the write to local memory at r_1 is executed before the read from local memory at r_2.

Synchronisations must not create a deadlock in the execution. Unfortunately, this is not easy to achieve as the following example illustrates. Suppose we have four reads $r_1, \ldots, r_4$ where $r_1 \in \mathcal{R}_{gl}$ and $r_i \xrightarrow{\text{in}} r_{i+1}$ for $1 \leq i \leq 3$. If

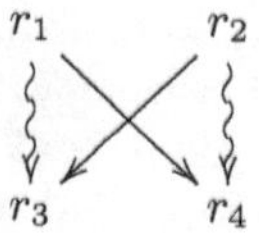

$r_1 \to r_4$ and $r_2 \to r_3$ are input dependences,
$r_1 \leadsto r_3$ and $r_2 \leadsto r_4$ denote control flow.

Figure 5.15: Deadlock situation for synchronisations introduced by different dependences

r_1, $\{r_2, r_3\}$, r_4 are mapped to three different processors (and to the same global time step t), then we must synchronise between the write to local memory of r_1 and the read in r_2, but we must also synchronise before r_3 and r_4 read. But we cannot issue a barrier synchronisation at all four operations, since r_2 and r_3 are on the same processor, so the barrier call at r_3 will be orphaned. We have to form appropriate groups for the synchronisations.

But even if we solve this problem, there remains another one. The synchronisations required for different input dependences may lead to a cyclic waiting relation (a "deadly embrace"). Figure 5.15 shows one such situation. r_3 is executed after r_1 in the same thread; likewise, r_4 is executed after r_2 by another thread. Due to the dependences $r_1 \xrightarrow{\text{in}} r_4$ and $r_2 \xrightarrow{\text{in}} r_3$, synchronisations are required which would require a reversal of control flow in one of the threads to complete. Hence, a deadlock is created.

Because of these difficulties, we do not consider synchronisation to order dependent read accesses any further. If a schedule which is computed to respect flow, output and anti dependences happens to respect the input dependences in addition, then the parallel program can be executed as is.

Let us now present an alternative to introducing synchronisations in the case that the schedule does not respect input dependences.

Reintroducing the Move-in Phase

Since doing without a move-in phase imposes an additional burden on either the parallelisation (the schedule must respect input dependences, too) or the code generation (additional, deadlock-free synchronisation), we pursue another solution. The problems arise from input dependences, i.e., from data which is read at least twice. To make sure that the read-in appears before the read accesses to local memory, we reintroduce a move-in phase which, however, only moves in elements which are read at least twice. The set of elements to move in is now defined by

$$I(t) = \{accelem(r) \mid r \in \mathcal{R}_{gl}, time(r) = t\},$$

i.e., we move in all the elements that are accessed by global-local reads at the beginning of the time step in which the access occurs. The global-local read accesses themselves are then handled like local reads: they simply read from local memory. This approach adds a slight overhead on the number of local memory accesses. Without a move-in phase, a global-local read has one read from global memory into a register, one write of the value to local memory and the computation can be performed on the value in the register. With a move-in phase, the move-in reads from global memory, writes to local memory and the use of the value at the global-local read performs an additional read from local memory.

But, since access to local memory is fast (on some architectures almost as fast as access to a register), the slight overhead is likely to be outweighed by the reduction in synchronisation costs or the ability to run the program with a better (less constrained) schedule.

Imprecise Dependence Information

The just presented dependence-based localisation computes precisely which elements to move into local storage and which accesses go to local or global memory, respectively, after the transformation. The assumption that has been made is that the dependence information is precise. Since not all programs allow a precise dependence analysis (or a precise analysis may be computationally too expensive), we briefly address the question what happens when the dependence information is inexact. Since the dependence information determines whether a transformed access goes to local or global memory, it is clear that an under-approximation of the actual dependences cannot be used. If a flow or input dependence is missing, the target access instance may go to global memory, although the data resides in local memory. A missing output or anti dependence may cause a write access to go to global memory instead of local storage and the next read access may read an out-of-date value from local storage.

Overestimating the dependences is dangerous, too. We must assume a dependence exists only between accesses instances that actually access the same memory cell. Otherwise, the localisation may rely on an access moving a value to local storage although the access goes to another element. Two problems remain even with this restriction:

(1) When an access instance has several possible sources, some sources may lie in the localisation window, others may be outside. Then, it is unclear at the target access instance whether the value can be found in local storage or has to be fetched from global storage.

(2) Likewise, if there are several possible writes for value, it is unclear which write access instance should write the value to global memory.

Problem (1) is solved by reintroducing the move-in phase. An approximation to solve Problem (2) is to write to global memory at every possible write but that is unsuitable for our goal of reducing the number of accesses to global memory. The other solution is to reintroduce a move-out phase. The set of elements to move out is given by

$$O(t) = \{accelem(r) \mid r \in \mathcal{W}_g, time(r) = t\}.$$

This may seem like being back at the localisation based on access instances. The difference is that a localisation based on dependences with a move-in and a move-out phase still takes care not to move elements to local storage which are not reused according to the dependences.

We should note that it is important to compute the sets $I(t)$, $O(t)$ and $C(t)$ precisely. For example, to compute $O(t)$ we have to determine precisely which access instances are actually executed at time t. If the access is guarded by a conditional $\gamma(t)$, we have to know at compile time when (for which t) $\gamma(t)$ holds. If this information is not available, a correct localisation cannot be performed. So, although dependence information may be an overapproximation, precise knowledge about which accesses are performed is still required.

5.4.6   Ordering the Reorganisation

As has been outlined in Section 5.4.4, a straight-forward implementation of the reorganisation phase requires two areas of local storage to avoid overwriting elements which have not yet been moved. Let us now prove that a single storage area is sufficient, i.e., the reorganisation can always be performed in-situ by adhering to a certain order in the intra-storage element moves. The key observation is that, if an element $L[y_1]$ has to be moved to $L[y_2]$ ($y_1 \neq y_2$) and $L[y_2]$ has in turn to be moved to $L[y_3]$, then $y_2 \neq y_3$ and $L[y_1]$ and $L[y_2]$ move in the same direction, i.e., $y_1 < y_2 \Leftrightarrow y_2 < y_3$.

Definition 5.3. Let $t \in \mathbb{Z}$ and $\mathbf{x} \in G(t)$. The *drift* $\delta(\mathbf{x}, t)$ of the element $L[\rho(\mathbf{x}, t)]$ is defined as $\delta(\mathbf{x}, t) := \rho(\mathbf{x}, t+1) - \rho(\mathbf{x}, t)$. We say that $L[\rho(\mathbf{x}, t)]$ moves *forward*, if $\delta(\mathbf{x}, t) > 0$, and *backward* if $\delta(\mathbf{x}, t) < 0$.

We now present the key idea introduced above formally and prove that, if an element moves from $L[y_1]$ to $L[y_2]$, the contents of $L[y_2]$ moves in the same direction as the contents of $L[y_1]$ (provided that $L[y_2]$ moves at all).

Proposition 5.4. Let $t \in \mathbb{Z}$ and $\mathbf{x}_1, \mathbf{x}_2 \in G(t)$ such that $\rho(\mathbf{x}_1, t+1) = \rho(\mathbf{x}_2, t)$. This validates the following two implications:

$$\delta(\mathbf{x}_1, t) > 0 \Rightarrow \delta(\mathbf{x}_2, t) > 0$$
$$\delta(\mathbf{x}_1, t) < 0 \Rightarrow \delta(\mathbf{x}_2, t) < 0$$

Proof. Let t, $\mathbf{x}_1, \mathbf{x}_2$ be as stated and $\delta(\mathbf{x}_1, t) > 0$, i.e., $\rho(\mathbf{x}_1, t+1) > \rho(\mathbf{x}_1, t)$. Since $\rho(\mathbf{x}_1, t+1) = \rho(\mathbf{x}_2, t)$ and $\mathbf{x}_1, \mathbf{x}_2 \in C(t)$, this implies (by Lemma 5.2) that $\mathbf{x}_1 \prec \mathbf{x}_2$. Again by Lemma 5.2 and since $\mathbf{x}_1, \mathbf{x}_2 \in C(t+1)$, this implies $\rho(\mathbf{x}_1, t+1) < \rho(\mathbf{x}_2, t+1)$ and, because of $\rho(\mathbf{x}_1, t+1) = \rho(\mathbf{x}_2, t)$, we get $\delta(\mathbf{x}_2, t) > 0$. Analogous reasoning applies to the second case with < 0 instead of > 0.   □

By this proposition, a way to reorganise local storage in-situ is quite obvious.

Corollary 5.5. *The reordering of elements in local storage L at the end of time step t can be achieved in-situ by a two-pass sweep over L.*

The in-situ reorganisation works by scanning $G(t)$ once in ascending lexicographic order and once in descending lexicographic order. In the ascending pass, it is guaranteed that, if $\delta(\mathbf{x}, t) < 0$ holds for an $\mathbf{x} \in G(t)$ being scanned, then its value (which corresponds to $A[\mathbf{x}]$) can safely be moved from $L[\rho(\mathbf{x}, t)]$ to $L[\rho(\mathbf{x}, t + 1)]$, since the target entry in L is either empty (because it contained an element from A which is not used at time step t) or it has been moved already, because its drift is negative, too. The descending scan, in turn, can safely move all the elements with a positive drift.

In many regular cases, in which the drift has the same sign for all moving data elements, a single pass is sufficient. In the very regular cases that the drift is identical for all elements in the local storage, there exists an alternative to moving the data around. We can change the addressing of the local storage to accomplish the same effect. Accesses $L[\rho(\mathbf{x}, t)]$ are replaced by $L[(\rho(\mathbf{x}, t) + o) \bmod S]$, where S is the size of the local storage and o is an offset which is initialised to 0 and incremented by the negated drift at the end of every time step. This round-robin addressing achieves the same effect as repeated movement. A precise formulation is given by the following lemma.

Lemma 5.6. *If $\big(\forall t, \mathbf{x}_1, \mathbf{x}_2 : t \in T, \mathbf{x}_1, \mathbf{x}_2 \in G(t) : \delta(\mathbf{x}_1, t) = \delta(\mathbf{x}_2, t) \big)$ holds, then one can, instead of reorganising the local storage, replace every $L[\rho(\mathbf{x}, t)]$ by $L[(\rho(\mathbf{x}, t) + o) \bmod S]$ where o is a variable initialised with 0 and incremented by $-\delta(\mathbf{x}, t)$ (for any $\mathbf{x} \in G(t)$) after every iteration of the loop on t, and S is the size of the local storage.*

The correctness of the lemma is obvious. When modulo addressing is possible instead of reorganising the data, it need not necessarily be the more efficient option. The cost of reorganisation is determined by the number of elements in the scratchpad, whereas the cost for modulo addressing is determined by the number of array accesses in the computation statements, since every access will contain a modulo operation. When comparing the two approaches, we have to bear in mind that, on a parallel architecture, the reorganisation can be done in parallel, too. Often, each thread moves a low, constant number of elements, because the size of the working set is proportional to the number of threads.

5.4.7 Adjusting the Granularity of the Localisation

To adjust the granularity of the localisation, i.e., the amount of data localised, we have to select an appropriate loop and a suitable localisation window w. Since localisation w.r.t. an outer loop l encompasses all the reuse that can be obtained by localising w.r.t. an inner loop l' (since one iteration of l contains all iterations of l' for this iteration of l), we simply want to localise w.r.t. the outermost loop which permits localisation. Let $C_l(t)$ denote the elements to be stored in the scratchpad in iteration t of loop l; $C_l(t) = \varnothing$ if t is not an iteration of loop l. To find the right granularity, we would like to select the outermost sequential loop l and a maximal $w \geq 1$ for which

$$\big(\max t : t \in D_l : s_l(t, w) \big) \leq S$$

where D_l is the iteration domain of l, S is the size of the scratchpad and

$$s_l(t, w) := |\bigcup_{i=0}^{w-1} C_l(t+i)|.$$

To solve this problem, we propose the following method. $C_l(t)$ is a Z-polyhedron, as we have already noted; hence, $|\bigcup_{i=0}^{w-1} C_l(t+i)|$ is a quasi-polynomial. Therefore, we can compute $s_l(t, w)$ for a given w. For each of the periodic cases of $s_l(t, w)$, we can find an approximation of its maximum by Bernstein expansion [CT04], i.e., we can approximate $m_l(w) := (\max t : t \in D_l : s_l(t, w))$. Obviously, $m_l(w+1) \geq m_l(w)$, so we can find a suitable loop l and an appropriate w by looking for the outermost sequential loop l with $m_l(1) \leq S$. For this loop, we look for the maximal w such that $m_l(w) \leq S$. If we cannot find a loop l with $m_l(1) \leq S$, then the scratchpad is too small to hold the reused elements from one iteration to another and our technique does not apply. We refer to the literature (cf. Section 3.4) for techniques to change the data layout and the working set size of a loop nest.

5.4.8 Code Generation Considerations

There are two non-trivial problems to solve to obtain efficient code. First, we have to take care of the possibly complex array subscripts $\rho(f_j(\mathbf{i}, t), t)$. Second, all iteration domains constructed are polyhedral, except for the in-situ reorganisation. Because of the condition $\delta(\mathbf{x}, t) > 0$ (or $\delta(\mathbf{x}, t) < 0$) in the description of the domain of the reorganisation statement, the domain need not be a polytope.

Generating Efficient Code

Let us assume that $\delta(\mathbf{x}, t)$ is an affine expression or that we are not using in-situ reorganisation. Since the iteration domains of the computation statements and the move-in, move-out, and reorganisation statements are Z-polyhedra, we can use a polyhedral code generator like CLooG [Bas04] to generate the transformed code. To obtain efficient code, we have to take care of the conditionals contained in the new access functions $L[\rho(f_j(\mathbf{i}, t), t)]$ ($1 \leq j \leq m$) in a statement. In general, $\rho(\mathbf{x}, t)$ is a case distinction on several conditions $c_1(\mathbf{x}, t), \ldots, c_q(\mathbf{x}, t)$. To avoid evaluating the conditions at every access, we partition the iteration domain $D(t)$ of the statement by the conditions such that in each of the partitions the truth values of the conditionals are constant. All in all, the transformed statement contains the conditionals

$$c_k(f_j(\mathbf{i}, t), t) \quad \text{for } 1 \leq k \leq q, \ 1 \leq j \leq m.$$

This gives rise to up to q^m partitions:

$$D_{(a_1, \ldots, a_m)}(t) := D(t) \cap \{\mathbf{i} \mid \bigwedge_{j=1}^{m} c_{a_j}(f_j(\mathbf{i}), t)\} \quad \text{for all } a_1, \ldots, a_m \in \{1, \ldots, q\}.$$

In each of the partitions, there is, for every $L\left[\rho\big(f_j(\mathbf{x},t)\big)\right]$, exactly one c_k which evaluates to true. So the index expression $\rho\big(f_j(\mathbf{x},t)\big)$ simplifies to a quasi-polynomial r_j (without case distinctions). Since all r_j have a fixed (and finite) period, one can additionally perform a periodic split of each partition of the domains by a common period of its r_j to obtain iteration domains in which each index expression is a polynomial and, hence, has no conditional expressions any more.

Generating Code for In-situ Reorganisation

The drift δ is a quasi-polynomial. The periodicity in the quasi-polynomial can be handled by case distinctions on the residue classes of $\mathbf{x}$ and t (as for the index expressions of L). Then, for each case, $\delta(\mathbf{x},t)$ is polynomial. With polynomial bounds, we are outside the polyhedron model. To generate code, we can use the techniques presented in Section 5.5 for non-linear bounds. Alternatively, we can generate code for the reorganisation phase using our generalised Fourier-Motzkin elimination if $\delta(\mathbf{x},t)$ is linear in $\mathbf{x}$. Because t is a parameter of the code generation for the reorganisation statements (we generate loops for $\mathbf{x}$), Fourier-Motzkin can be applied for each of the two cases $\delta(\mathbf{x},t) > 0$ and $\delta(\mathbf{x},t) < 0$ to obtain the loop nests for enumerating the elements to be reorganised.

5.4.9   Examples

Let us now present some examples demonstrating the effectiveness of our transformation. We have implemented a prototype tool for the localisation based on access instances. We have used this prototype to compute the localisation for the parallel code examples presented here. We have not implemented our method based on dependences because we would require a dependence analysis based on access instances, which we did not have available.

The parallel benchmarks have been performed on an NVIDIA® GeForce® GTX 9800 GPU with a 1944 MHz shader clock and a 1150 MHz memory clock. The programming environment is NVIDIA's CUDA technology [NVI09] (cf. Section 2.2.2). Each multiprocessor has 16 KB of local memory which can be accessed within one clock cycle simultaneously by the threads of a warp provided that some alignment restrictions are obeyed. Access to main memory is much slower, but the thread scheduler in a multiprocessor tries to hide memory latency by overlapping computation and memory access. Therefore, the higher latency of the main memory can be hidden partly if enough threads are available. Our experiments use only one multiprocessor at a time since there is no way to share scratchpad memory between multiprocessors.

Example 5.7 (1d-SOR). As an example of a scientific code, let us look at one-dimensional successive over-relaxation (1d-SOR) which we have already studied w.r.t. tiling in Section 5.3.1. The code of a sequential implementation is again given in Figure 5.16(a). Since we are interested in the effect of localisation (and tiling does not improve the code for a single multiprocessor), we use an

```
for (k=1; k<=m; k++)
  for (i=1; i<=n-1; i++)
    A[i] = (A[i-1]+A[i+1])*0.5;
        (a) original code
```

```
for (k=1; k<=m; k++) {
  l0 = A[0];           // move in
  for (i=1; i<=n-1; i++) {
    l2 = A[i+1];       // move in
    l1 = (l0 + l2) * 0.5;
    A[i-1] = l0;       // move out
    l0 = l1;           // reorganise
  }
  A[n-1]=l0; A[n]=l1; // move out
}
```
(b) access-based localisation

```
for (k=1; k<=m; k++) {
  for (i=1; i<=n-1; i++) {
    (i==1 ? l0:l1) = A[i] =
      ((i==1 ? A[i-1] : l0)
         + A[i+1]) * 0.5;
    if (i >= 2) l0 = l1;
  }
}
```
(c) dependence-based localisation

```
for (k=1; k<=m; k++) {
  l = (A[0]+A[2])*0.5;
  for (i=2; i<=n-1; i++)
    l = A[i] = (1+A[i+1])*0.5;
}
```
(d) dependence-based localisation with loop optimisations

Figure 5.16: 1d-SOR: sequential codes

untiled parallel code which is shown in Figure 5.17(a) as the basis for the transformation. Notice the synchronous parallelism expressed by the parallel loop on p inside the sequential loop on t. Before we apply our techniques to the parallel code, we briefly note that the sequential code can be improved slightly using the localisation transformation. We also use this example to compare the localisation based on access instances and on dependences.

Localisation based on access instances

Considering the loop on i in the sequential code as the time loop, we obtain $C(i) = \{i - 1, i, i + 1\}$, i.e., at time i, the accessed elements are $A[i - 1]$, $A[i]$, and $A[i + 1]$. This yields $\rho(x, i) = x - i + 1$, i.e., $A[i - 1]$ is mapped to $L[0]$, $A[i]$ to $L[1]$, and $A[i + 1]$ to $L[2]$. Since the drift $\delta(x, i) = \rho(x, i + 1) - \rho(x, i)$ is

$m =$	128	256	384	512
original	1095	2168	3111	4139
localised	723	1595	2150	2865
speedup	1.52	1.36	1.45	1.44

Table 5.3: 1d-SOR: benchmarks for sequential code for $n = 10^6$ on an AMD Opteron[TM] 275 processor with 2.2 GHz using GCC 4.2

```
for (t=0; t<=n+2*m-4; t++) {
  parfor (p=max(0,(t-n+3)/2); p<=min(m-1,t/2); p++) {
    int i = t+1-2*p;
    A[i] = (A[i-1] + A[i+1]) * 0.5;
  }
}
```

(a) parallel code

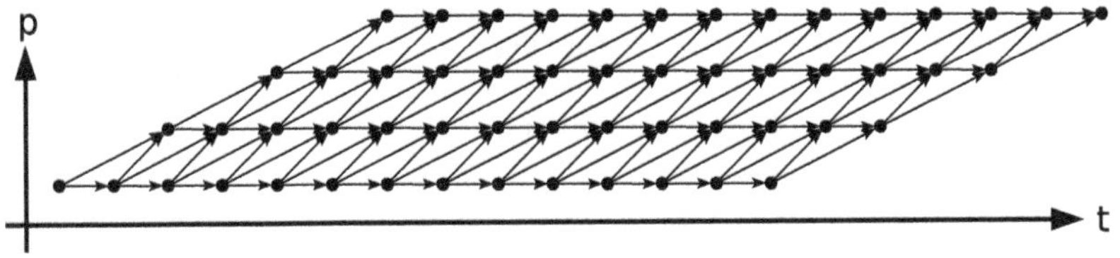

(b) iteration domain for $m = 4$, $n = 16$

Figure 5.17: 1d-SOR: parallel version

constantly -1, we obtain the simple transformed code shown in Figure 5.16(b). Since the indices into L are fixed at 0, 1, 2, the array L can be replaced by three local variables for the array elements.

Localisation based on dependences

Localisation based on dependences takes into account which elements are reused, i.e., are read again after having been read or written. In this example, the write to $A[i]$ is local, since it is reused at the next time step, and global, since it is not overwritten later. $A[i-1]$ is in the local read set for $i \geq 2$. It is in the global read set for $i = 1$ since no input dependence to $A[i-1]$ for $i = 1$ exists. Since there is no relevant input dependence, the global-local read set $\mathcal{R}_{gl}$ is empty.

$m =$	1	64	128	192	256	320	384	448	512
parallel code	381	709	1089	1456	1759	2135	2416	2807	3082
intra-thread	–	545	758	964	1125	1322	1515	1766	2019
inter-thread	–	525	539	587	652	684	784	856	1002
full, moves	–	504	518	559	611	647	735	800	X
full, modulos	–	498	534	621	710	789	905	X	X

Table 5.4: 1d-SOR: benchmark for parallel codes, $n = 10^6$ on GPU, number of threads equal to m, run times in milliseconds. "X" means code could not be executed due to too many divergent threads or not enough registers.

$p =$	64	128	192	256	320	384
not localised	0.29s	0.99s	2.10s	3.54s	5.42s	8.03s
fully localised	0.30s	0.74s	1.42s	2.18s	3.10s	4.21s
speedup	0.99	1.35	1.48	1.62	1.75	1.91

Table 5.5: 2d-Gauss-Seidel: run times for $m = 1000$, $n = 2p + 1$ on GPU

Thus, we find the sets $C(i)$ and $G(i)$ and the function $\rho(x, i)$:

$$C(i) = \begin{cases} \{i\} & \text{if } i = 1 \\ \{i - 1, i\} & \text{if } 2 \leq i \leq n - 2 \\ \{i - 1\} & \text{if } i = n - 1 \\ \varnothing & \text{otherwise} \end{cases}$$

$$G(i) = C(i) \cap C(i + 1) = \begin{cases} \{i\} & \text{if } 1 \leq i \leq n - 1 \\ \varnothing & \text{otherwise} \end{cases}$$

$$\rho(x, i) = \begin{cases} x - i & \text{if } i = 1 \\ x - i + 1 & \text{if } 2 \leq i \leq n - 1 \end{cases}$$

The code obtained (we again exploit the fact that the indices into L turn out to be constants) is shown in Figure 5.16(c). A polyhedral code generator can unroll the first iteration of the loop on i to avoid the conditionals $i = 1$ and $i \geq 2$; additionally, traditional compiler data flow analysis reveals that l_0 and l_1 can be stored in the same memory cell l, thus, saving the reorganisation. The resulting code is shown in Figure 5.16(d). Running the sequential code and the transformed code on an AMD Opteron^{TM} 275 processor yields the run times shown in Table 5.3.

The index set (with dependences) of the parallel code is shown in Figure 5.17(b). Note that the number of parallel threads that can be used equals the parameter m. We use our prototype to apply localisation based on access instances. Localisation based on access instances is not inferior to localisation based on dependences in this example as the working set is contiguous and shifts by one element in each iteration of the loop on t.

In the parallel code, we can localise twice. First, we can perform localisation on each thread of the inner parallel loop w.r.t. the loop on t, i.e., exploit the intra-thread reuse of data (similarly to the localisation of the sequential code). A dependence-based localisation reveals that the value written by $A[i]$ in iteration t is read again by $A[i - 1]$ in the iteration $t + 1$ in the same thread.

The second localisation is again w.r.t. the loop on t for all threads, exploiting also inter-thread data reuse. With all m threads active, $2m + 1$ array elements are accessed in one iteration of the loop on t and there is an overlap of $2m - 1$ elements with the next iteration. Although this second localisation encompasses the first in principle, it is worthwhile to apply the intra-thread localisation first, because it reveals the reuse within the same thread and, in this example, the one value which is reused can be put into a register. The code resulting from both transformations together (with simplifications for readability) is shown in Figure 5.18. Note the variable l which stores the value reused within each thread. Table 5.4 shows the run times of the unlocalised and the localised codes. The fully localised code (both localisations applied) performs best with speedups of up to 3.5; explicit data moves in the reorganisation phase outperform modulo addressing. On a GPU with slower main memory (NVIDIA Quadro® NVS 135M, 800 MHz shader clock, 600 MHz memory clock), we observed speedups of up to 4.7.

Example 5.8 (2d-Gauss-Seidel). Let us now consider a two-dimensional Gauss-Seidel algorithm with rowwise alternating even-odd updates on an $(n+1)^2$ matrix with m iterations and p parallel threads. The sequential code is shown in Figure 5.19 and a localised version is presented in Figure 5.20. The localised code shown has been written by hand for readability.[3] The macros AA and LL are used to show two-dimensional accesses instead of the underlying (but visually more challenging) one-dimensional addressing. The localisation based on dependences is performed with a localisation window encompassing the updates to both even and odd elements of a row. The localised part of the matrix consists of two successive rows progressing row by row with the computation (i.e., with the loop on i in the code shown). The comparison of the run times of the original and localised codes is shown in Table 5.5.

5.5 Code Generation

5.5.1 Introduction to Code Generation

When we speak of code generation, we mean the generation of loops that enumerate index sets and execute statements (loop bodies) for each enumerated point. For example, let us generate code for two statements T_1 and T_2, where T_1 is executed at every point in $D_1 = \{x \mid 2 \leq x \leq 8\}$ and T_2 at every point in $D_2 = \{x \mid 2 \leq x \leq p\}$. Since T_1 is to be executed for $x = 2, \ldots, 8$ and T_2 for $2, \ldots, p$ (for $p \in \mathbb{Z}$), we have to generate loops with the index variable x which enumerate the respective x-values and execute T_1 and T_2 at the respective index points. Unfortunately, enumerating the x-values for the two statements independently, as in the following sequence of loops:

```
for (x=2; x<=8; x++)
  T1;
for (x=2; x<=p; x++)
  T2;
```

is not the solution we desire, because the enumeration of the index points has to respect the ordering on the index variable x. For example, the execution of T_2

---

[3]In addition, computational complexity and correctness issues in the polyhedral library used to implement our prototype make it difficult to generate a correct localisation automatically.

```
#define RHO1(x) (x)
#define RHO2(x) ((x)-t+2*m-2)
#define LOAD1L { int i=t+1-2*self; if (i==1) l=L[0]; }
#define BODY1L { int i=t+1-2*self; L[RHO1(i)] = l = (1+L[RHO1(i+1)])*0.5f; }
#define BODY2L { int i=t+1-2*self; L[RHO2(i)] = l = (1+L[RHO2(i+1)])*0.5f; }

void sor1d_cuda_fully_localised(float *A, int m, int n) {
    int self = threadIdx.x;  // index number of the thread
    int np = m;              // number of threads
    int t, x;                // loop iterators
    float l;                 // value localised to a register

    for (t=0; t<=0; t++) {
        for (x=0+self; x<=2; x+=np) L[RHO1(x)] = A[x];
        __syncthreads();
        LOAD1L;
        if (self <= t/2) BODY1L;
        __syncthreads();
    }
    for (t=1; t<=2*m-3; t++) {
        if (self == 0) L[RHO1(t+2)] = A[t+2];
        __syncthreads();
        LOAD1L;
        if (self <= t/2) BODY1L;
        __syncthreads();
    }
    t=2*m-2;
    LOAD1L;
    for (t=2*m-2; t<=n-2; t++) {
        if (self == 0) L[RHO2(t+2)] = A[t+2];
        __syncthreads();
        BODY2L;
        __syncthreads();
        if (self == 0) A[t-2*m+2] = L[RHO2(t-2*m+2)];
        float reorg0 = L[1+self], reorg1 = L[1+np+self];
        __syncthreads();
        L[0+self] = reorg0; L[0+np+self] = reorg1;
    }
    for (t=n-1; t<=n+2*m-5; t++) {
        if ((t-n+3)/2 <= self) BODY2L;
        __syncthreads();
        if (self == m-1) A[t-2*m+2] = L[RHO2(t-2*m+2)];
        int lb = RHO2(t-2*m+3), ub = RHO2(n);
        for (int r=0; r<=(ub-lb)/np; r++) {
            x = lb + r*np + self;
            if (x <= ub) v = L[x];
            __syncthreads();
            if (x <= ub) L[x-1] = v;
        }
    }
    for (t=n+2*m-4; t<=n+2*m-4; t++) {
        if ((t-n+3)/2 <= self) BODY2L;
        __syncthreads();
        for (x=n-2+self; x<=n; x+=np) A[x] = L[RHO2(x)];
        __syncthreads();
    }
}
```

Figure 5.18: 1d-SOR: fully localised parallel code with reorganisation (localisation based on access instances)

```
#define AA(ii,jj) (A[(ii)*n1+(jj)])

void rb_orig(float *A, int m, int n) {
    int k, i, j;
    int n1 = n + 1;
    for (k=1; k<=m; k++) {
        for (i=1; i<=n-1; i++) {
            for (j=1; j<=n-1; j+=2)
                AA(i,j) = (4.0f*AA(i,j) + AA(i-1,j) + AA(i+1,j)
                                + AA(i,j-1) + AA(i,j+1)) * 0.125f;
            for (j=2; j<=n-1; j+=2)
                AA(i,j) = (4.0f*AA(i,j) + AA(i-1,j) + AA(i+1,j)
                                + AA(i,j-1) + AA(i,j+1)) * 0.125f;
        }
    }
}
```

Figure 5.19: Gauss-Seidel: original code

```
#define AA(ii,jj) (A[(ii)*n1+(jj)])
#define LL(ii,jj) (L[lw*((ii)-i+1)+(jj)-1])

void redblack_cuda_localised(float *A, int m, int n) {
    const int np   = blockDim.x;   // number of threads
    const int self = threadIdx.x;  // index of "this" thread
    int k, i, j;

    const int n1 = n + 1;
    const int lw = 2*(np-1)+2;
    for (k=1; k<=m; k++) {
        i=1;
        LL(0,2*self+1) = A[2*self+1];
        LL(0,2*self+2) = A[2*self+2];
        __syncthreads();
        for (i=1; i<=n-1; i++) {
            j = 2*self + 1;
            LL(i,j)   = AA(i,j);
            LL(i,j+1) = AA(i,j+1);
            __syncthreads();
            AA(i,j) = LL(i,j) = (4.0f*LL(i,j) + LL(i-1,j) + AA(i+1,j)
                            + (j==1 ? AA(i,j-1) : LL(i,j-1)) + LL(i,j+1)) * 0.125f;
            __syncthreads();

            j = 2*self + 2;
            AA(i,j) = LL(i,j) = (4.0f * LL(i,j) + LL(i-1,j) + AA(i+1,j) + LL(i,j-1)
                            + (j==n-1?AA(i,j+1):LL(i,j+1))) * 0.125f;
            __syncthreads();
            L[2*self]   = L[lw+2*self];
            L[2*self+1] = L[lw+2*self+1];
            __syncthreads();
        }
    }
}
```

Figure 5.20: Gauss-Seidel: localised parallel code (localisation based on access instances)

```
for (x=2; x<=max(8,p); x++) {
  if (2 <= x && x <= 8)
    T1;
  if (2 <= x && x <= p)
    T2;
}
```

(a) simple code with conditionals

```
for (x=2; x<=min(8,p); x++)
  { T1; T2; }
for (x=max(p+1,2); x<=8; x++)
  T1;
for (x=9; x<=p; x++)
  T2;
```

(b) tricky loop bounds

```
if (p >= 9) {
  for (x=2; x<=8; x++)
    { T1; T2; }
  for (x=9; x<=p; x++)
    T2;
} else if (p == 8) {
  for (x=2; x<=8; x++)
    { T1; T2; }
} else if (p >= 2) {
  for (x=2; x<=p; x++)
    { T1; T2; }
  for (x=p+1; x<=8; x++)
    T1;
} else {
  for (x=2; x<=8; x++)
    T1;
}
```

(c) case distinctions on p

Figure 5.21: Three possible codes for the two domains $D_1 = \{x \mid 2 \leq x \leq 8\}$ and $D_2 = \{x \mid 2 \leq x \leq p\}$

for $x = 2$ may happen before or after T_1 for $x = 2$, but it must happen before any execution of T_1 or T_2 for $x \geq 3$. The generation of correct code is complicated by the fact that we do not know the value of the upper bound p at code generation time, so the emitted code must work for all possible (integral) values of p. Figure 5.21 shows three possible codes which enumerate the index sets correctly. The figure illustrates that there is a tradeoff between code size and efficiency of the generated code. The code in Figure 5.21(a) specifies the evaluation of two conditionals (in the if statements) in every iteration of the loop. The codes in Figures 5.21(b) and 5.21(c) have no overhead for evaluating conditions inside the loops. With the case distinctions on p, the code in Figure 5.21(c) never executes an empty loop, i.e., when a loop is reached, the upper bound is guaranteed to be greater than or equal to the lower bound. This property comes at the price of an increased code length. The code in Figure 5.21(b) is shorter and there are no case distinctions in p apart from the loop bounds, but loops may be empty, for example, the last loop is empty for $p \leq 8$. The algorithm we present subsequently produces code without conditionals inside the loops.

In general, the ordering of the operations follows the lexicographic order of the index set points. For example, in the case of a two-dimensional index set with (x, y) coordinates, the outer loop of the generated code enumerates the x-dimension, and an inner loop enumerates the y-dimension in dependence of x, i.e., for given x, all values y such that (x, y) is in the index set are enumerated. The main task of code generation is to partition the index sets of the statements such that each partition can be scanned by a loop nest. In the above example, a suitable disjoint union of the domains $D_1 \cup D_2 = U_1 \; \dot\cup \; U_2 \; \dot\cup \; U_3$ is given by the following three sets:

$$U_1 = \{x \mid 2 \leq x \leq \min(8, p)\}$$
$$U_2 = \{x \mid \max(p{+}1, 2) \leq x \leq 8\}$$
$$U_3 = \{x \mid 9 \leq x \leq p\}$$

Note that a statement executes either at every point or not at all in U_i. T_1 executes in $U_1 \; \dot\cup \; U_2$ and T_2 executes in $U_1 \; \dot\cup \; U_3$. In addition, the sets U_i are convex, which implies that each set can be enumerated by a single **for** loop. This scheme generalises to the case of n-dimensional polytopes as index sets, i.e., the index sets of the statements can always be represented as a disjoint union of polytopes such that each partition is either a subset of a given index set or disjoint from it and each partition can be enumerated by a single nest of **for** loops. The reason is that intersection and difference of polytopes can, again, be represented by (a finite union of) polytopes, and polytopes are convex sets. In the generalisation we are pursuing, this is not true. In general, index sets with arbitrary multivariate polynomial bounds cannot be represented as a finite union of convex sets.

5.5.2   Non-linearity and Non-convexity

Let $D = \{(x, y) \mid 1 \leq x \leq 7, 1 \leq y \leq 9, (y - 4)^2 + 12 - 3x \geq 0\}$ be a non-convex index set. D is depicted in Figure 5.22(a). It is non-convex due to the parabolic piece of the border. Code generators for the polyhedron model treat non-convexities arising from differences of polytopes by representing the domain as a finite union of convex domains, but this is not possible here. D cannot be represented as a finite union of convex sets. Instead, the code generation has to handle non-convexity directly in the general code generation procedure. All loop bounds that are needed to enumerate the domain correctly are roots of (multivariate) polynomials. For example, the roots of $(y - 4)^2 + 12 - 3x$, namely $4 \pm \sqrt{3x - 12}$, are bounds of respective inner loops in the code shown in Figure 5.22(b). Our main result (cf. Theorem 5.14) states that the needed polynomials and their roots can be computed, if the index sets are described by polynomial inequalities.

We are aware of three frequent sources of non-linearities:

1. The source program contains non-linear loop bounds. This is the case, e.g., in the Sieve of Eratosthenes (cf. Section 5.5.9). The outermost loop has a non-linear bound and can be written as a **for** loop, in C-like languages as **for (i=2; i*i<=n; i++)**.

2. The source program has non-constant strides. Before transformations are applied to the program model, the loop strides are normalised to unit strides, such that every integral point in the index set represents an execution of the loop body. For example, the loop **for (j=0; j<=n; j+=i)** is normalised to **for (k=0; k*i<=n; k++)**, replacing j by k*i in the loop

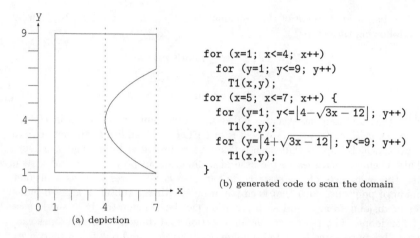

```
for (x=1; x<=4; x++)
  for (y=1; y<=9; y++)
    T1(x,y);
for (x=5; x<=7; x++) {
  for (y=1; y<=⌊4−√3x − 12⌋; y++)
    T1(x,y);
  for (y=⌈4+√3x − 12⌉; y<=9; y++)
    T1(x,y);
}
```

(b) generated code to scan the domain

(a) depiction

Figure 5.22: Index set $D = \{(x,y) \mid 1 \leq x \leq 7, 1 \leq y \leq 9, (y-4)^2 + 12 - 3x \geq 0\}$ which is non-convex due to the parabolic piece of the border

body. Normalisation is a necessary step in automatic loop program transformation, since code generators usually generate code which scans every integral point in the index sets (cf. the definition of the code generation problem, Definition 5.11).

3. A non-linear transformation can be applied to the program. For example, it has been shown that non-linear schedules can improve the performance of solving affine recurrence equalities substantially over linear schedules. An example is presented in Section 5.5.9.

All these cases could not be handled by a general procedure so far, since no code could be generated in the presence of non-linearities. We illustrate here the feasibility of code generation for non-linear, non-convex domains, although the efficiency of the code generation procedure has to be improved to be applicable to bigger examples (cf. Section 5.5.9).

An objection to non-linear code generation, which is sometimes raised, is that the set of integral points described by semi-algebraic sets can be described by a union of polyhedra. Figure 5.23 shows the iteration domain for $x, y \in \mathbb{Z}$, $0 \leq x \leq p \wedge 0 \leq y \leq \sqrt{x}$ (the bound $y = \sqrt{x}$ is marked with (a)) and the integer hull defined by an inscribed polytope (upper bound on y marked with (b)) and an even tighter inscribed union of rectangles (marked with (c)). But one can only inscribe the integer hull polytope(s) for a given value of the parameter p. With growing p, the number of facets/polytopes increases without limit. There is no way to describe the integer hull with finitely many parametric polyhedra.

Lemma 5.9. *The set* $D(p) := \{(x,y) \in \mathbb{Z}^2 \mid 0 \leq x \leq p \wedge 0 \leq y \leq \sqrt{x}\}$ *cannot be described by a finite union of parametric polyhedra, i.e., there exists no* $m \in \mathbb{N}_+$ *and polyhedra* $P_1(p), \ldots, P_m(p)$ *such that* $D(p) = \mathbb{Z}^2 \cap \bigcup_{i=1}^{m} P_i(p)$.

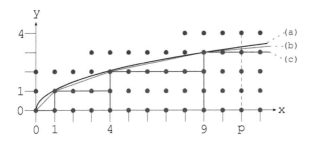

Figure 5.23: Integer points in $\{(x,y) \mid 0 \leq x \wedge 0 \leq y \leq \sqrt{x}\}$

Proof. Assume that $m \in \mathbb{N}_+$ and polyhedra $P_1(p), \ldots, P_m(p)$ exist such that $D(p) = \mathbb{Z}^2 \cap \bigcup_{i=1}^{m} P_i(p)$. Then, by Ehrhart theory (cf. Section 2.1.7) since $D(p)$ is a finite union of $\mathbb{Z}$-polyhedra, $\text{card}(D(p))$ must be a piecewise quasi-polynomial. Since there can only be finitely many case distinctions in the piecewise quasi-polynomials, there exists a quasi-polynomial $c \in \mathcal{P}[X]$ such that $\text{card}(D(p)) = c(p)$ for infinitely many $p \in \mathbb{N}$ where $p = q^2$ is square (and $q \in \mathbb{N}$). Let us now compute $\text{card}(D(q^2))$ by summing up the number of integral points in the inscribed rectangles (marked with (c) in Figure 5.23). Observe that the ith rectangle ($i \in \mathbb{N}_+$) starts at $x = (i-1)^2$ and is i integer points high. The width of the ith rectangle (without the right-hand border which is counted through the $(i+1)^{\text{th}}$ rectangle) is $i^2 - (i-1)^2 = 2i - 1$. At $x = p = q^2$, there are additional $q + 1$ integer points.

$$
\begin{aligned}
\text{card}(D(q^2)) &= q + 1 + \sum_{i=1}^{q} i(2i - 1) \\
&= q + 1 + \frac{1}{6}(4q^3 + 3q^2 - q) \\
&= \frac{2}{3}q^3 + \frac{1}{2}q^2 + \frac{5}{6}q + 1 \\
&= \frac{2}{3}p^{\frac{3}{2}} + \frac{1}{2}p + \frac{5}{6}\sqrt{p} + 1
\end{aligned}
$$

Every constituent $\text{con}_l(c, i)$ for $0 \leq i \leq l - 1$ (with $l := \text{lp}(c)$) is a polynomial from $\mathbb{Z}[X]$. At least one of these finitely many polynomials would have to coincide with the just computed expression for $\text{card}(D(p))$ for infinitely many p, but this is impossible as the computed expression is not a polynomial in p (it has fractional exponents). Hence, the assumption that $D(p)$ can be written as a finite union of parametric polyhedra is false. □

5.5.3 Definition of the Code Generation Problem

Definition 5.10. A *statement* $T(\mathbf{x})$ is a piece of code (in a given programming language) which depends on a number of variables $\mathbf{x} = (x_1, \ldots, x_n)$ ($n \in \mathbb{N}$).

We need not specify statements $T(x)$ more concretely, because we are only concerned with the generation of code for scanning the index sets of the statements, i.e., loops, and the statements themselves have no influence on the structure of the generated loops. The loops are determined by the index sets of the statements. We consider only bounded index sets, because unbounded index sets cannot be enumerated by proper **for** loops with a finite lower and upper bound. Our code generation algorithm works, in principle, also for unbounded index sets; only outputting code with proper **for** loops is, obviously, impossible then.

We can now define the code generation problem.

Definition 5.11. Let $k, n, m \in \mathbb{N}$, $C \subseteq \mathbb{Z}^k$. Given statements $T_1(\mathbf{x}), \ldots, T_m(\mathbf{x})$ and domains $D_1(\mathbf{p}), \ldots, D_m(\mathbf{p}) \subseteq \mathbb{Z}^n$, the problem of *code generation* is to generate a program P which, for any given $\mathbf{p} \in C$, executes all (and no more) operations $T_i(\mathbf{x})$ with $\mathbf{x} \in D_i(\mathbf{p})$ for $1 \leq i \leq m$, such that $T_i(\mathbf{x})$ is executed before $T_j(\mathbf{y})$ if $\mathbf{x} \prec \mathbf{y}$ for $1 \leq j \leq m$, $\mathbf{y} \in D_j(\mathbf{p})$.

Note that our definition of the code generation problem requires the dimensionality of the domains to agree and does not mention so-called scattering functions (where the index sets to enumerate are given as affine images of polytopes) as are supported by CLooG [Bas04], for example. But this is no principal restriction, because scattering functions (even non-invertible ones) and variations in dimensionality can be encoded in the general definition – possibly losing efficiency both in the generation of the code and in the execution of the generated code. Improving the algorithm for such special cases is on our future agenda.

5.5.4   Code Generation by Cylindrical Algebraic Decomposition

Having seen an introductory examples in Section 5.5.1, let us now state precisely for which index sets we can generate code and that the generated code is efficient in the sense that it does not enumerate an integer superset of the given domains. We start by giving the definitions we need for our main theorem and the algorithm.

5.5.5   Code Generation as Cylindrical Decomposition

A program solving the code generation problem has to enumerate the points of the index sets of the statements in lexicographic order. This implies that the outermost dimension is enumerated by one or a sequence of several loops and, inside every loop, the next dimension is enumerated in dependence of the outer dimensions, etc. The concept of a loop nest that scans a union of index sets lexicographically is captured by the following definition.

Definition 5.12. A loop nest is called *cylindrical* for $(x_1, \ldots, x_n)$ in context C, if $n = 0$ and it is the empty loop nest (i.e., it consists only of a loop body), or $n \geq 1$ and it is a sequence of $r \in \mathbb{N}$ loops in x_1

```
for (x₁ = l₁(p); x₁ ≤ u₁(p); x₁++)
    P₁;
...
for (x₁ = lᵣ(p); x₁ ≤ uᵣ(p); x₁++)
    Pᵣ;
```

such that all l_i and u_i are continuous functions in $\mathbf{p}$, $l_i(\mathbf{p}) \leq u_i(\mathbf{p})$ for every $\mathbf{p} \in C$, $1 \leq i \leq r$ and $u_i(\mathbf{p}) < l_{i+1}(\mathbf{p})$ for every $\mathbf{p} \in C$, $1 \leq i \leq r-1$ and, for every $1 \leq i \leq r$, P_i is cylindrical for $(x_2, \ldots, x_n)$ in context $C \times [l_i(\mathbf{p}), u_i(\mathbf{p})]$ (note that x_1 becomes a parameter in the subprograms $P_1, \ldots, P_r$).

We call this kind of loop nest *cylindrical*, because the bounds of the loops define a cylindrical decomposition of $\mathbb{R}^n$. The lower bounds $l_1, \ldots, l_r$ and upper bounds $u_1, \ldots, u_r$ of the loops in Definition 5.12 define a stack in $\mathbb{R}$ (given by the sections $(l_1, u_1, \ldots, l_r, u_r)$) and, since the requirements for the inner dimensions are the same, the loops define a cylindrical decomposition of $\mathbb{R}^n$. Note that the loops do not scan every cell of the decomposition; for example, the cell between the upper bound of a loop and the lower bound of its successor is not scanned. The code generation problem can now be reduced to computing a cylindrical decomposition of $\mathbb{R}^n$ such that every cell in the decomposition is, for every index set, either a subset of this index set or disjoint from it. The code generated by code generators for the polyhedron model like CLooG is, in fact, cylindrical. The solution to generating code for the more general case with non-linear index set bounds relies on an algorithm for computing a cylindrical decomposition of $\mathbb{R}^n$. The algorithm cannot, in general, compute a cylindrical decomposition with a minimal set of cells, because it computes a cylindrical *algebraic* decomposition which has the additional restriction that the functions f_i (which define the sections of a stack) are polynomials or root expressions. Polyhedral code generators generate loop bounds which are maxima or minima of linear expressions for the lower or upper bound of a polytope, respectively. Since the minimum or maximum of two expressions is, in general, not a polynomial or a root expression, the code generated by our algorithm for polyhedral input is longer than the code generated by polyhedral techniques (for an example, cf. Section 5.5.9).

5.5.6 The Efficiency of a Solution

The definition of code generation (Definition 5.11) does not take efficiency into account. For example, all examples shown in Figure 5.21 are solutions to the code generation problem stated there, but obviously the code in Figure 5.21(a) is less efficient because it evaluates two conditionals in the `if` statements in every iteration of the loop. A different source of inefficiency are inner loops which have empty iteration sets for some iterations of the outer loops, i.e., the outer loops enumerate points (in the outer coordinates) which do not belong to integer solutions of the index sets. Very inefficient code can be generated for a large class of code generation problems. To obtain some solution, it is sufficient to enumerate some arbitrarily large but finite superset of the union of all index sets $\bigcup D_i(\mathbf{p})$ and to test for every enumerated point $\mathbf{x}$ whether $\mathbf{x} \in D_i(\mathbf{p})$ and execute $T_i(\mathbf{x})$ if this is the case (like in Figure 5.21(a)).

To capture the notion of an efficient program, which does not enumerate integral values from a superset of the domains, we introduce the concept of a proper scan in $\mathbb{R}$ and $\mathbb{Z}$ for cylindrical loop nests. The idea is to call a loop nest a proper $\mathbb{Z}$-scan, if, for some values enumerated by r outer loops of a loop nest, we can be sure that there is an integral point in the domain that matches the enumerated values and, hence, the body of the loop nest will be executed for the choice of the outer r dimensions. A less strict property, called a proper $\mathbb{R}$-scan, is that there exists any value (maybe with real values for the inner dimensions) that matches the outer dimensions.

Definition 5.13. Let P be a cylindrical loop nest solving the code generation problem for some domains and statements without if statements inside its loops. P is said to perform a *proper* $\mathbb{R}$-*scan* or a *proper* $\mathbb{Z}$-*scan*, respectively, of the domains if, for every loop nest

for $(x_1 = l_1(\mathbf{p})$; $x_1 \leq u_1(\mathbf{p})$; x_1++)

$\cdot \cdot \cdot$

   for $(x_n = l_n(\mathbf{p}, x_1, \ldots, x_{n-1})$; $x_n \leq u_n(\mathbf{p}, x_1, \ldots, x_{n-1})$; x_n++)
   $T_j(x_1, \ldots, x_n)$;

surrounding an occurrence of T_j in P, for every $0 \leq r \leq n-1$, and $X = \mathbb{R}$ or $X = \mathbb{Z}$, respectively, the following condition holds:

$$\mathbf{p} \in C \wedge \bigwedge_{i=1}^{r} \left(x_i \in \mathbb{Z} \wedge l_i(\mathbf{p}, x_1, \ldots, x_{i-1}) \leq x_i \leq u_i(\mathbf{p}, x_1, \ldots, x_{i-1}) \right)$$

$$\implies \left(\exists x_{r+1}, \ldots, x_n : x_{r+1}, \ldots, x_n \in X : (x_1, \ldots, x_n) \in D_j(\mathbf{p}) \right)$$

Note that, since the program is cylindrical, it is impossible for two distinct parts of the program to enumerate the same values $(x_1, \ldots, x_r)$ for the outer dimensions (this would violate the cylindricality of the program).

It is desirable to have programs which perform proper $\mathbb{Z}$-scans, because this guarantees that every iteration an outer loop performs will lead to at least one execution of the body. In contrast, the proper $\mathbb{R}$-scan property only guarantees that the program does not enumerate integer points from a superset of the domains of the statements, but outer loops may perform superfluous iterations which have empty inner loops. For example, the program

```
for (x=0; x<=p; x++)
    for (y=ceil(x/(2*p)); y<=1-floor(x/(2*p)); y++)
        T(x,y);
```

performs a proper $\mathbb{R}$-scan of the domain

$$D(p) = \{(x,y) \mid 0 \leq x \leq p, 2x \leq 2py + x \leq 2p\}$$

for $p \geq 0$, because for every x-value with $0 \leq x \leq p$ there exists $y \in \mathbb{R}$ such that $2x \leq 2py + x \leq 2p$, for example, $y = 0.5$. Only the iteration $x = 0$ has a non-empty loop on y with $y \in \{0,1\}$ but, for $x \geq 1$, the real y-values of D lie only in the open interval between 0 and 1. Cases like these do occur in practise when two index variables are linked by an equality or a system of equalities which has integer "holes" in its solution set, as in the Sieve of Eratosthenes and related example (cf. Section 5.5.9). On the other hand, the problem is rarely caused by inequalities, i.e., inequalities with real solutions but without integral solutions are infrequent in practise.

5.5.7   Code Generation for Semi-algebraic Sets

Theorem 5.14. *Let C and D_i be as in Definition 5.11, where the D_i are bounded index sets. The code generation problem can be solved with a cylindrical loop nest which performs a proper $\mathbb{R}$-scan of the domains if the extended index sets $\widehat{D}_i = \{(\mathbf{p}, \mathbf{x}) \mid \mathbf{p} \in C, \mathbf{x} \in D_i(\mathbf{p})\}$ are semi-algebraic. A solution can be computed algorithmically from the defining formulas with polynomial (in)equalities for $D_1(\mathbf{p}), \dots, D_m(\mathbf{p})$ and C from a sign-invariant cylindrical algebraic decomposition of $\mathbb{R}^n$ for the formulas defining the $\widehat{D}_i$ and Algorithm 5.1. The generated code performs a proper $\mathbb{R}$-scan of the domains.*

Proof. Let Ψ be the set of all polynomials in the formulas defining the $\widehat{D}_i$. A sign-invariant cylindrical algebraic decomposition of $\mathbb{R}^{k+n}$ for Ψ can be computed by well-known algorithms, cf. Section 2.1.8. This yields decompositions P_j of $\mathbb{R}^j$ for $1 \leq j \leq k+n$ with two important properties:

(1) For every $1 \leq i \leq m$ and $S \in P_{k+n}$, either $S \subseteq \widehat{D}_i$ or $S \cap \widehat{D}_i = \varnothing$. This is due to the sign invariance of the decomposition. All $\psi \in \Psi$ have constant sign on S and, therefore, the truth value of the formula defining $\widehat{D}_i$ is constant on S.

(2) Due to the cylindrical nature of the decomposition, there exists a total order $\lhd$ on the cells of P_j such that for $\mathbf{w} \in \mathbb{R}^{j-1}$ and cells $S_1, S_2 \in P_j$, $S_1 \neq S_2$, and

$$A_1 := \{x_j \in \mathbb{R} \mid (\mathbf{w}, x_j) \in S_1\},$$
$$A_2 := \{x_j \in \mathbb{R} \mid (\mathbf{w}, x_j) \in S_2\},$$

(that is, A_1 and A_2 are the x_j-coordinates of points "above" $\mathbf{w}$ in S_1 and S_2, respectively) the implication $S_1 \lhd S_2 \Rightarrow (\forall a_1, a_2 : a_1 \in A_1, a_2 \in A_2 : a_1 < a_2)$ holds.

Code is generated as specified by Algorithm 5.1. It is a recursive procedure which, in each step of the recursion, generates the loops for the next dimension. The main code generation function is `code_gen`(S, t, d), where d is the number of the current dimension, S a sector or section from the decomposition of $\mathbb{R}^{d-1}$ and $t \in S$, a so-called test point which is used (in the base case of the recursion) to test whether a domain $\widehat{D}_i$ is a subset of the current cell (for which loops are generated). These properties of S, d and t are an invariant of the recursion.

Code generation starts with $S = \{()\}$, $t = ()$, $d = 1$. Note that S is the only sector of a decomposition of $\mathbb{R}^0$ ($d - 1 = 0$), and $t \in S$ holds. In each step of the recursion, code is generated for the f_i-sections and (f_i, f_{i+1})-sectors over S in the functions `section_code` and `sector_code`, respectively. Note that the code is composed such that the lexicographic ordering is respected due to property (2) of the decompositions. The code generated is different depending on whether the current dimension d is a parameter dimension ($1 \leq d \leq k$) or an index set variable ($k + 1 \leq d \leq k + n$). For a parameter dimension, a conditional statement is generated that checks that the actual value of the parameter satisfies the constraint imposed by the current section or sector. For an index set dimension, the code generated is a loop that enumerates the integral points between the two sections of a sector (if code for a sector is generated), or a loop with exactly one iteration if and only if the section has an integral value (for the given values of the outer dimensions). Note that, in the course of the recursion, a test point $t \in S$ is constructed. The function `rational_between`(a,b) is used to compute a rational point between a and b (note that $a, b \in \mathbb{A}$ in general).

The base case of the recursion is $d = n + k + 1$, in which no more loops are generated and the loop body is written. If $t \in \widehat{D}_i$ for a domain $\widehat{D}_i$, then $S \subseteq \widehat{D}_i$; otherwise $S \cap \widehat{D}_i = \varnothing$ (due to property (1) of the decomposition). That is, the body of the loop nest generated has to contain exactly the statements T_i for which $t \in \widehat{D}_i$ holds.   □

Note that our algorithm generates code which has exactly one lower and one upper bound in each loop generated.

Let us illustrate the relation between the index set, a cylindrical algebraic decomposition and the code generated for the example shown in Figure 5.24. The roots (i.e., sections) for x defining P_1 are $1, 4, 7$, i.e., we have to handle the cases $x = 1$, $1 < x < 4$, $x = 4$, $4 < x < 7$, and $x = 7$. For $1 \leq x < 4$, the decompositions of $\{1\} \times \mathbb{R}$ and $]1,4[\times \mathbb{R}$ are given by the roots 1 and 9 for y. For $x = 4$, the roots for y are given by 1, 4, and 9. For $4 < x < 7$, the roots for y are 1, $4 - \sqrt{3x - 12}$, $4 + \sqrt{3x + 12}$, and 9 and, for $x = 7$, we have the roots 1, $4 + \sqrt{3x + 12}$, and 9. The sections and test points (i.e., points which lie on each of the sections and in each of the sectors and are used to test whether the respective cell is part of a domain) for the domain are shown in Figure 5.24(b). The roots correspond directly to the loop bounds of the code in Figure 5.24(c).

5.5.8   Improving the Code

The example in Figure 5.24 shows that the code generated by the algorithm is quite lengthy. The key insight to reducing the code size is that the loops for neighbouring cells (sections and sectors) in a stack often contain the same inner loops and loop bodies. For example, the loops on x for $1 \leq x \leq 1$ and $1 < x < 4$ contain syntactically identical code. These two loops on x could be combined straight away into one loop for $1 \leq x < 4$. Combing this loop with the loop for $4 \leq x \leq 4$ is not possible at first, since at $x = 4$, there is an additional case

```
// Generate loops from a cylindrical decomposition
//    n:  dimensionality of the index sets
//    k:  number of parameters
//    T₁,...,Tₘ:  statements
//    D̂₁,...,D̂ₘ:  extended index sets of the statements
// Parameters of code_gen:
//    S: generate loops for the cylinder over this section or sector
//    t: a test point from S
//    d: level of the loops to be generated
code_gen(S,t,d):
  code = "";
  if d = n + k + 1 then
     for i:=1 to m
        if t ∈ D̂ᵢ then code += "Tᵢ(x₁,...,xₙ);";
     end for
  else
     let f₁,...,fᵣ be the sections defining the stack over S
     f₀ = -∞;
     for i:=1 to r - 1
        code += sector_code(S,fᵢ₋₁,fᵢ,t,d);
        code += section_code(S,fᵢ,t,d);
     end for
     code += sector_code(S,fᵣ,+∞,t,d);
  end if
  return code;
section_code(S,f,t,d):
  inner = code_gen(section(S,f),(t,f(t)),d+1);
  if inner ≠ "" then
     if d ≤ k then
        head = "if (pᵈ = f)";
     else
        head = "for (x_{d-k}=ceil(f); x_{d-k} ≤floor(f); x_{d-k}++)";
     end if
     return (head + "{" + inner + "}");
  end if
  return "";
sector_code(S,f,g,t,d):
  t' = (t,rational_between(f(t),g(t)));
  inner = code_gen(sector(S,f,g),t',d+1);
  if inner ≠ "" then
     if d ≤ k then
        head = "if (pᵈ > f and pᵈ < g)";
     else
        if f ≠ -∞ then f = ⌊f⌋ + 1;
        if g ≠ +∞ then g = ⌈g⌉ - 1;
        head = "for (x_{d-k}=f; x_{d-k} ≤ g; x_{d-k}++)";
     end if
     return (head + "{" + inner + "}");
  end if
  return "";
```

Algorithm 5.1: Code generation by cylindrical algebraic decomposition

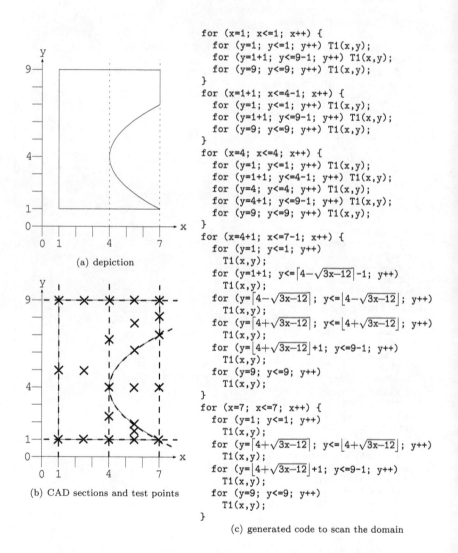

(a) depiction

(b) CAD sections and test points

```
for (x=1; x<=1; x++) {
    for (y=1; y<=1; y++) T1(x,y);
    for (y=1+1; y<=9-1; y++) T1(x,y);
    for (y=9; y<=9; y++) T1(x,y);
}
for (x=1+1; x<=4-1; x++) {
    for (y=1; y<=1; y++) T1(x,y);
    for (y=1+1; y<=9-1; y++) T1(x,y);
    for (y=9; y<=9; y++) T1(x,y);
}
for (x=4; x<=4; x++) {
    for (y=1; y<=1; y++) T1(x,y);
    for (y=1+1; y<=4-1; y++) T1(x,y);
    for (y=4; y<=4; y++) T1(x,y);
    for (y=4+1; y<=9-1; y++) T1(x,y);
    for (y=9; y<=9; y++) T1(x,y);
}
for (x=4+1; x<=7-1; x++) {
    for (y=1; y<=1; y++)
        T1(x,y);
    for (y=1+1; y<=⌈4-√3x-12⌉-1; y++)
        T1(x,y);
    for (y=⌈4-√3x-12⌉; y<=⌊4-√3x-12⌋; y++)
        T1(x,y);
    for (y=⌈4+√3x-12⌉; y<=⌊4+√3x-12⌋; y++)
        T1(x,y);
    for (y=⌊4+√3x-12⌋+1; y<=9-1; y++)
        T1(x,y);
    for (y=9; y<=9; y++)
        T1(x,y);
}
for (x=7; x<=7; x++) {
    for (y=1; y<=1; y++)
        T1(x,y);
    for (y=⌈4+√3x-12⌉; y<=⌊4+√3x-12⌋; y++)
        T1(x,y);
    for (y=⌊4+√3x-12⌋+1; y<=9-1; y++)
        T1(x,y);
    for (y=9; y<=9; y++)
        T1(x,y);
}
```

(c) generated code to scan the domain

Figure 5.24: Code for domain $\{(x,y) \mid 1 \leq x \leq 7, 1 \leq y \leq 9, (y-4)^2 + 12 - 3x \geq 0\}$ according to Algorithm 5.1

distinction for $y = 4$ (the apex of the parabolic piece of the border). But, of course, if we combine the loops on y inside the loops on x first, the first three loops an x only contain a loop on y for $1 \leq y \leq 9$ in their respective bodies, and $1 \leq x \leq 4$ can be scanned by a single loop on x (with a single loop on y inside).

The situation is more complex with the two loops on x for $4 < x \leq 7$. Combining the loops on y inside the loops on x yields the following two loop nests:

```
for (x=4+1; x<=7-1; x++) {        for (x=7; x<=7; x++) {
  for (y=1; y<=⌊4−√3x−12⌋; y++)     for (y=1; y<=1; y++)
    T1(x,y);                          T1(x,y);
  for (y=⌈4+√3x−12⌉; y<=9; y++)     for (y=⌈4+√3x−12⌉; y<=9; y++)
    T1(x,y);                          T1(x,y);
}                                  }
```

The obvious problem which prevents us from combining these two loops is that the upper bounds of the respective first loops on y are different, namely $\lfloor 4-\sqrt{3x-12} \rfloor$ and 1. But the values of the bounds are the same for $x = 7$, namely 1. This happens since both expressions are roots of polynomials which define the respective section and an implementation of a CAD algorithm naturally selects the root with the lower degree if two roots coincide in a stack (here: the stack over $x = 7$). This problem occurs whenever roots of different polynomials cross. We have to note that "crossing polynomials" excludes polynomials which vanish on an entire cylinder (i.e., which are called *identically zero* in a term used in the CAD literature). For example, the polynomial $x - 1$, whose root $x = 1$ crosses the roots $y = 1$ and $y = 7$ (and which vanishes on $\{1\} \times \mathbb{R}$), does not inhibit the combining of the loops for $x = 1$ and $1 < x < 4$. To be able to combine loops in the general case that several polynomials have coinciding roots in a stack, the CAD procedure must retain all the roots which can be used as bounds (i.e., which define the sections), and the code generation procedure selects those which achieve a maximum of combining possibilities. So the intermediate code (after combining the loops on y) is

```
for (x=4+1; x<=7-1; x++) {
  for (y=1; y<=⌊4−√3x−12⌋; y++)
    T1(x,y);
  for (y=⌈4+√3x−12⌉; y<=9; y++)
    T1(x,y);
}
for (x=7; x<=7; x++) {
  for (y=OneOf{1,⌈4−√3x−12⌉}; y<=OneOf{1,⌊4−√3x−12⌋}; y++)
    T1(x,y);
  for (y=⌈4+√3x−12⌉; y<=9; y++)
    T1(x,y);
}
```

where OneOf means that the code output procedure is free to choose either of the given roots. Combining loops as much as possible yields the desired simple code which has already been shown in Figure 5.22(b).

5.5.9   Examples

In this section we give several examples of the code generated by our procedure outlined in Section 5.5.7. We start by comparing the code generated to that generated by polyhedral code generators for polyhedral input before we show some non-polyhedral cases.

Comparison with Polyhedral Code Generation

A Triangular Index Set   As a first example, consider the triangular domain $D = \{(x, y) \mid y \geq 1, y \leq x, y \leq -x+p\}$ depicted in Figure 5.25. Polyhedral code generators like CLooG have no difficulty combining parts of index sets bounded by different upper (or lower) bounds, like the bounds $y \leq x$ and $y \leq -x + p$ in the example. CLooG implicitly computed a cylindrical decomposition of $\mathbb{R}^2$ with the two sections $x_1 = 1$ and $x_2 = p$ to decompose $\mathbb{R}$ and the two sections

$$y_1(x) = 1$$

$$\text{and} \qquad y_2(x) = \begin{cases} x & \text{if } 1 \leq x \leq \frac{p}{2} \\ -x+p & \text{if } \frac{p}{2} < x \leq p \end{cases}$$

to decompose $[1, p] \times \mathbb{R}$. Note that this decomposition is *not* algebraic (cf. Definition 2.45), because y_2 is not a root of a polynomial (due to its non-smoothness at $x = \frac{p}{2}$). Therefore, a cylindrical algebraic decomposition must have an additional section at $x_3 = \frac{p}{2}$ and the scanning of the x-dimension in the code generated by our method is divided into two loops for both halves of the triangle. This is a slight optimisation in terms of loop bound evaluation costs, because the polyhedral code has to evaluates two upper bounds for y and take their minimum for every value of x. But, since loop bounds are usually only evaluated rarely compared to the number of executions of the loop body, the polyhedral code is to be considered superior, because it does not duplicate the loop body.

Quilleré's Example   As a second example, we consider the problem given (and solved) by Quilleré et al. [QRW00] with

$$D_1(m, n) = \{(x, y) \mid 1 \leq x \leq n, 1 \leq y \leq m\}$$
$$D_2(m, n) = \{(x, y) \mid x = y, 3 \leq x \leq n\}$$

shown in Figure 5.26. The codes were generated assuming that $m, n \geq 4$. Again, the polyhedral code is shorter. The reason here is that our algorithm only generates loops which are non-empty in the reals (a proper $\mathbb{R}$-scan does not guarantee non-emptiness in the integers, though), but CLooG's code can contain empty loops for certain parameter constellations. For example, the last loop on x in CLooG's code is empty for $m \geq n$.

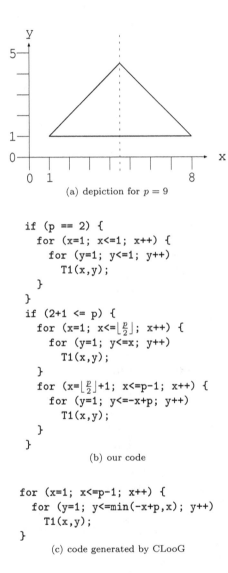

(a) depiction for $p = 9$

```
if (p == 2) {
  for (x=1; x<=1; x++) {
    for (y=1; y<=1; y++)
      T1(x,y);
  }
}
if (2+1 <= p) {
  for (x=1; x<=⌊p/2⌋; x++) {
    for (y=1; y<=x; y++)
      T1(x,y);
  }
  for (x=⌊p/2⌋+1; x<=p-1; x++) {
    for (y=1; y<=-x+p; y++)
      T1(x,y);
  }
}
```

(b) our code

```
for (x=1; x<=p-1; x++) {
  for (y=1; y<=min(-x+p,x); y++)
    T1(x,y);
}
```

(c) code generated by CLooG

Figure 5.25: Example: domain $D = \{(x,y) \mid y \geq 1, y \leq x, y \leq -x + p\}$

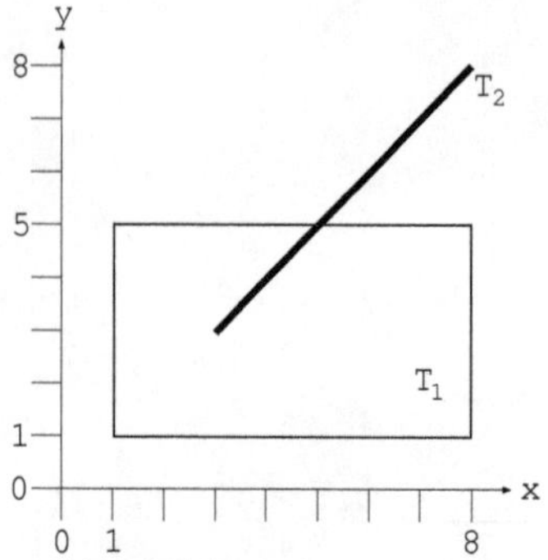

(a) depiction for $m = 5$, $n = 8$

```
for (x=1; x<=2; x++)
    for (y=1; y<=m; y++) T1(x,y);
for (x=3; x<=min(m-1,n); x++) {
    for (y=1; y<=x-1; y++) T1(x,y);
    T1(x,x); T2(x,x);
    for (y=x+1; y<=m; y++) T1(x,y);
}
if (m <= n) {
    for (y=1; y<=m-1; y++) T1(m,y);
    T1(m,m); T2(m,m);
}
for (x=m+1; x<=n; x++) {
    for (y=1; y<=m; y++) T1(x,y);
    T2(x,x);
}
```

(b) CLooG code

```
if (n <= m-1) {
  for (x=1; x<=3-1; x++) { for (y=1; y<=m; y++) T1(x,y); }
  for (x=3; x<=n; x++) {
    for (y=1; y<=x-1; y++) T1(x,y);
    for (y=x; y<=x; y++) { T1(x,y); T2(x,y); }
    for (y=x+1; y<=m; y++) T1(x,y);    }
} else if (n == m) {
  for (x=1; x<=3-1; x++) { for (y=1; y<=OneOf(m,n); y++) T1(x,y); }
  for (x=3; x<=OneOf(n,m)-1; x++) {
    for (y=1; y<=x-1; y++) T1(x,y);
    for (y=x; y<=x; y++) { T1(x,y); T2(x,y); }
    for (y=x+1; y<=OneOf(m,n); y++) T1(x,y);    }
  for (x=OneOf(n,m); x<=OneOf(n,m); x++) {
    for (y=1; y<=OneOf(m,x,n)-1; y++) T1(x,y);
    for (y=OneOf(m,x,n); y<=OneOf(m,x,n); y++) { T1(x,y); T2(x,y); }  }
} else if (m+1 <= n) {
  for (x=1; x<=3-1; x++) { for (y=1; y<=m; y++) T1(x,y); }
  for (x=3; x<=m-1; x++) {
    for (y=1; y<=x-1; y++) T1(x,y);
    for (y=x; y<=x; y++) { T1(x,y); T2(x,y); }
    for (y=x+1; y<=m; y++) T1(x,y);    }
  for (x=m; x<=m; x++) {
    for (y=1; y<=OneOf(m,x)-1; y++) T1(x,y);
    for (y=OneOf(m,x); y<=OneOf(m,x); y++) { T1(x,y); T2(x,y); }  }
  for (x=m+1; x<=n; x++) {
    for (y=1; y<=m; y++) T1(x,y);
    for (y=x; y<=x; y++) T2(x,y);    }
}
```

(c) our code

Figure 5.26: Example from [QRW00] (under the assumption $m, n \geq 4$)

Non-polyhedral Examples

A Quadratic Schedule It has been argued [AZ00] that non-linear schedules found by quadratic programming can provide substantially shorter overall execution times. An example used by Achtziger et al. [AZ00, Example 2.2], for which we presented the computation of a schedule linear in the variables in Section 5.2.1, is a recurrence equality with the index set $D(n)$ defined by

$$2 \leq x \leq n$$
$$4 \leq y \leq n$$
$$n - x \leq y$$

for $n \geq 7$ and the following dependences:

$$(x - 1, x) \rightarrow (x, y)$$
$$(x, y - 1) \rightarrow (x, y)$$

Achtziger et al. compute $\theta_1(x, y) = (n-3) \cdot x + y$ as a linear (in x and y) schedule and $\theta_2(x, y) = \frac{1}{2}x^2 - \frac{5}{2}x + y - 4$ as a quadratic, nearly optimal schedule. To generate code for a parallel execution, we use the equality defining the schedule (i.e., $t = \theta_i(x, y)$) and the original index set to define the domain of the statement and generate code for the variable ordering (t, x, y). For θ_1, we can compare the code generated by our algorithm with code generated by applying our generalised version of Fourier-Motzkin elimination [GGL04], since there is only one index set which is, in addition, a conjunction of formulas linear in the variables. Both codes are shown in Figures 5.27(a) and 5.27(b). The code generated by Fourier-Motzkin elimination is shorter because it generates several lower and upper bounds for each loop, if required. Our CAD based code is longer, but incurs less overhead in the loop bounds. For the quadratic θ_2, the code generated by CAD is depicted in Figure 5.28.

Schedule $\theta(i) = \lfloor \frac{i}{n} \rfloor$ Let us again consider an example from Section 5.2 shown again in Figure 5.29(a). Section 5.2 computes the schedule $\theta(i) = \lfloor \frac{i}{n} \rfloor$ for this program and notes that a suitable description for code generation is given by:

$$0 \leq i \leq m$$
$$n \cdot t + r = i$$
$$0 \leq r \leq n - 1$$

where t is the time coordinate and r is an additional iterator whose value equals $i \bmod n$. The codes generated for $m \geq n \geq 1$ by generalised Fourier-Motzkin elimination and CAD are shown in Figures 5.29(b) and 5.29(c), respectively. The unnecessary assignment r=i-n*t (i.e., a loop on r with only one iteration) will be optimised away by an optimising compiler; to reduce the size of the code shown, we omitted these statements in the code generated by CAD entirely. The main difference between the Fourier-Motzkin and CAD code is the reduced loop overhead achieved by increased code size.

```
for (t=3*n-8+1; t<=3*n-6; t++)
  parfor (x=2; x<=⌊ t−n/n−4 ⌋; x++)
    for (y=(-n+3)*x+t; y<=(-n+3)*x+t; y++)
      T1(x,y);
for (t=3*n-6+1; t<=n*n-7*n+16; t++)
  parfor (x=⌈ t−n/n−3 ⌉; x<=⌊ t−n/n−4 ⌋; x++)
    for (y=(-n+3)*x+t; y<=(-n+3)*x+t; y++)
      T1(x,y);
for (t=n*n-7*n+16+1; t<=n*n-3*n+4; t++)
  parfor (x=⌈ t−n/n−3 ⌉; x<=⌊ t−4/n−3 ⌋; x++)
    for (y=(-n+3)*x+t; y<=(-n+3)*x+t; y++)
      T1(x,y);
for (t=n*n-3*n+4+1; t<=n*n-2*n; t++)
  parfor (x=⌈ t−n/n−3 ⌉; x<=n; x++)
    for (y=(-n+3)*x+t; y<=(-n+3)*x+t; y++)
      T1(x,y);
```

(a) code generated by CAD for $n \geq 7$

```
for (t=3*n-8; t<=n*n-2*n; t++)
  parfor (x=max(2,⌈ t−n/n−3 ⌉); x<=min(min(n,⌊ t−4/n−3 ⌋),⌊ t−n/n−4 ⌋); x++)
    for (y=max(max(-4,-x+n),t+(-n+3)*x); y<=min(n,t+(-n+3)*x); y++)
      T1(x,y);
```

(b) code generated by Fourier-Motzkin elimination for $n \geq 7$

Figure 5.27: Example 2.2 from [AZ00] with schedule $\theta(x,y) = (n-3) \cdot x + y$

```
inline void T1(int t, int x) { int y=-x*x+5*x+2*t+4; ... }
```

```
for (t=⌈n-13/2⌉; t<=⌊n-13/2⌋; t++)
  parfor (x=⌈3 - √(2t - n + 13)⌉; x<=⌊3 - √(2t - n + 13)⌋; x++)
    T1(t,x);
for (t=⌊n-13/2⌋+1; t<=⌊n-12/2⌋; t++)
  parfor (x=⌈3 - √(2t - n + 13)⌉; x<=⌊3 + √(2t - n + 13)⌋; x++)
    T1(t,x);
for (t=⌊n-12/2⌋+1; t<=⌊4*n-41/8⌋; t++)
  parfor (x=2; x<=⌊3 + √(2t - n + 13)⌋; x++)
    T1(t,x);
for (t=⌊4n-41/8⌋+1; t<=⌊n-10/2⌋; t++) {
  parfor (x=2; x<=⌊5-√(8t-4n+41)/2⌋; x++)
    T1(t,x);
  parfor (x=⌈5+√(8t-4n+41)/2⌉; x<=⌊3 + √(2t - n + 13)⌋; x++)
    T1(t,x);
}
for (t=⌊n-10/2⌋+1; t<=⌈n-4/2⌉-1; t++)
  parfor (x=⌈5+√(8t-4n+41)/2⌉; x<=⌊3 + √(2t - n + 13)⌋; x++)
    T1(t,x);
for (t=⌊n-4/2⌋+1; t<=⌊n²-13n+36/2⌋; t++)
  parfor (x=⌈5+√(8t-4n+41)/2⌉; x<=⌊3 + √(2t - n + 13)⌋; x++)
    T1(t,x);
for (t=⌊n²-13n+36/2⌋+1; t<=⌊n²-5n/2⌋; t++)
  parfor (x=⌈5+√(8t-4n+41)/2⌉; x<=⌊5+√(8t-4n+41)/2⌋; x++)
    T1(t,x);
for (t=⌊n²-5n/2⌋+1; t<=⌊n²-4n-4/2⌋; t++)
  parfor (x=⌈5+√(8t-4n+41)/2⌉; x<=n; x++)
    T1(t,x);
```

Figure 5.28: Code generated by CAD for Example 2.2 from [AZ00] with schedule $\theta_2(x,y) = \frac{1}{2}x^2 - \frac{5}{2}x + y - 4$

```
for (i=0; i<=m; i++)
    A[i+n] = f(A[i]);
```

(a) Original program

```
for (t=⌈(1-n)/n⌉; t<=⌊m/n⌋; i++) {
    parfor (i=max(n*t,0); i<=min(n*t+n-1,m); i++) {
        r = i-n*t;
        A[i+n] = f(A[i]);
    }
}
```

(b) Parallel code generated by Fourier-Motzkin

```
for (t=⌈(1-n)/n⌉; t<=0; t++)
    parfor (i=0; i<=n*t+n-1; i++)
        A[i+n] = f(A[i]);
for (t=1; t<=⌊(m-n+1)/n⌋; t++)
    parfor (i=n*t; i<=n*t+n-1; i++)
        A[i+n] = f(A[i]);
for (t=⌊(m-n+1)/n⌋+1; t<=⌊m/n⌋; t++)
    parfor (i=n*t; i<=m; i++)
        A[i+n] = f(A[i]);
```

(c) Parallel code generated by CAD

Figure 5.29: Example program for non-linear schedule

```
                                    for (i=2; i*i<=n; i++) {
   for (i=2; i*i<=n; i++) {           for (k=i; k*i<=n; k++) {
     for (j=i*i; j<=n; j+=i)             j=k*i;
       A[j]++;                           A[j]++;
   }                                   }
                                    }
          (a) sequential code     }
                                        (b) normalised sequential code
```

```
   parfor (j=4; j<=n; j++) {
     for (i=2; i<=⌊√j⌋; i++) {
       for (k=⌈j/i⌉; k<=⌊j/i⌋; k++)
         A[j]++;
     }
   }
```

(c) parallel code

Figure 5.30: Example: computing the number of 2-factorisations

2-Factorisations   The Sieve of Eratosthenes is a well-known algorithm for computing the prime numbers in $2, \ldots, n$. A related, but slightly different, problem is to compute the number of factorisations of the numbers $2, \ldots, n$ into two factors (excluding 1) not considering the ordering of the factors. For example, 96 can be factored as $2 \cdot 48$, $3 \cdot 32$, $4 \cdot 24$, $6 \cdot 16$, and $8 \cdot 12$. The sequential code for computing the number of factorisations into two factors is given in Figure 5.30(a). At the end of the program, $A[j]$ will contain the number of factorisations of j (assuming that A is initialised with all zeros). Obviously, the loop on j can be executed in parallel for a given i, since different j iterations access different elements of A. But such a parallel execution requires a synchronisation after the loop on j for every iteration of i. It is desirable to exchange the loops on i and j in order to make the outer loop the parallel loop. To do so, we first have to normalise the program such that all loops have unit stride. This is achieved by applying the substitution $j := k \cdot i$ on the loop on j. The resulting normalised program is shown in Figure 5.30(b). Now, code generation for the domain defined by:

$$2 \le i \wedge i^2 \le n$$
$$i \le k \wedge k \cdot i \le n$$
$$j = k \cdot i$$

with the variable ordering (j, i, k) can be applied. This yields the code shown in Figure 5.30(c). The loop on j, which is now the outermost loop, is marked as parallel. We have to point out that the transformed code is less efficient than the original code because, by exchanging the loops on i and j, it is not guaranteed (by the construction of the loops) that j is a multiple of i. That is why the loop on k, whose only function is to check whether i divides j, has to be present in the code, and it has many iterations which are empty in the integers. So a substantial number of processors is required to achieve a speedup.

5.5.10   Combining Polyhedral Code Generation with CAD

Cylindrical algebraic decomposition is less efficient than applying a polyhedral code generator. In addition, we expect many bounds in code generation problems to be affine and only a few to be non-linear. This motivates the desire for a combined code generation procedure, i.e., a procedure which handles the polyhedral parts of a problem by polyhedral code generation techniques and applies cylindrical algebraic decomposition only to the non-linear parts.

In order to avoid a modification of existing polyhedral code generators, we have tried to develop a procedure which uses a polyhedral code generator like CLooG [Bas04] as a plug-in to handle the detected polyhedral parts. An alternative, which we have not been pursuing further, would be to enhance a polyhedral code generation technique to take non-linear bounds into account, e.g., when computing projections of iteration domains by computing an appropriate cylindrical decomposition. Let us now define the concept of a linear relaxation of a given quantifier-free formula.

Definition 5.15. Let $\varphi \in Qf(\mathcal{V})$ be a conjunction of atomic formulas, i.e., $\varphi = \bigwedge_{i=1}^{m} \alpha_i$ with atomic formulas $\alpha_1, \ldots, \alpha_m \in At(\mathcal{V})$. Then, we call φ^l defined by

$$\varphi^l := \bigwedge \{\alpha_i \mid 1 \leq i \leq m, \alpha_i \in Aff(\mathcal{V})\}$$

the *linear relaxation* of φ. For an arbitrary $\psi \in Qf(\mathcal{V})$, we define its linear relaxation ψ^l by

$$\psi^l := \bigvee_{i=1}^{r} \beta_i^l \quad \text{with} \quad \psi^{+\vee} = \bigvee_{i=1}^{r} \beta_i,$$

i.e., the linear relaxation is given by the disjunction of the linear relaxations of every disjunct in the positive disjunctive normal form $\varphi^{+\vee}$.

The relaxation of a conjunction removes any conjuncts which are not affine. Thus, the feasible set of the formula can only grow, i.e., $\varphi \to \varphi^l$ holds in $\mathbb{R}$, and that is why we call φ^l a relaxation of φ. For arbitrary quantifier-free formulas, we define the linear relaxation via a positive disjunctive normal form since, in arbitrary formulas, a removal of subformulas can shrink the feasible set and then the test in the algorithm of whether a non-linear bound is "sharp" would not work.

The code generation procedure is shown in Algorithm 5.2. It starts with iteration domains φ_i and "tags" (statement identifiers) T_i (for $1 \leq i \leq m$), the iteration variables $(x_1, \ldots, x_n)$ and a context C which provides conditions on the parameters. The idea behind this recursive algorithm is that, if the problem contains non-linearities, to project the iteration domains to the outer dimensions $(x_1, \ldots, x_{n-1})$ by eliminating x_n and splitting the projected sets according to whether the stack in the cylinder above them is defined by linear bounds only, or not. If $\mathbf{x} = (x_1, \ldots, x_{n-1})$ satisfies η_i (for given values of the parameters), then, in the cylinder above $\mathbf{x}$, the domain φ_i is defined by linear

---

Input: $\{(\varphi_1, T_1), \ldots, (\varphi_m, T_m)\}$, $(x_1, \ldots, x_n)$, C where the φ_i are the domains of the statements T_i, $x_1, \ldots, x_n$ are the loop iterators with x_1 being the outermost loop and C is the context (assumptions on the parameters).

a) Simplify all φ_i w.r.t. C.

b) If all φ_i are polyhedral, apply polyhedral code generator and problem is solved.

c) Let ψ_i be a quantifier-free equivalent of $\exists x_n \, (\varphi_i)$.

d) Compute η_i as a positive quantifier-free equivalent of $\forall x_n \, \left(\varphi_i \leftrightarrow \varphi_i^l\right)$ simplified under C.

e) Generate code for the outer dimensions by calling the code generation procedure recursively for
$\{(\eta_i \wedge \psi_i, T_{i,l}) \mid 1 \leq i \leq m\} \ \cup \ \{(\neg\eta_i \wedge \psi_i, T_{i,\neg l}) \mid 1 \leq i \leq m\}$,
$(x_1, \ldots, x_{n-1})$, C

f) In the generated code, replace every body with tags T for a cell defined by κ by the 1-dimensional code generated for $\{(\varphi_i^l, T_i) \mid T_{i,l} \in T\} \ \cup \ \{(\varphi_i, T_i) \mid T_{i,\neg l} \in T\}$, x_n, $C \cup \{\kappa\}$ according to the below subalgorithm.

g) Split the outer loops by the conditionals generated in the previous step to eliminate these conditionals.

Subalgorithm to generate 1-dimensional code:

Input: $\{(\varphi_i, T_i) \mid 1 \leq i \leq m\}$, x, C

a) Simplify all φ_i w.r.t. C.

b) If all φ_i are polyhedral, call polyhedral code generation.

c) Otherwise, use CAD to generate code exploiting the context C to compute a CAD of the relevant cells only.

Algorithm 5.2: Combined polyhedral and CAD code generation procedure

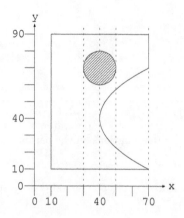

Figure 5.31: Example for combined polyhedral/CAD code generation

bounds, i.e., the non-linear bounds impose weaker restrictions than the linear bounds. By recursion, code is generated for all projections $\eta_i \wedge \psi_i$ and $\neg \eta_i \wedge \psi_i$ for the outer dimensions $(x_1, \ldots, x_{n-1})$. As soon as all bounds are linear, the problem is handed over to a polyhedral code generator. After generating code for the outer dimensions, the loops for the innermost dimension x_n are generated. Depending on whether the domain above a certain cell has non-linear bounds or not, the innermost loop is generated either by a polyhedral code generator or by cylindrical algebraic decomposition. By looking at whether the statement identifier is tagged with l or $\neg l$, we know whether we can use φ_i^l or must use φ_i as bounds. The code generated for the innermost dimension x_n may contain case distinctions (if statements) on the outer dimensions $x_1, \ldots, x_{n-1}$ and the parameters. To obtain efficient code, i.e., code without if statements inside the loops, we finally split the outer loops according to the conditions on $x_1, \ldots, x_{n-1}$. Splitting the outer loops is easy if the conditions are cylindrical themselves. This is guaranteed if the inner code has been generated by CAD. If the inner code has been generated by a polyhedral code generator, all conditionals are affine and we can apply Fourier-Motzkin elimination to them to obtain a cylindrical form.

Example 5.16. Consider the following code generation problem with two domains defined by φ_1 and φ_2 for dimensions (x, y) with context $C = \varnothing$, depicted in Figure 5.31:

$$\varphi_1 = \left(10 \leq x \leq 70 \wedge 10 \leq y \leq 90 \wedge (y - 40)^2 + 1200 - 30x \geq 0 \right)$$
$$\varphi_2 = \left((x - 40)^2 + (y - 70)^2 \leq 10^2 \right)$$

Since there are non-linearities in the domains, we cannot apply a polyhedral code generation. Projecting onto the x-dimension yields the formulas:

$$\psi_1 = \left(10 \leq x \leq 70 \right), \quad \psi_2 = \left(30 \leq x \leq 50 \right)$$

The linear relaxations of the original domains are:

$$\varphi_1^l = \left(10 \leq x \leq 70 \land 10 \leq y \leq 90\right)$$
$$\varphi_2^l = \left(\text{true}\right)$$

and the formulas η_i (the quantifier-free equivalent of $\forall y(\varphi_i \leftrightarrow \varphi_i^l)$) are given by:

$$\eta_1 = \left(10 \leq x \leq 40\right), \qquad \eta_2 = \left(\text{false}\right)$$

So the code generation continues for x with input:

$$\{(\eta_1 \land \psi_1, T_{1,l}), (\neg \eta_1 \land \psi_1, T_{1,\neg l}), (\eta_2 \land \psi_2, T_{2,l}), (\neg \eta_2 \land \psi_2, T_{2,\neg l})\}$$

which is (after simplification) equivalent to

$$\{(1 \leq x \leq 40, T_{1,l}), (41 \leq x \leq 70, T_{1,\neg l}), (30 \leq x \leq 50, T_{2,\neg l})\}.$$

Since the projected domains are all polyhedral, we can apply polyhedral code generation and obtain:

```
for (x=10; x<=29; x++)
    T₁,ₗ;
for (x=30; x<=40; x++) {
    T₁,ₗ;
    T₂,₋ₗ;
}
for (x=41; x<=50; x++) {
    T₁,₋ₗ;
    T₂,₋ₗ;
}
for (x=51; x<=70; x++)
    T₁,₋ₗ;
```

as preliminary code for the outer dimension. Code generation continues for the inner dimension after returning from the recursive invocation of the procedure for the outer dimension. In this example, we have four invocations of code generation for the inner dimension, one for each of the loops on x generated for the outer dimension. For the case $10 \leq x \leq 29$, the constraints on y are equivalent to φ_1^l (because T_1 is additionally tagged with l) and we call a polyhedral code generator for the loops on y with the new context $C \cup \{10 \leq x \leq 29\}$. In the three cases with $x \geq 30$, there are non-linear constraints involved, so we call CAD-based code generation for each part. To reduce the number of computations to be made, we exploit the new context (e.g., $C \cup \{30 \leq x \leq 40\}$) to compute a CAD of the relevant subset of $\mathbb{R}^2$ only. For example, for $30 \leq x \leq 40$, we only need to compute sections and test points which actually satisfy $30 \leq x \leq 40$. Inserting the generated codes for y, we obtain the final code which is shown in Figure 5.32.

```
for (x=10; x<=29; x++)
  for (y=10; y<=90; y++)
    T₁(x,y);
for (x=30; x<=40; x++) {
  for (y=10; y<=⌈69 − √(10 − (x − 40)²)⌉; y++)
    T₁(x,y);
  for (y=⌈70 − √(10 − (x − 40)²)⌉; y<=⌊70 + √(10 − (x − 40)²)⌋; y++) {
    T₁(x,y);
    T₂(x,y);
  }
  for (y=⌊71 + √(10 − (x − 40)²)⌋; y<=90; y++)
    T₁(x,y);
}
for (x=41; x<=50; x++) {
  for (y=10; y<=⌊40 − √(30x − 1200)⌋; x++)
    T₁(x,y);
  for (y=⌈40 + √(30x − 1200)⌉; y<=⌈69 − √(10 − (x − 40)²)⌉; y++)
    T₁(x,y);
  for (y=⌈70 − √(10 − (x − 40)²)⌉; y<=⌊70 + √(10 − (x − 40)²)⌋; y++) {
    T₁(x,y);
    T₂(x,y);
  }
  for (y=⌊71 + √(10 − (x − 40)²)⌋; y<=90; y++)
    T₁(x,y);
}
for (x=51; x<=70; x++) {
  for (y=10; y<=⌊40 − √(30x − 1200)⌋; x++)
    T₁(x,y);
  for (y=⌈40 + √(30x − 1200)⌉; y<=90; y++)
    T₁(x,y);
}
```

Figure 5.32: Code generated for input shown in Figure 5.31

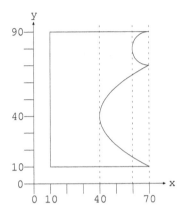

Figure 5.33: A domain which needs an additional split

In this example, code generation for the inner dimension (after the recursion) does not produce a case distinction in the outer dimensions. Let us present another example to illustrate why splitting the outer loops by conditionals created by the generation of the inner loops is necessary in the general case.

Example 5.17. Consider the following domain, depicted in Figure 5.33:

$$\varphi = \left(10 \leq x \wedge 10 \leq y \leq 90 \wedge (y - 40)^2 + 1200 - 30x \geq 0 \wedge \right.$$
$$\left. (x - 70)^2 + (y - 80)^2 \leq 10^2\right)$$

Obviously, the formula ψ is $10 \leq x \leq 70$ and η is $10 \leq x \leq 40$. Therefore, the code generation continues with:

$$\{(10 \leq x \leq 40, T_{1,l}), (41 \leq x \leq 70, T_{1,\neg l})\}$$

and we obtain the following code after generating the outer loops on x and the inner loop on y for $10 \leq x \leq 40$ by polyhedral code generation and the inner loops on y for $41 \leq x \leq 70$ by CAD:

```
for (x=10; x<=40; x++)
  for (y=10; y<=90; y++)
    T₁(x,y);
for (x=41; x<=70; x++) {
  if (x<=60) {
```
$$\text{for } (y=10; \; y<=\lfloor 40 - \sqrt{30x - 1200}\rfloor; \; x++)$$
$$T_1(x,y);$$
$$\text{for } (y=\lceil 40 + \sqrt{30x - 1200}\rceil; \; y<=90; \; y++)$$
$$T_1(x,y);$$
```
  } else if (x>=61) {
```
$$\text{for } (y=10; \; y<=\lfloor 40 - \sqrt{30x - 1200}\rfloor; \; x++)$$
$$T_1(x,y);$$
$$\text{for } (y=\lceil 40 + \sqrt{30x - 1200}\rceil; \; y<=\lfloor 80 - \sqrt{100 - (x - 70)^2}\rfloor; \; y++)$$
$$T_1(x,y);$$
$$\text{for } (y=\lceil 80 + \sqrt{100 - (x - 70)^2}\rceil; \; y<=90; \; y++)$$
$$T_1(x,y);$$
```
  }
}
```

As we can see, the non-linear part of the iteration domain $(41 \leq x \leq 70)$ needs a split at $x = 60$, but the formula η does not provide this split as it only separates linear and non-linear parts. By partitioning the loop on x by the two conditionals $x \leq 60$ and $x \geq 61$, we obtain the final code:

```
for (x=10; x<=40; x++)
  for (y=10; y<=90; y++)
    T₁(x,y);
for (x=41; x<=60; x++) {
```
$$\text{for } (y=10; \; y<=\lfloor 40 - \sqrt{30x - 1200}\rfloor; \; x++)$$
$$T_1(x,y);$$
$$\text{for } (y=\lceil 40 + \sqrt{30x - 1200}\rceil; \; y<=90; \; y++)$$
$$T_1(x,y);$$
```
}
for (x=61; x<=70; x++) {
```
$$\text{for } (y=10; \; y<=\lfloor 40 - \sqrt{30x - 1200}\rfloor; \; x++)$$
$$T_1(x,y);$$
$$\text{for } (y=\lceil 40 + \sqrt{30x - 1200}\rceil; \; y<=\lfloor 80 - \sqrt{100 - (x - 70)^2}\rfloor; \; y++)$$
$$T_1(x,y);$$
$$\text{for } (y=\lceil 80 + \sqrt{100 - (x - 70)^2}\rceil; \; y<=90; \; y++)$$
$$T_1(x,y);$$
```
}
```

5.5.11   Generalising a Polyhedral Code Generator to Non-linear Parameters

As a alternative to code generation based on cylindrical algebraic decomposition, it is worthwhile to try to generalise a polyhedral code generation algorithm to non-linear parameters. Such a code generation procedure is less general than one based on cylindrical algebraic decomposition as it cannot handle non-linear variables. But with non-linear parameters alone, the code generator can solve problems that go beyond the classical case. For example, generating tiled loop code with parametric tile sizes for several statements is one such problem.

We have implemented a code generator for non-linear parameters by generalising a simple polyhedral code generator to non-linear parameters. Unfortunately, we did not have enough time, yet, to advance this prototype far enough to present examples which allow a comparison against the CLooG code generator.

To discuss the generalisation, let us review the operations a polyhedral code generation relies on:

(1) Given two polyhedral iteration sets $D(\mathbf{p})$ and $E(\mathbf{p})$, a partitioning[4] of $D(\mathbf{p}) \cup E(\mathbf{p})$ can be computed such that:

   (a) each partition $F(\mathbf{p})$ is a parametric polyhedron and is a subset of exactly one of $D(\mathbf{p}) \cap E(\mathbf{p})$, $D(\mathbf{p}) - E(\mathbf{p})$ or $E(\mathbf{p}) - D(\mathbf{p})$, and

   (b) the partitions can be ordered by a partial order $\lhd$ such that for two partitions $F(\mathbf{p})$, $G(\mathbf{p})$, $F(\mathbf{p}) \neq G(\mathbf{p})$ with $F(\mathbf{p}) \lhd G(\mathbf{p})$ the following condition holds:
   $$(x_1, \ldots, x_{n-1}, x_n) \in F(\mathbf{p}), (x_1, \ldots, x_{n-1}, y_n) \in G(\mathbf{p}) \implies x_n < y_n \, (*)$$

(2) Given a polyhedral index set $D(\mathbf{p}) \subseteq \mathbb{R}^n$, its projection to the outer $n - 1$ dimensions $\Pi(D(\mathbf{p})) \subseteq \mathbb{R}^{n-1}$ can be computed and $\Pi(D(\mathbf{p}))$ is a parametric polyhedron.

To fulfil (1a), (1b) and (2), no case distinctions on the linear parameters are required. The partitioning and the projections can be computed while treating the parameters like additional variables. Only in (1b), we may want to make case distinctions for efficiency because we want to remove partitions which are empty for certain values of the parameters from the generated code.

We can generalise these operations to non-linear parameters. To compute the required disjoint union in (1a), we can use the disjoint union algorithm given in our own previous work [Grö03]. This requires no case distinctions even in the case with non-linear parameters. The projections in (2) can be computed by our generalised Fourier-Motzkin elimination (cf. Section 4.4) or the algorithm from Section 4.3.1 (Corollary 4.15). With both approaches, case distinctions on the parameters become necessary. The ordering in (1b) can be computed by quantifier elimination by asking for which condition on the parameters property (*) holds, i.e., computing the quantifier-free equivalent of

$$\forall x_1 \cdots \forall x_n \forall y_n \left((x_1, \ldots, x_{n-1}, x_n) \in F(\mathbf{p}) \wedge (x_1, \ldots, x_{n-1}, y_n) \in G(\mathbf{p}) \right.$$
$$\left. \longrightarrow x_n < y_n \right)$$

---

[4]Due to the requirement that each partition is polyhedral in (1a), some strict bounds ($f > 0$) have to be replaced by weak bounds ($f \geq 1$) when computing the partitioning. This does not change the set of integral points (if f is denominator-free), but omits some points in the reals.

```
if (n >= 0 && m >= 0) {
  for (i=0; i<=min(p*n,m); i++) {
    S1(i);
    if (i%p == 0)
      S2(i/p);
  }
}
if (m <= p*n-1 && n >= 0) {
  for (i=max(m+1,0); i<=p*n; i++) {
    if (i%p == 0)
      S2(i/p);
  }
}
if (m >= p*n-1 && m >= 0) {
  for (i=max(p*n+1,0); i<=m; i++)
    S1(i);
}
```

Figure 5.34: Example code for a problem with non-linear scattering $i = p \cdot x$ for S_2

or, as an alternative, this question can be answered using our generalised simplex (cf. Section 4.4) by minimising the target function $y_n - x_n$ over the domain defined by $(x_1, \ldots, x_{n-1}, x_n) \in F(\mathbf{p}) \wedge (x_1, \ldots, x_{n-1}, y_n) \in G(\mathbf{p})$ and checking whether the minimum is positive.

From these building blocks, we can implement a code generator for non-linear parameters. But, to achieve an efficient generation, the same engineering effort has to be made as has been done for code generators for the linearly parametric case. To achieve results comparable to, for example, the CLooG code generator, many improvements have to be made in the generator. With our prototype, we made a few observations that will have to be examined in more detail when the prototype has matured. Our impression is that for step (1b), quantifier elimination is faster than applying the generalised simplex, whereas for (2) Fourier-Motzkin (to eliminate one dimension) is faster than using quantifier elimination. In addition, the prototype for code generation with non-linear parameters seems to outperform our prototype for code generation based on cylindrical algebraic decomposition; but, since both prototypes have to be improved, the question of whether CAD can compete or not cannot be answered at the moment.

As one example which our prototype can solve already, consider the following code generation problem:

$$D_1(m,n,p) = \{i \mid 0 \le x \le m, i = x\}$$
$$D_2(m,n,p) = \{i \mid 0 \le x \le n, i = p \cdot x\}$$

The functions $i = x$ and $i = p \cdot x$ are so-called *scattering functions* which are used by CLooG, for example. Our prototype handles scattering functions (this may be one reason why it outperforms our code generator based on CAD). Note that the scattering function for $D_2(m, n, p)$ is non-linear. The code generated under the assumption $p \geq 1$ is shown in Figure 5.34. The statements are executed for each point i in their domain; the argument of S_1 and S_2 is the value of x which corresponds to the enumerated i-value.

5.5.12   Code Generation as a Formula Simplification Problem

Instead of computing a cylindrical algebraic decomposition, we can also generate code if we express the domains of the statements as logical formulas and let a formula simplifier "simplify" or, more precisely, transform the formula with a suitable simplification objective.

To be able to partition the domains into cells of a cylindrical decomposition, the result formula must be of a certain structure. The required structure is related to the concept of GEOFORM formulas [Bro99], but not quite the same. We need formulas that are of a certain syntactic structure, namely formulas which correspond directly to cylindrical loop nests (cf. Definition 5.12). Therefore, non-adjacent cells of the CAD induced by the bound polynomials must not be combined into one. For example, the formula $x_1^2 \geq 2$ is unsuitable, because we need the information that the feasible set is composed of the two cells:

$$x_1 \leq -\sqrt{2} \ \vee \ x_1 \geq \sqrt{2}.$$

At the moment, no formula simplifier which produces the required formulas seems to be available. Maybe such a procedure can be implemented in a formula simplifier based on CAD, like the QEPCAD/SLFQ system.

5.5.13   Improvements of the Basic Algorithm

Our algorithm produces code which has the properties that it is a proper $\mathbb{R}$-scan and that every loop generated has exactly one lower and one upper bound. Both properties offer room for improvement. Since the theory of integers with addition and multiplication is undecidable, there cannot be a general improvement over proper $\mathbb{R}$-scans. But there are many special cases in practical code generation. Therefore, it is worthwhile to invest in integral non-emptiness tests for common cases, e.g., linear formulas. If a cell (section or sector) is bounded by linear formulas only, its integral feasibility can be tested. This improvement for linear cases is obtained "for free" in some cases if CAD based code generation is combined with polyhedral code generation and the polyhedral code generator is optimised in this respect (cf. Section 5.5.10).

The other direction for improvement is to reduce the code size by combining inner loops with different upper or lower bounds by using minima and maxima in the bounds. For example, in the triangular index set example (cf. Figure 5.25), the two loops on x cannot be combined because of the different inner loops on y. But the upper bounds of the loops on y are compatible in the sense that each bound is stricter than the other bound in its respective x-cell, i.e., because the implications

$$1 \leq x \leq \frac{p}{2} \Rightarrow x \leq -x + p$$
$$\frac{p}{2} < x \leq p \Rightarrow -x + p \leq x$$

hold, it could be detected that the loops on y can be combined into the loop nest generated by polyhedral code generation. This is a *semantic* test that goes beyond the syntactic test we perform on the roots defining the sections of two neighbouring stacks when deciding whether the codes for the two stacks can be merged into a single code. This optimisation may be achieved by letting a formula simplifier compute a formula representing a suitable cylindrical decomposition (cf. Section 5.5.12).

Chapter 6

Conclusions

6.1 Summary

The polyhedron model has been used to describe transformations of programs with a certain regular structure. To go beyond the restriction of affine expressions as loop bounds and array indices we have studied different algorithms and approaches to extending the model to non-linear domains. Since non-linearity implies that the coefficients of variables need not be fixed rational (or integral) numbers, but can be expressions in the structural parameters, dealing with case distinctions on such expressions is central to a generalisation. How we deal with these expressions depends on the application, i.e., on the phase in the transformation process which we want to extend to non-linearities.

6.1.1 Dependence Analysis

In dependence analysis, it is of utmost importance to compute the integral solutions of the conflict equality system, and not a rational or real overapproximation of the solution set. We have been able to show that one can solve the conflict equality system exactly if there is exactly one non-linear parameter. The coefficient expressions allowed are not only polynomials in this parameter, but encompass also floor operations and (by equivalence) periodic case distinctions on the value of the parameter, i.e., quasi-polynomials.

The feasibility of a dependence analysis in this more general situation relies on the fact that it is possible to generalise the computation of greatest common divisors, which lies at the heart of solving linear Diophantine equality systems. Using entire quasi-polynomials, we can describe the pointwise greatest common divisor of polynomials from $\mathbb{Z}[X]$ (i.e., a function whose return value corresponds to the GCD of the function values of two given polynomials) and, more generally, in the entire quasi-polynomials themselves. With this generalised dependence analysis procedure, it is possible to analyse the data dependences of a wider class of programs than in the polyhedron model.

6.1.2 Computing Schedules

In the transformation phase, non-linearities arise or are of use in different situations. When computing schedules and placements, it is often sufficient to deal with real solutions of the problem considered, since integral solutions can be obtained from a real solution (e.g., by rounding down a fractional schedule) and a slight deviation from the optimal solution is negligible for practical applications.

Our main tool for achieving the generalisation here is quantifier elimination in the real numbers. The parametric coefficients of the inequality systems studied are handled using logical formulas in the language of ordered rings over the reals. Since there exists a quantifier elimination procedure for this structure, some problems, like finding a legal schedule, can be expressed as a formula and quantifier elimination computes a solution.

In addition, we have shown that some algorithms used in the polyhedron model can be generalised to handle non-linear parameters by a syntactic transformation and the use of quantifier elimination to make the arising case distinctions finite. This enables to use a generalised simplex algorithm to compute schedules which are linear in the variables but probably non-linear in the parameters.

6.1.3 Tiling

Even if the source program does not contain non-linear parameters, we may want or need to introduce non-linearities during the transformation. Tiling, which is used to control the granularity of, e.g., the parallelism or the cache usage of a transformed program, can only be expressed with static tile sizes in the polyhedron model. There are solutions for special cases with parametric tile sizes.

Using non-linearities, we can express arbitrary parametric tilings. We have even shown that, in the common case of parallelepiped tiles, no case distinctions occur when applying Fourier-Motzkin elimination to generate code for a single statement (i.e., in this case, no quantifier elimination tool is necessary). Although the generated loop bounds are usually quite complex compared to the source program, the code executes efficiently without large overhead to compute the loop bounds, since the innermost loops remain "simple" in the sense that optimising compilers need only a few instructions to express the update on the loop iterator from one iteration to the next by performing induction variable detection and related optimisation techniques.

Tiling is indispensable to accommodate execution parameters, like the number of processors, which are unknown at compile time. Two problems which often spoil performance are load imbalance, due to a varying number of tiles in the parallel dimension, and the presence of incomplete tiles at the borders of the index space. Load imbalance could nominally be reduced by using smaller tiles, but this would lead to an increased overhead of the tile enumeration. When tile sizes are chosen such that the number of tiles in the parallel dimension is of the same order of magnitude as the number of available processor cores, dealing with load imbalances and irregularities at the index space bounds becomes indispensable. Both problems need to be researched further; we have offered basic ideas of solutions and made some promising experiments.

Another factor limiting performance is memory bandwidth. With the NUMA architecture becoming more common, replicating data in the local memory areas of each physical processor unit is another topic for future research.

6.1.4 Array Localisation

Another application of non-linearities in the transformation phase is accelerating programs by exploiting the fact that some architectures have, in addition to main memory, an explicitly addressable fast memory area, the so-called scratchpad. By way of precise data dependence information, we are able to compute exactly which data items to copy to fast memory to exploit temporal locality. We determine exactly when to copy a value to fast memory, when to copy an updated value back to main memory and when to relocate a value in fast memory.

The transformed program will contain non-linearities, because some loops need non-linear bounds. Since the data held in fast storage is stored in a compact fashion without holes, the access functions can be complex (piecewise conditional quasi-polynomials), but our experiments suggest that, by using advanced code generation techniques, the overhead can be eliminated by partitioning the iteration domains according to the conditions in the new access functions. In our experiments on a GPU, we observed accelerations of factors up to 3.5 compared to parallel code which uses main memory only.

If no dependence information is available, a simpler transformation based on access instances which may move more elements to fast storage than necessary can be applied.

6.1.5 Code Generation

The third phase of the transformation process must generate code from the index sets of the transformed model. Cylindrical algebraic decomposition enables the generation of target loop code for index sets with arbitrary polynomial bounds. We have presented a basic algorithm. The algorithm relies on the computation of a cylindrical algebraic decomposition (CAD) of $\mathbb{R}^n$ (for n-dimensional index sets).

The requirement of the decomposition to be algebraic causes the generated code to be quite lengthy. But we have shown that loops can be combined by syntactic reasoning (provided that the CAD procedure emits all polynomials whose roots coincide over a cell). Each loop generated has exactly one lower and one upper bound and, when a loop is reached, the lower bound is less than or equal to the upper bound, i.e., the loop is non-empty in the reals, but there is no guarantee of integral non-emptiness. Integral non-emptiness is undecidable in the general case but may be checked for common cases like linear bounds in a future version of the algorithm. Further reduction of the code size is another goal which may be achieved by combining suitable loops and thereby introducing minima and maxima of bounds in the new loop bounds.

We have also given an algorithm for a combined code generation procedure which checks, during each projection, which parts of the problem are polyhedral and can be offloaded to a polyhedral code generator. CAD is applied only for the parts which are defined by some non-linear bounds. This is a first step in the direction of reducing code size and improving generation efficiency. Another approach, for the case with linear variables and non-linear parameters only, is to generalise the operations used in polyhedral code generation to non-linear parameters. We have implemented a prototype for this approach, too, but more engineering effort is required to improve it such that it becomes competitive to code generators like CLooG.

6.2   Future Directions

We hope that the ideas and algorithms presented in this thesis are starting points for further research. Let us now present a few directions for further research in the three main phases of the transformation process.

6.2.1   Dependence Analysis

Being able to solve systems of linear Diophantine equalities which are non-linear in one parameter is the basis for a generalisation of Banerjee's dependence analysis (Section 5.1). To be able to implement more advanced analyses, like the Feautrier dependence analysis, we must be able to handle inequalities and perform integral linear optimisation, i.e., optimise a target function w.r.t. a given polyhedron or compute the lexicographic minimum in a polyhedron (with one non-linear parameter). This is, of course, inherently more difficult than solving a linear equality system and, at the moment, it is unclear whether this problem is decidable and, if it is undecidable, whether interesting decidable special cases exist.

If we think in the direction of using a generalised simplex algorithm (to find the real optimum) and branching (to generate subproblems with tighter bounds to find the integral optimum eventually), we need the arithmetic operations $+$, $-$, $\cdot$, $/$ (in the simplex) and $\lfloor \cdot \rfloor$ (for the branching). Because of the divisions used by simplex, the coefficients cannot be quasi-polynomials from EQP, but must be fractions of quasi-polynomials, i.e., $\frac{f}{g}$ with $f, g \in EQP$. It turns out that we can even describe floor operations $\lfloor \frac{f}{g} \rfloor$ on such fractions. The reason is that, by polynomial division, we can compute $e, r \in \mathcal{P}[X]$ such that:

$$\frac{f}{g} = e + \frac{r}{g} \quad \text{with} \quad \deg(r) < \deg(g)$$

and, therefore:

$$\lim_{p \to \pm\infty} \frac{r(p)}{g(p)} \to 0$$

This implies that $\lfloor \frac{f(p)}{g(p)} \rfloor$ is equal to $\lfloor e \rfloor(p)$ or $\lfloor e \rfloor(p) - 1$, depending on the sign of $\frac{r(p)}{g(p)}$) for $|p| \geq b$ for some $b \in \mathbb{N}$ (except in the vanishing constituents of g). Therefore, $\lfloor \frac{f(p)}{g(p)} \rfloor$ can be described by a sixtuple (b, e_-, k, e_+, l, U), where $e_-, e_+ \in EQP$ are the floor values for $p \leq -b$ and $p \geq b$ (either $\lfloor e \rfloor$ or $\lfloor e \rfloor - 1$), respectively, $k : \{-b+1, \ldots, b-1\} \to \mathbb{Z}$ is a tabulated function representing the values of $\lfloor \frac{f(p)}{g(p)} \rfloor$ for $-b < p < b$, $l \in \mathbb{N}_+$ is the period of g, and $U = \{i \mid 0 \leq i \leq l - 1, \text{con}_l(g, i) = 0\}$ lists the constituents in which the fraction $\frac{f}{g}$ is undefined. The set of all such objects is closed under $+$, $-$, $\cdot$, $/$, $\lfloor \div \rfloor$. Therefore, these objects may be a starting point for exploring the possibilities to compute the integral optimum of a target function w.r.t. a polyhedron in the presence of one non-linear parameter.

6.2.2 Transformations

We have presented transformations which introduce non-linearities, namely non-linear schedules, parametric tiling and array localisation. Computing schedules and tiling is possible for inputs which are already non-linear because quantifier elimination, which is used to compute schedules, can handle them. Tiling is possible because it only adds some dimensions and constraints to the iteration domains; thus, handling the non-linearities is (only) a problem of code generation.

But other transformations are not ready to cope with non-linear input. One example is our array localisation. It relies on counting the integral points in polytopes, which is done using Ehrhart theory. It has to be investigated whether computing Ehrhart polynomials (or a suitable generalisation of them) is possible in the presence of non-linear parameters. All transformations that rely on counting are affected by this problem. In addition, we cannot compute integral optima of a target function w.r.t. to a polyhedron in the presence of non-linear parameters (see also Section 6.2.1). Therefore, all transformations that require to solve an ILP problem will run into difficulties, too. Future research will have to address the question whether we can build a rich set of viable transformations which handles non-linear input programs.

6.2.3 Code Generation

Our code generation technique, which uses cylindrical algebraic decomposition, can only be a first step. The efficiency is worse than that of polyhedral code generators since computing a CAD is doubly-exponential in the number of dimensions in the worst case. Although we have outlined a procedure which uses a polyhedral code generator as a plug-in to offload code generation for polyhedral parts of the index space, this offloading requires that, by projection, a cylinder is obtained with only polyhedral bounds in it. Better applicability and a higher efficiency, we expect, can be obtained using an integrated code generation procedure which augments a polyhedral code generator with the necessary routines to handle non-linear bounds by computing a CAD in the respective cylinders. Such an integrated code generator may be a next goal for research in the code generation area. Testing integral non-emptiness (where possible) to avoid enumerating iteration sets which are only non-empty in the reals is another aspect to consider.

Another future challenge in code generation may be the question of whether we can go beyond polynomial bounds. For example, CAD does not enable us to generate loops with bounds like $0 \leq y \leq \log_2 x$, which can occur in tree algorithms (because of the logarithmic tree depth).

Bibliography

[ABRY01]   Rumen Andonov, Stefan Balev, Sanjay Rajopadhye, and Nicola
            Yanev. Optimal semi-oblique tiling. In *Proc. 13th Ann. ACM
            Symp. on Parallel Algorithms and Architectures (SPAA 2001)*,
            pages 153–162. ACM Press, July 2001. Extended version available
            as technical report: IRISA, nr. 1392, December 2001.

[ACM98]   Dennis S. Arnon, George E. Collins, and Scott McCallum. Cylin-
            drical Algebraic Decompositions I: The Basic Algorithm. In Bob F.
            Caviness and Jeremy R. Johnson, editors, *Quantifier Elimination
            and Cylindrical Algebraic Decomposition*, pages 136–151. Springer-
            Verlag, 1998.

[AI91]   Corinne Ancourt and François Irigoin. Scanning Polyhedra with
            DO Loops. *Third ACM SIGPLAN Symposium on Priciples & Prac-
            tice of Parallel Programming*, 26(7):39–50, July 1991.

[AZ00]   Wolfgang Achtziger and Karl-Heinz Zimmermann. Finding
            quadratic schedules for affine recurrence equations via nonsmooth
            optimization. *J. VLSI Signal Process. Syst.*, 25(3):235–260, 2000.

[Ban93]   Utpal K. Banerjee. *Loop Transformations for Restructuring Com-
            pilers: The Foundations*. Kluwer Academic Publishers, Norwell,
            MA, USA, 1993.

[Bar98]   Denis Barthou. *Array Dataflow Analysis in Presence of Non-affine
            Constraints*. PhD thesis, Université de Versailles St-Quentin, Ver-
            sailles, February 1998. http://www.prism.uvsq.fr/users/bad/
            Research/ps/these.pdf.

[Bas04]   Cédric Bastoul. Code generation in the polyhedral model is easier
            than you think. In *PACT '04: Proceedings of the 13th International
            Conference on Parallel Architectures and Compilation Techniques*,
            pages 7–16, Washington, DC, USA, 2004. IEEE Computer Society.

[BBK+08a]   Muthu M. Baskaran, Uday Bondhugula, Sriram Krishnamoorthy,
            J. Ramanujam, Atanas Rountev, and P. Sadayappan. Automatic

data movement and computation mapping for multi-level parallel architectures with explicitly managed memories. In *PPoPP '08: Proc. of the 13th ACM SIGPLAN Symposium on Principles and Practice of Parallel Programming*, pages 1–10, New York, NY, USA, 2008. ACM.

[BBK$^+$08b] Uday Bondhugula, Muthu M. Baskaran, Sriram Krishnamoorthy, J. Ramanujam, Atanas Rountev, and P. Sadayappan. Automatic transformations for communication-minimized parallelization and locality optimization in the polyhedral model. In *Int. Conf. on Compiler Construction (ETAPS CC)*, April 2008.

[BF03] Cédric Bastoul and Paul Feautrier. Improving data locality by chunking. In *CC'12 Int. Conf. on Compiler Construction, LNCS 2622*, pages 320–335, Warsaw, April 2003.

[BFT01] Alberto Bemporad, Komei Fukuda, and Fabio D. Torrisi. Convexity recognition of the union of polyhedra. *Computational Geometry*, 18(3):141–154, 2001.

[Bla77] Robert G. Bland. New finite pivoting rules for the simplex method. *Mathematics of Operations Research*, 2:103–107, 1977.

[BR07] Matthias Beck and Sinai Robins. *Computing the Continuous Discretely: Integer-Point Enumeration in Polyhedra*. Springer, July 2007.

[Bro99] Christopher W. Brown. *Solution Formula Construction For Truth-Invariant CADs*. PhD thesis, University of Delaware, 1999.

[Bro01a] Christopher W. Brown. Improved projection for cylindrical algebraic decomposition. *J. Symb. Comput.*, 32(5):447–465, November 2001.

[Bro01b] Christopher W. Brown. Simple cad construction and its applications. *J. Symb. Comput.*, 31(5):521–547, 2001.

[Bro03] Christopher W. Brown. Qepcad b: a program for computing with semi-algebraic sets using cads. *SIGSAM Bull.*, 37(4):97–108, 2003.

[CF93] Jean-François Collard and Paul Feautrier. Automatic generation of data parallel code. In Henk J. Sips, editor, *Proc. of the Fourth International Workshop on Compilers for Parallel Computers*, pages 321–332, December 1993.

[Chv83] Vašek Chvátal. *Linear Programming*. W. H. Freeman and Company, 1983.

[CK08] Guangyu Chen and Mahmut T. Kandemir. Compiler-directed code restructuring for improving performance of MPSoCs. *IEEE Transactions on Parallel and Distributed Systems*, 19(9):1201–1214, September 2008.

[CM00] Philippe Clauss and Benoît Meister. Automatic memory layout transformations to optimize spatial locality in parameterized loop nests. In *4th Annual Workshop on Interaction between Compilers and Computer Architectures, INTERACT-4, Toulouse, France*, January 2000.

[CT04] Philippe Clauss and Irina Tchoupaeva. A symbolic approach to bernstein expansion for program analysis and optimization. In *13th International Conference on Compiler Construction, CC 2004*, pages 120–133. Springer, 2004.

[Dav73] Martin Davis. Hilbert's tenth problem is unsolvable. *American Mathematical Monthly*, 80, 1973.

[DH88] James H. Davenport and Joos Heintz. Real quantifier elimination is doubly exponential. *J. Symb. Comput.*, 5(1-2):29–35, 1988.

[DR95] Alain Darte and Yves Robert. Affine-by-statement scheduling of uniform and affine loop nests over parametric domains. *J. Parallel Distrib. Comput.*, 29(1):43–59, 1995.

[DRV00] Alain Darte, Yves Robert, and Frederic Vivien. *Scheduling and Automatic Parallelization*. Birkhäuser, 2000.

[DS97] Andreas Dolzmann and Thomas Sturm. REDLOG: computer algebra meets computer logic. *SIGSAM Bull.*, 31(2):2–9, 1997.

[DV97] Alain Darte and Frédéric Vivien. Optimal fine and medium grain parallelism detection in polyhedral reduced dependence graphs. *Int. J. Parallel Programming*, 25(6):447–496, December 1997.

[Fea91] Paul Feautrier. Dataflow analysis of array and scalar references. *Int. J. Parallel Programming*, 20(1):23–53, February 1991.

[Fea92a] Paul Feautrier. Some efficient solutions to the affine scheduling problem: I. one-dimensional time. *Int. J. Parallel Program.*, 21(5):313–348, 1992.

[Fea92b] Paul Feautrier. Some efficient solutions to the affine scheduling problem: II. multidimensional time. *Int. J. Parallel Program.*, 21(5):389–420, 1992.

[GFG05] Martin Griebl, Paul Feautrier, and Armin Größlinger. Forward communication only placements and their use for parallel program construction. In *Languages and Compilers for Parallel Computing, 15th International Workshop, LCPC'02. Revised Papers*, Lecture Notes in Computer Science 2481, pages 16–30. Springer-Verlag, 2005.

[GFL04]   Martin Griebl, Peter Faber, and Christian Lengauer. Space-time mapping and tiling: A helpful combination. *Concurrency and Computation: Practice and Experience*, 16(3):221–246, March 2004.

[GGL04]   Armin Größlinger, Martin Griebl, and Christian Lengauer. Introducing non-linear parameters to the polyhedron model. In Michael Gerndt and Edmond Kereku, editors, *Proc. 11th Workshop on Compilers for Parallel Computers (CPC 2004)*, Research Report Series, pages 1–12. LRR-TUM, Technische Universität München, July 2004.

[GL97]   Martin Griebl and Christian Lengauer. The loop parallelizer LooPo—Announcement. In David Sehr et al., editors, *Ninth Workshop on Languages and Compilers for Parallel Computing*, volume 1239 of *Lecture Notes in Computer Science*, pages 603–604. Springer-Verlag, 1997. More details at `http://www.infosun.fim.uni-passau.de/cl/loopo`.

[Gri04]   Martin Griebl. *Automatic Parallelization of Loop Programs for Distributed Memory Architectures*. Fakultät für Mathematik und Informatik, Universität Passau, 2004. Habilitation thesis.

[Grö03]   Armin Größlinger. Extending the Polyhedron Model to Inequality Systems with Non-linear Parameters using Quantifier Elimination. Diploma thesis, Universität Passau, September 2003. `http://www.infosun.fim.uni-passau.de/cl/arbeiten/groesslinger.ps.gz`.

[Grö09]   Armin Größlinger. Precise management of scratchpad memories for localising array accesses in scientific codes. In O. de Moor and M. Schwartzbach, editors, *Proceedings of the International Conference on Compiler Construction (CC 2009)*, number 5501 in Lecture Notes in Computer Science, pages 236–250. Springer-Verlag, 2009.

[GS08]   Armin Größlinger and Stefan Schuster. On computing solutions of linear diophantine equations with one non-linear parameter. In *Proceedings of the 10th International Symposium on Symbolic and Numeric Algorithms for Scientific Computing (SYNASC 2008)*, pages 69–76. IEEE Computer Society, September 2008.

[Hea68]   Anthony C. Hearn. REDUCE: A user-oriented interactive system for algebraic simplification. In M. Klerer and J. Reinfelds, editors, *Interactive Systems for Experimental Applied Mathematics*, pages 79–90. Academic Press, New York, 1968.

[Hon98]   Hoon Hong. An Improvement of the Projection Operator in Cylindrical Algebraic Decomposition. In Bob F. Caviness and Jeremy R. Johnson, editors, *Quantifier Elimination and Cylindrical Algebraic Decomposition*, pages 166–173. Springer-Verlag, 1998.

[IBMD04] Ilya Issenin, Erik Brockmeyer, Miguel Miranda, and Nikil D. Dutt. Data reuse analysis technique for software-controlled memory hierarchies. In *DATE '04: Proc. of the Conf. on Design, Automation and Test in Europe*, pages 202–207, Washington, DC, USA, 2004. IEEE Computer Society.

[Int99]   Intel Corporation. *Instruction Set Reference*, volume 2 of *Intel Architecture Software Developer's Manual*. Intel Corporation, 1999. http://developer.intel.com/design/pentiumii/manuals/243191.htm.

[Iri88]   François Irigoin. Code generation for the hyperplane method and for loop interchange. Technical Report ENSMP-CAI-88-E102/CAI/I, Ecole Normale Supérieure des Mines de Paris, October 1988.

[IT88]   François Irigoin and Rémi Triolet. Supernode partitioning. In *Proceedings of the Fifteenth Annual ACM SIGACT-SIGPLAN Symposium on Principles of Programming Language s*, pages 319–329. ACM Press, January 1988.

[KC02]   Mahmut T. Kandemir and Alok N. Choudhary. Compiler-directed scratch pad memory hierarchy design and management. In *DAC '02: Proc. of the 39th Conf. on Design Automation*, pages 628–633, New York, NY, USA, 2002. ACM.

[KMW67]   Richard M. Karp, Raymond E. Miller, and Shmuel Winograd. The organization of computations for uniform recurrence equations. *Journal of the ACM*, 14(3):563–590, July 1967.

[KP09]   Konstantinos Kyriakopoulos and Kleanthis Psarris. Nonlinear symbolic analysis for advanced program parallelization. *IEEE Transactions on Parallel and Distributed Systems*, 20(5):623–640, May 2009.

[KPR95]   Wayne Kelly, William Pugh, and Evan Rosser. Code generation for multiple mappings. In *FRONTIERS '95: Proceedings of the Fifth Symposium on the Frontiers of Massively Parallel Computation*, pages 321–332, Washington, DC, USA, 1995. IEEE Computer Society.

[KRC97]   Mahmut T. Kandemir, J. Ramanujam, and Alok N. Choudhary. A compiler algorithm for optimizing locality in loop nests. In *Proc. of the 11th Int. Conf. on Supercomputing (ICS)*, pages 269–276, July 1997.

[KRI+01]   Mahmut T. Kandemir, J. Ramanujam, Mary J. Irwin, Narayanan
           Vijaykrishnan, Ismail Kadayif, and Amisha Parikh. Dynamic man-
           agement of scratch-pad memory space. In *DAC '01: Proc. of the
           38th Conf. on Design Automation*, pages 690–695, New York, NY,
           USA, 2001. ACM.

[Lam74]   Leslie Lamport. The parallel execution of DO loops. *Communica-
           tions of the ACM*, 17(2):83–93, February 1974.

[Len93]   Christian Lengauer. Loop parallelization in the polytope model.
           In Eike Best, editor, *CONCUR'93*, LNCS 715, pages 398–416.
           Springer-Verlag, 1993.

[LL98]   Amy W. Lim and Monica S. Lam. Maximizing parallelism and min-
           imizing synchronization with affine partitions. *Parallel Computing*,
           24(3-4):445–475, 1998.

[LMC02]   Vincent Loechner, Benoît Meister, and Philippe Clauss. Pre-
           cise data locality optimization of nested loops. *J. Supercomput.*,
           21(1):37–76, 2002.

[Loo83]   Rüdiger Loos. Computing in Algebraic Extensions. In Bruno
           Buchberger, George E. Collins, and Rüdiger Loos, editors, *Com-
           puter Algebra, Symbolic and Algebraic Computation*, pages 173–
           187. Springer-Verlag, New York, second edition, 1983.

[LW93]   Rüdiger Loos and Volker Weispfenning. Applying Linear Quantifier
           Elimination. *The Computer Journal*, 36(5):450–462, 1993. Special
           issue on computational quantifier elimination.

[Mes08]   Message Passing Interface Forum. *MPI: A Message-Passing Inter-
           face Standard, Version 2.1*. High Performance Computing Center
           Stuttgart (HLRS), June 2008.

[NS07]   Nicholas Nethercote and Julian Seward. Valgrind: a framework for
           heavyweight dynamic binary instrumentation. In *PLDI '07: Pro-
           ceedings of the 2007 ACM SIGPLAN conference on Programming
           language design and implementation*, pages 89–100, New York, NY,
           USA, 2007. ACM.

[NVI09]   NVIDIA Corporation. NVIDIA CUDA™ Programming Guide
           Version 2.2, 2009. http://www.nvidia.com/cuda.

[Ope08]   OpenMP Architecture Review Board. OpenMP Application Pro-
           gram Interface, Version 3.0, May 2008. http://openmp.org/wp/
           openmp-specifications/.

[PDN97]   Preeti R. Panda, Nikil D. Dutt, and Alexandru Nicolau. Efficient
           utilization of scratch-pad memory in embedded processor applica-
           tions. In *EDTC '97: Proc. of the 1997 European Conf. on Design
           and Test*, page 7, Washington, DC, USA, 1997. IEEE Computer
           Society.

[PW92]   William Pugh and David Wonnacott. Eliminating false data depen-
           dences using the Omega test. *ACM SIGPLAN Notices*, 27(7):140–
           151, July 1992. *Proc. ACM SIGPLAN Conf. on Programming Lan-
           guage Design and Implementation (PLDI'92)*.

[PW95]   William Pugh and David Wonnacott. Nonlinear array dependence
           analysis. In B. K. Szymanski and B. Sinharoy, editors, *Languages,
           Compilers and Run-Time Systems for Scalable Computers*, pages
           1–14. Kluwer Academic Publishers, Boston, 1995.

[QRW00]   Fabien Quilleré, Sanjay Rajopadhye, and Doran Wilde. Generation
           of efficient nested loops from polyhedra. *Int. J. Parallel Program-
           ming*, 28(5):469–498, October 2000.

[RKRS07]   Lakshminarayanan Renganarayanan, DaeGon Kim, Sanjay Ra-
           jopadhye, and Michelle Mills Strout. Parameterized tiled loops
           for free. In *PLDI '07: Proceedings of the 2007 ACM SIGPLAN
           conference on Programming language design and implementation*,
           pages 405–414, New York, NY, USA, 2007. ACM.

[Sch07]   Stefan Schuster. On algorithmic and heuristic approaches to in-
           tegral problems in the polyhedron model with non-linear parame-
           ters. Diploma thesis, Universität Passau, June 2007. http://www.
           infosun.fim.uni-passau.de/cl/arbeiten/schuster-d.pdf.

[Tar51]   Alfred Tarski. A Decision Method for Elementary Algebra and Ge-
           ometry. Technical report, University of Califonia Press, 2nd edition,
           revised, 1951.

[vdD03]   Lou van den Dries. Generating the greatest common divisor, and
           limitations of primitive recursive algorithms. *Foundations of Com-
           putational Mathematics*, 3(3):297–324, 2003.

[vEBS+04] Robert A. van Engelen, Johnnie Birch, Yixin Shou, Burt Walsh,
           and Kyle A. Gallivan. A unified framework for nonlinear depen-
           dence testing and symbolic analysis. In *ICS '04: Proceedings of
           the 18th annual international conference on Supercomputing*, pages
           106–115, New York, NY, USA, 2004. ACM.

[VSB+04]   Sven Verdoolaege, Rachid Seghir, Kristof Beyls, Vincent Loechner,
           and Maurice Bruynooghe. Analytical computation of ehrhart poly-
           nomials: Enabling more compiler analyses and optimizations. In
           M. J. Irwin, W. Zhao, L. Lavagno, and S. Mahlke, editors, *Proc.*

148

of the 2004 Int. Conf. on Compilers, Architecture, and Synthesis for Embedded Systems (CASES), pages 248–258, Washington DC, USA, 9 2004. ACM.

[VSB⁺07]   Sven Verdoolaege, Rachid Seghir, Kristof Beyls, Vincent Loechner, and Maurice Bruynooghe. Counting integer points in parametric polytopes using Barvinok's rational functions. *Algorithmica*, 48(1):37–66, June 2007.

[Wei88]   Volker Weispfenning. The Complexity of Linear Problems in Fields. *J. Symb. Comput.*, 5(1&2):3–27, February–April 1988.

[Wei97]   Volker Weispfenning. Quantifier elimination for real algebra—the quadratic case and beyond. *Applicable Algebra in Engineering Communication and Computing*, 8(2):85–101, February 1997.

[Wet95]   Sabine Wetzel. Automatic code generation in the polyhedron model. Master's thesis, Fakultät für Mathematik und Informatik, Universität Passau, November 1995. http://www.fmi. uni-passau.de/loopo/doc/wetzel-d.ps.gz.

[WL91]   Michael E. Wolf and Monica S. Lam. A data locality optimizing algorithm. In *PLDI '91: Proc. of the ACM SIGPLAN 1991 Conf. on Programming Language Design and Implementation*, pages 30–44, New York, NY, USA, 1991. ACM.

[XH97]   Jingling Xue and Chua-Huang Huang. Reuse-driven tiling for data locality. In Zhijuan Li, Pen-Chung Yew, Siddharta Chatterjee, Chua-Huang Huang, P. Sadajappan, and David Sehr, editors, *Languages and Compilers for Parallel Computing*, pages 17–33. Springer, August 1997.

[Xue97a]   Jingling Xue. Communication-minimal tiling of uniform dependence loops. *J. Parallel and Distributed Computing*, 42(1):42–59, April 1997.

[Xue97b]   Jingling Xue. On tiling as a loop transformation. *Parallel Processing Letters*, 7(4):409–424, 1997.

[ZZ08]   Jing Zhou and Guosun Zeng. A general data dependence analysis for parallelizing compilers. *J. Supercomput.*, 45(2):236–252, 2008.